Public defender

DATE			
DEC 17 '74	DEC 10		
MAR 11 '75	NOV 2		
OCT 23 '75	JAN 10		
MAY 19 '76			
OCT 6 '76			
NOV 5 '76			
FEB 16 '77			
FEB 23 '77			
MAR 13			
DEC 1			
NOV 2			
FEB 15			

Public Defender

BOOKS BY JAMES PRESLEY

Center of the Storm: Memoirs of John T. Scopes
(in collaboration with John T. Scopes)

"Please, Doctor, Do Something!"
(in collaboration with Joe D. Nichols, M.D.)

Vitamin B_6: The Doctor's Report
(in collaboration with John M. Ellis, M.D.)

PUBLIC DEFENDER

GERALD W. GETTY and
JAMES PRESLEY

GROSSET & DUNLAP, PUBLISHERS
New York

Published simultaneously in Canada
Library of Congress catalog card number: 73–14130
ISBN 0-448-01023-2
First printing
Printed in the United States of America

For L. Michael, Muriel, Marie Therese, and Gracia

–G.W.P.

For Fran, Alex, Gilbert, and Cora

–J.P.

ACKNOWLEDGMENTS

The public defender's office relies on the efforts of many people. In the course of my years as head of the Cook County office, there were many outstanding assistants — lawyers who helped me defend cases and investigators who helped us learn all the facts. Some of them are mentioned in this book because they happen to have worked on the cases that we have written about. Other assistants who became prominent in the legal profession include Stanton Bloom, Cornelius J. Collins, David Dillner, John T. Duffy, Joe Fitzgerald, William Fitzpatrick, John M. Flaherty, Joseph Gill, Robert Harrington, Ted Kowalski, John McDonald, Joseph McGovern, James Oakey, Shelvin Singer, Joseph Solan, and Cornelius Toole. Among the fine investigators in our office not mentioned in the book were Charles Cook and Julius Mesko.

Many people helped to bring this book to completion; we can only name a few here. Our appreciation to Lee Schryver, our editor at Grosset & Dunlap, who got it all started and kept us going; to Helene Mandelbaum, for her helpful editorial suggestions; to Donald S. Engel, for reviewing the manuscript; and to our valued friend and agent, Blanche C. Gregory, who played a major role in the book's making from inception to publication and was a constant source of encouragement.

Gerald W. Getty
James Presley

The Public Defender, as directed by the court, shall act as attorney and counsellor-at-law, without fee, before any court of record within any county of less than 500,000 inhabitants and before any court of record exercising general criminal jurisdiction in counties of 500,000 or more inhabitants for all persons who are held in custody or who are charged with the commission of any criminal offense, and who the court finds are unable to employ counsel.

— ILLINOIS CODE, CH. 34, 5604

CONTENTS

AUTHORS' NOTE

To protect the privacy of individuals still alive, some names of those officially connected with the various legal proceedings, as well as others mentioned in the proceedings, have been changed.

CHAPTER I

Defense of the Despised

"IN THE NAME OF GOD, *what are you trying to do?*"

It was a tough case, maybe the toughest a defense lawyer has ever faced, and the hate mail came early. A Connecticut man started with "Dear Bastard," then got mean. Others rained blunt, ugly curses upon me and my family. Several hoped my tongue would rot. Some flung words of excrement. One man termed me a "thing" and ranted, "How can you sleep nights? I see where you defended 402 murdering *bastards,* and none got the death sentence. I suppose you feel good with a record like that, you lousy S.O.B." Others, always refusing to give their names, telephoned threats upon my life. Another writer, who classified me as "the worst person that ever walked," thought my client (my 403rd in a jury trial) and I should both be shot, but especially me for defending him!

"How in the world can you bear to defend such a monster who has contributed nothing to the world but has snuffed out the lives of eight young women who had dedicated themselves to serving humanity as nurses?"

My client was not only a monster but, judging from the early mail, had already been convicted without a trial. He was Richard F. Speck, an indigent drifter and unemployed seaman.

He had been charged with the July 14, 1966, murders of eight student nurses on Chicago's South Side. Newspapers heralded it as the crime of the century.

Why was I defending this "monster"? For one simple reason: he was poor. He was unable to hire a lawyer, and I was the public defender in Cook County, Illinois, where he was charged with the murders. The court had appointed me personally to represent Speck. It was my job, as an employee of the county, to make certain that every person accused of a criminal act and too poor to afford an attorney was properly represented. In our legal adversary system the public defender's role is to provide a defense equal to the state's prosecution. Speck was merely one of thousands of indigent defendants I have represented.

The Sixth Amendment of the United States Constitution stipulates: "In all criminal prosecution, the accused shall have the right . . . to have the assistance of counsel for his defense." If the poorest man in the country, charged with the most heinous, repulsive crime, does not have proper legal counsel to insure the safeguarding of all his constitutional rights, then the rights of all of us are in jeopardy. The defense is as integral a part of law enforcement as the police, the prosecution, and the courts. We need them all in a democratic society. And the poor deserve the same constitutional guarantees as the rich.

I thought by defending Speck I was helping make democracy work. Before the trial was over a lot of other people thought so, too. Soon the mail became two-to-one in my favor. I received congratulations for my efforts. Eventually some wrote that they believed my client was innocent. These were people who realized that our court system would be a mockery if I had not put forth every effort to defend Speck.

* * *

But what exactly is a public defender? And what is the public defender system? How does it work? Where and how did it start?

In at least four leading encyclopedias there are no entries between *Puberty* and *Public Domain* where you would expect to find *Public Defender*. Yet the idea has been around since the time of Columbus, when Queen Isabella provided for an "Advocate for the Poor." But although Scotland, Hungary, Argentina, Norway, Denmark, Belgium, France, and Mexico have had public defenders at various times in their histories, the concept did not come to the United States until the late nineteenth century, at which time it was mainly a controversial ideal.

The first public defender office in the United States was established in Los Angeles County, California, in 1913. Soon afterward Portland, Omaha, and Columbus set up offices. In 1921, San Francisco and Alameda Counties in California adopted the idea, as did Bridgeport, Hartford, and New Haven in Connecticut.[1] Today Illinois and at least thirty-four other states have made statutory provisions for the office of public defender, and fourteen have statewide offices. According to the National Legal Aid and Defender Association, in 1973 there were 400 public defender offices in the United States.

Although all public defender offices are supported entirely by public funds, the method of selecting the chief defender varies from one locale to another. In Florida, for example, he is elected; in Massachusetts and Oregon, he is selected by a committee of private citizens. In Los Angeles County and Memphis, the chief is chosen by the county commissioners; in Rhode Island, by the governor; in Illinois, Connecticut, and Oklahoma, by the judges; and in Long Beach and the City of Los Angeles, by the city council.[2] In some places the public defender's job is part-time.

The Cook County public defender's office goes back to October 1, 1930, when it was created by the Illinois legislature's

[1]Philip Kraus, "The Office of Public Defender in Los Angeles County" (M.A. thesis, University of California at Los Angeles, 1937), pp. 2 ff.

[2]L. Silverstein, *Denfense of the Poor in Criminal Cases in American State Courts: A Field Study and Report* (American Bar Foundation, 1965), Vol. 1, National Report, pp. 39–40, 57–58.

statutory enactment. This followed an extensive study by the Chicago Bar Association's Committee on the defense of prisoners and the Judicial Advisory Council of Cook County during the years 1927 to 1929. Before then Cook County followed the usual practice of appointing lawyers for the indigent directly from the trial bar. Most of the appointed lawyers served without compensation. In Cook County the only fee was for death penalty cases, and then it was only $250.

The system was unsatisfactory. In great metropolitan centers like my native Chicago it produced chaos in the legal machinery. It was a drain on the time of experienced attorneys, and defendants resented the appointment of younger, less experienced lawyers. And though a young lawyer might gain much needed experience, it was always at the expense of his client, whose liberty or perhaps life was at stake. The old method led to crowded dockets, slow prosecutions because of continuances, and the wasting of money. All too often, defendants lingered unnecessarily in the county jail, awaiting trial. The accused didn't like it; neither did the lawyers.

Beginning in 1930 the judges of the circuit court chose the public defender and the county board allocated funds from the county treasury for the running of the office. This *modus operandi* has continued to the present day.

The first public defender of Cook County was Benjamin Bachrach. His office soon was defending more than half of those indicted for felonies for which a conviction might result in a prison sentence or death. Since then the public defender has continued to represent approximately half of the criminal defendants in Cook County. We have a lot of poor people, and a lot of them get into trouble.

There are six million persons in Cook County. Three and a half million of them are in Chicago itself. In some years my office represented as many as 60 percent of the criminal defendants. This sprawling, polyglot, ever-changing county has been the scene of murder, rape, and all varieties of the lesser crimes. Since its incorporation as a city on March 4, 1837, Chicago has seen it all. The city of Carl Sandburg, Al Capone, Jane Addams, Big Bill Thompson, Clarence Darrow, Nelson Algren, Boss Ed Kelly, Gwendolyn Brooks, Saul Alinsky and Richard J. Daley is steeped in history and violence: the Haymarket Riots, the St. Valentine's Day massacre, the Great Chicago Fire and the Loeb-Leopold trial. But most of all, Chicago is a city of the present and future: a city with an eternally mobile face, a city kept in motion by demolition crews razing huge old buildings to be replaced by huge new buildings. It is a city of confrontation and contrast, with the ugly, the violent, and the beautiful in one bulging, sometimes incongruous package: smoke-belching factories and ritzy Michigan Avenue and century-old quarry pits and top-ranking educational and cultural institutions and slummy flophouses and the stunning Loop skyline.

Chicago is one of the great ethnic melting pots of the world. All ethnic groups that exist are probably found here. This fact is personally symbolized in my own family by the surname of my son, his wife's maiden name, and the surnames of my two married daughters: Getty, Cerri, Ranachowski, and Goldberg. In the old days, Chicago was a city of ethnic enclaves; today, most of the ''melting'' has already occurred. Chicago is still a city of neighborhoods, but now the city is surrounded by burgeoning suburbs, some of them reaching into adjacent counties.

Whatever their ethnic background, my clients have had in common their poverty. The black people of Chicago have been the poorest and, as might be expected, that vast, teeming South Side black ghetto, especially the crime-infested Lawndale and Kenwood sections, has produced from 60 to 70 percent of the public defender's caseload. The Italians, Irish, Puerto Ricans, Polish, and other ethnic groups haunt the office in descending order. There is one ethnic group I don't believe has ever been represented by the public defender in Cook County: The Chinese almost never get into trouble, and if they do, they are apt to have the funds to provide their own defense.

* * *

My clients have all been poor. They have been the penniless and the friendless, the dregs of society, the ones nobody cares about. A few have had families who cared very much. But most of them have had nobody. In many cases society was arrayed against them, breathing down their necks and clamoring for their lives before the trial.

I have not spent time defending doctors, businessmen, or comfortable working-class people. Such defendants invariably have someone to come through for them in one way or another. The indigent are another story. They are apt to be involved in the worst of cases and they are the hardest of clients to defend. As Lee Silverstein, a scholar of our legal system, has observed, "Poor people may be less skillful at committing crime and therefore more likely to be caught in open and shut cases."[3] It is the poor person, in criminal courts around the world, whose life or liberty most often is at stake.

People expect a wealthy man to obtain his freedom by exercising his constitutional rights. But if a poor man escapes the electric chair, full public condemnation may follow. We often do not take the time to remember that a poor man should have the same chance of maintaining his life and liberty as his rich counterpart.

Even Cook County, with one of the earliest public defender offices in the nation, has an underlying, unspoken theme of the local government: The Poor Be Damned.

Most of my office's clients have come from what I call the "vulnerable group," those between eighteen and twenty-six years of age. (Richard Speck was twenty-four when I defended him.) But some have been younger than eighteen and many have been over thirty. The people who commit murder cannot be placed in a single age grouping. In the black ghetto, homicide frequently occurs over a seemingly trivial matter. One man was killed in a dispute over a turkey leg at Thanksgiving Day dinner. This is the kind of case that invariably winds up in the public defender's office in Cook County where poor men

[3] *Ibid.*, p. 53.

and women have committed some of the most absurd and atrocious crimes of our era.

You will not find in these pages a glittering parade of not guilties designed to prove that I am a great lawyer — a kind of super-Darrow. Any lawyer can carefully select his cases in order to prove his skill or success. That approach would be misleading in this book. Out of the 412 jury trials and more than 1,100 bench trials as public defender of Cook County, I was fortunate enough to win approximately 65 percent of the cases that were contested before a judge or jury. That amounts to 267 not guilty jury verdicts. But for this memoir I have chosen from the guilty as well as the not guilty verdicts. Any attempt to present only the not guilty verdicts would make the public defender's job appear relatively easy. It isn't.

As public defender, I have represented several thousand clients over the years. About 70 percent have pleaded guilty. Others have had trials. Most have been despised. Many have been despicable. Many have been guilty. A good number of the cases have been senational ones, tried in an atmosphere of inflamed public opinion.

The odds have almost always been against the client. Often he has admitted his act. Often he has had a hopeless case. In these, the guilty verdict came as no surprise. The only victory in many instances was in keeping the defendant out of Cook County's electric chair, one of the busiest in the nation, or in holding his sentence to a reasonable term. In the toughest cases you don't expect total victory. And this book will feature some of the toughest cases I have seen.

A lawyer in private practice would never touch some of these cases. Not only are the cases more challenging, but the clients frequently inspire little or no sympathy from the public. However, unlike the attorney in private practice, the public defender cannot select his cases; the court assigns them to him. It is an order. When the public defender is appointed to a case he must not do a half-hearted job. It is his duty to do his best, as if he had been paid a $100,000 or $200,000 fee by a wealthy client.

In this book I hope to depict the many aspects of the public defender system by using cases and experiences from my own career. Some of these experiences will evoke memories of similar cases in other cities where public defenders represented indigents. This is particularly likely to be true in Los Angeles, where, over the years, Ellery E. Cuff, Erling J. Hovden, and Richard S. Buckley, the present chief defender, have faced a volume of cases comparable to mine in Chicago. The Los Angeles office, the oldest in this country, has, like Chicago's, seen some of the toughest cases. The only reason the Los Angeles public defender didn't wind up with the Charles Manson "family" case in the La Bianca murders is that the office was already representing a member of Manson's "family." This was in another case, but the client had given evidence against Manson. Representing in both cases would have constituted a conflict of interest, so the public defender had to withdraw from the larger case involving Manson himself.

Wilbur F. Littlefield, chief of the branch and area offices division in the Los Angeles public defender's office, has seen his share of hard cases during a busy career in court. In 1959 he represented the alleged triggerman in the murder of the reputed head of the Mafia in San Diego. His client — indigent by then — was, of four defendants, the one with the most serious accusation against him. The killing had occurred in San Diego, but the trial was transferred to Los Angeles on a change of venue. Originally there had been five defendants, but one had turned state's evidence, testifying against Littlefield's client. The prosecutor, a leading trial lawyer in that part of California, strenuously sought the death penalty. Littlefield attempted to bring in testimony about the Mafia, which would have possibly helped his client; he was unsuccessful. The defendants received life sentences. In a case like that, particularly for Littlefield's client, it was a victory.

Most of the public defender's work goes unpublicized. In Boston, for example, where a statewide defender system has its central office, there have been few headline cases, according to

Scott Harshberger, deputy chief counsel for Massachusetts. Part of the reason for this is that first degree murder — or murder one — cases in Massachusetts, even when the defendant is indigent, are traditionally defended by appointed counsels rather than by the public defender. But the caseload, ranging from the "smaller" crimes to rape and robbery, has been consistently heavy enough to keep Chief Counsel Jerald Schaefer — it was Edgar A. Rimbold before him — and his ninety-five attorneys busy.

In Pittsburgh, the Stanley Hoss case made national headlines. It was only one of many difficult cases in the office headed by George H. Ross, public defender, and Ralph Cappy, his deputy, but it was probably the most sensational. The defendant Hoss, an inmate of the Allegheny County Jail, escaped and shot a policeman fatally. During his flight he allegedly kidnapped a woman and her baby in Maryland. Their bodies were never found. Hoss was tried in Pittsburgh in the policeman's death. Fred Baxter, Jr., an assistant public defender, represented Hoss. During the highly publicized trial, the prosecutor brought in the kidnapping, even though Hoss was not on trial for that. Hoss was convicted of the killing of the policeman and sentenced to death. Baxter appealed the sentence of death on the basis that, over Baxter's timely objection at the trial, the prosecution had been permitted to admit into evidence facts and allegations concerning the alleged Maryland kidnapping. Baxter successfully argued that evidence of the Maryland kidnapping was totally irrelevant to the murder case at issue and thus prejudicial to the minds of the jury, thereby resulting in the death sentence. The Pennsylvania Supreme Court agreed. Hoss is now doing life in prison.

Public defenders in other cities have seen cases similar to some of those I handled and have described in this book. William J. Shaw, public defender of St. Louis County, Missouri, for instance, has had two cases of mistaken identification in his office in recent years. One client, charged with rape, was picked out of a lineup in 1972 by three victims. They were positive he was the man. But Frank Rouse, an investigator in Shaw's office, noted the defendant's similarity to another man arrested for sex violations. Each of the accused men wore dark-framed glasses, had wavy hair and tattoos on the left arm. The look-alike client, represented by Shaw's assistant, Joseph R. Aubuchon, protested his innocence. At his place of employment, his time card showed he was at work on the days the crimes were committed. Further investigation revealed the rapist had driven an old blue car; the client did not own a blue automobile. Confronted by the photos of both men at once, the witnesses grew less positive and became confused. Charges were dropped. An innocent man went free.

Earlier, in a 1967 case in St. Louis County, an ex-convict on parole for robbery in another state was positively identified by eyewitnesses as one of two gunmen in a holdup in which an off-duty police sergeant was fatally shot. The client insisted he was innocent and was not even in the St. Louis area at the time. At considerable expense, the public defender's office checked out the alibi, located the client's aunt and uncle in Kentucky. They confirmed that the defendant had spent the night of the murder with them. After Shaw's assistant, Charles R. Abele, emphasized the highly credible alibi and other weaknesses in the state's case, the jury found the defendant not guilty.

In Nashville, Tennessee, James Tyre Havron, an elected public defender, cites the Gammon case as one of his toughest. Raymond Gammon, a man with a previous record, was charged with murdering two women. It was a headline case in which community feeling was running high. Before Gammon was arrested, rewards had been offered by the news media. It was a terrible crime, with no apparent motive. One of the women had been stabbed, the other beaten to death with a tire jack. The bodies were found in a field near the municipal airport. It was a case in which, as Jim Havron has commented, the police were under pressure to make an arrest, and the prosecutor to win a conviction. The defendant had had a dozen or so mixed drinks on the night of the crime. He had encountered two women at 2 or 3 A.M. but he didn't remember anything more. Later, he came to as he was falling down an embankment. He had a pistol that had been fired once, and there was blood on him. Yet neither of the victims had been shot, and the defendant had no knife. There were many unanswered questions in Havron's mind — as there were in my mind during the trying of the Speck case. For the first time, many teen-agers appeared on the jury rolls, an unknown factor. Havron sought *all* teen-aged jurors, but the prosecutor avoided that, and the jury ended up half teen-aged and half middle-aged. In a pressure-filled case involving circumstantial evidence, the jury's alternatives were clear: find the defendent not guilty, or find him guilty of first degree murder. There was no middle ground. They found him guilty. He received two 99-year terms, to run consecutively.

Public defenders have been in the forefront of the legal evolution of our civil liberties. They have taken a number of cases to the U.S. Supreme Court. One such case that I handled in Cook County is described in this book. On several occasions the Defender Section of the National Legal Aid and Defender Association has filed briefs as *amicus curia* in Constitutional cases.

Oregon State Public Defender Gary Babcock's office made new law in 1973 with the *Wardius* v. *Oregon* decision of the U.S. Supreme Court. The *Wardius* appeal, handled by Marvin Kuhn, Babcock's deputy, established the principle of reciprocal disclosure as to a defendant's alibi. In this instance, the defendant, charged with selling marijuana to an undercover policeman, claimed he was at a drive-in movie with his girl friend at the time of the alleged crime. But he did not file his alibi, as required by Oregon law, and in the ensuing bench trial the court would not allow him or his girl friend to testify as to his alibi. Convicted, he was sentenced to eighteen months. Deputy Public Defender Kuhn sought a reversal in the Oregon higher courts, to no avail. Then he took it to the nation's highest tribunal, where he won. The Supreme Court ruled that if the defendant is required to present his alibi before trial, then the state must present its rebuttal evidence to the defendant at that time. This procedure had not been complied with.

In Miami, Public Defender Phillip A. Hubbart took *Smith* v. *Florida* to the U.S. Supreme Court in 1972 and won, in a case that was instrumental in striking down Florida's vagrancy statute as unconstitutional. In its various trial divisions as well as its busy appellate division headed by Bennett Brummer, the Miami office has been as active as any in protecting the rights of the poor. Assistant Public Defender William Aaron, a trial lawyer who generally defends against felony charges, took *Rollins* v. *State* to the Florida Supreme Court where it was held that the incarceration of an indigent defendant for failure to pay a fine constituted a violation of the right to counsel as established by the U.S. Supreme Court in *Argersinger* v. *Hamlin*. The high court required that a new trial be held in such cases. A rehearing is now pending, however, as a result of the state's request.

Rollie R. Rogers, who directs the state public defender system of Colorado, also personally handles a large number of the cases that are processed through his office in Denver. Like public defenders elsewhere, Rogers has had the notorious ones too. In a case that the community followed avidly, he represented a black man accused of murdering a white policeman in 1971. The policeman had been shot in the back outside a Denver restaurant during a 4 A.M. hassle with a group of black persons who had come from an after-hours club. Trying the case with his assistant, J.D. MacFarlane, Rogers went all-out in his pre-trial preparations. In the courtroom, he bore down hard on the question of identification. Was this, indeed, the man who had fired the fatal shot? Before the evidence had been presented, it had looked like a shoo-in for the prosecution, but Rogers won an acquittal, as the jury agreed the defendant had not been proved guilty beyond a reasonable doubt.

Women lawyers have also played significant roles in the public defender system. At least two have served as heads of their offices. In Indianapolis, Mrs. Harriette Bailey Conn is public defender of Indiana, supervising the state office that handles post-conviction matters only, and taking her turn in court along with the other attorneys on her staff. Mrs. Conn, a former deputy attorney general, deputy prosecutor, and state representative, was appointed to the post by the Indiana Supreme Court.

In Washington, Barbara Allen Babcock directed the Public Defender Service for the District of Columbia from 1968 until 1972, when she accepted an associate professorship in Stanford University's law school. During her tenure Babcock saw the office grow from a staff of 26 to one of 140 that included 44 lawyers.

While she was director, her office represented one of the defendants in the notorious Carwash Murders case. The victims of the 1968 triple slaying were a white man who owned the carwash, a black man, and a black woman. All were brutally beaten to death. Two black men were charged and tried. One was represented by lawyers appointed from the private bar; the other was represented by assistant public defenders Sanford Berman and John Perazich. The government's case involved circumstantial evidence. The defense bore down on the elements of doubt in the prosecution's case. The jury agreed that the defendants had not been proved guilty beyond a reasonable doubt and brought in an acquittal.

During her years in the office, Babcock herself defended in ten to eleven trials a year in addition to her administrative duties. Among the felony cases in which she represented were an estimated ten to fifteen rape cases. During her last few years in Washington she tried only murder cases. "They weren't headline cases," she said, "but in all I handled thirty to forty murder trials, with good success, involving every kind of human situation." In many instances, the defendants were very young, eighteen or nineteen, charged with first degree murder. In one street killing, three witnesses claimed to have seen the defendant commit the fatal act. But at the trial, held before Federal Judge John J. Sirica of Watergate fame, Babcock concentrated on what she considered "tremendous" flaws in the government's case. The government's witnesses were alleged heroin pushers, "the worst kind of witnesses," who were having charges dropped against them in return for their testimony. She dwelt upon these witnesses' "unhealthy, cozy relationship with the police" that reflected deeply upon their credibility. The result was a hung jury. The case was not retried. Subsequently the defendant pleaded guilty to a count of unarmed robbery, which closed the case.

In New York City, there is no public defender system such as we have in Chicago. Instead of a public defender, the Legal Aid Society, which is a private, non-profit organization, sends lawyers to the criminal courts, and the city pays for this service. Until the past ten years of its 98-year existence in New York, the Legal Aid Society, which is supported by private donations, had concentrated on providing services to the poor in civil law, such as child custody and support, divorce, and rent cases. At the present time, however, according to Alan Friess, attorney-in-charge of the Criminal Courts Branch in Manhattan, the criminal division in New York carries Legal Aid's caseload by a six-to-one ratio. William Gallagher is in overall charge of the criminal division in New York City.

Martin Erdmann, executive attorney for the criminal defense division, noted that in the early 1960s the work of the Legal Aid Society in New York City was almost equally divided between civil and criminal cases. Virtually all funds came from private sources. Shortly after *Gideon* v. *Wainwright* in 1963, which invested the state with the responsibility of providing free legal assistance to all indigent persons charged with felonies, New York State enacted legislation permitting local governments to decide the manner in which to provide these services. New York City chose to utilize the already existing Legal Aid Society. Since then, New York City has entered into annual contracts with the Legal Aid Society and has provided about 95 percent of the funding for the Society's criminal defense division. The Society, of course, remains a private organization with its own board of directors. In 1963 there were 50 lawyers in the criminal defense division; in 1973, the figure had shot up to 444 — a staff almost three times as large as the civil branch and the family court branch combined.

The New York City arrangement with Legal Aid for the defense of indigents in criminal cases is an exception to the general rule. Although there are other similar exceptions in other areas, particularly in some Ohio cities, Legal Aid is primarily private and remains in civil law.

In many places chief defenders direct statewide systems. James H. McDermott is state public defender for Wisconsin; Lawrence M. Sullivan, for Delaware; Stanley C. Van Ness, for New Jersey; and James Cardono, for Rhode Island. As a result of the *Gideon* v. *Wainwright* Supreme Court decision in 1963, Florida now has a statewide system, divided into judicial circuits. Louis O. Frost, Jr., for example, represents the poor of Jacksonville, while attorneys like Maynard W. Schryver of Collier County have defended in areas that are predominantly rural. In other states, Charles Gill is chief public defender of the Circuit Court of Connecticut; Norman Lefstein directs the defender service for the District of Columbia. Occasionally the title changes, as in Fort Wayne, Indiana, where Bruce E. Bloom is officially the Allen County Poor Attorney, but the job is the same.

In the larger cities, public defenders have directed staffs that varied in size in proportion to population: Edward T. Mancuso in San Francisco, Ross P. Lee in Phoenix, Myzell Sowell in Detroit, Robert C. Legakes in Las Vegas, Harry E. Youtt in Cleveland, Don Anderson in Oklahoma City, Vincent J. Ziccardi in Philadelphia, John W. Williams, Jr., in Columbia, South Carolina, John M. Darrah in Seattle, Charles Kitchin in the City of St. Louis, and Willard B. Bunch in Kansas City.

The list could go on and on. Whoever they are, in whichever city, I believe that every one of these fellow public defenders will know what I mean when I say that I would not have swapped my job for that of any of the other 14,000 lawyers in Cook County. It was like sitting in a hot seat, where the pressures could mount unbelievably, but I was in the midst of the action, and I loved it. I had taken my oath seriously when I swore upon a Bible to ". . . protect the rights and privileges of all the persons charged with the commission of any criminal offense, whom the court has found to be unable to employ counsel and for whom I shall be appointed as attorney, to the best of my ability, so help me God." That oath spelled out for me what San Francisco Public Defender Edward T. Mancuso has said of the public defender's office: [it is] "a modern instrument created to make, in the administration of criminal justice, a realistic and practical application of our Christian and democratic belief of the dignity and importance of the individual."[4]

Whoever they are or were, whatever they may have done, my clients are human beings and I have dedicated myself to seeing that they have received fair trials under our state and federal constitutions.

That, in the name of God and justice, is what I sincerely tried to do.

[4]Edward T. Mancuso, *The Public Defender System in the State of California* (Chicago: National Legal Aid and Defender Association, 1963).

CHAPTER 2
Getting Started

LOOKING BACK, it isn't surprising at all that I became a public defender. Some factors in my choosing this career I can remember as vividly as if they were headlines in this morning's newspaper.

The notorious Loeb-Leopold case was the talk of Chicago and the nation when I was in grade school at St. Philip Neri on Chicago's South Shore. The defendants both lived on the South Side where I was born and grew up. The body of their victim, Bobby Franks, had been found in the Burnham area near where I was born. It was sensational and close to home, with the famous Clarence Darrow, Chicago's own, defending in what was one of America's greatest trials. I could never forget it.

In high school I read about some of Abraham Lincoln's trials as a young lawyer and I was left forever impressed by the character of that revered son of Illinois.

But the most important influence of all in my decision to study law was probably my maternal grandfather, George Winkler, whose surname is my middle name. He always talked about how he would have liked to have been a lawyer. He wanted me to become one. I respected him. Add to these the fact that I grew up with a feeling for the underdog, without which I could scarcely have lasted long as a public defender.

Now as I ponder those early influences, all that followed seems as logical and natural and pre-designed as the rib-like veins on the underside of a tree leaf, as if it could have happened no other way.

I was born to a German-American (my mother was also English and Irish) family on June 17, 1911, in a two-story frame house at 9447 Burnside Avenue that my paternal grandparents had built around the turn of the century. It is not far from the focal point of the Speck case. Now the house is gone; on the site is a large slab of asphalt serving as a Chicago Transit Authority bus parking and turning area. This is typical of Chicago; a city in continual motion, tearing down, rebuilding, always changing.

Change came often. We moved a number of times, always on the South Side, which was expanding then, and I went to a variety of schools: kindergarten on Burnside Avenue; primary grades in Calumet City public schools and a Catholic school in Hammond, Indiana, a mile away; later St. Philip Neri until the eighth grade; and then Mt. Carmel High School, where I graduated at seventeen. My parents separated when I was in the third grade. Kenneth, my brother four years younger, went to live with our mother; my father and I lived with his parents on the South Shore. My paternal great-grandparents had come from Germany in 1848 and my grandparents spoke German, which my father, their firstborn, understood. They always used English with me. If my grandmother didn't want me to understand something, she would say it in German. We were melting fast.

My playmates were children of various backgrounds. The South Shore area, like St. Philip Neri parish, was predominantly Irish and rather well-to-do. Some areas were comparatively wealthy. When my father remarried we moved to Avalon Park, a new neighborhood near Eighty-Fourth and Blackstone, which was mainly Swedish and Irish, and I played with kids with names like Petersen, Lindstrom and Carlson.

In 1930, the year the public defender's office was set up in Chicago, I entered the University of Illinois to study business administration, planning to enter law school later. But the great depression caused me to later transfer to DePaul University in downtown Chicago in order to cut down on expenses. When I had accumulated three years' credit, I was admitted to the DePaul University law school where I received my Bachelor of Laws degree in February, 1938. I took the Illinois exam on December 16, 1938, and was admitted to the Bar of Illinois along with 295 others.

I found an office in Avalon Park at Eighty-Second and Stony Island that I shared with a real estate firm. Interested in real estate myself, I handled some of the broker's legal work and, because I wanted all the experience I could get, I volunteered with the Legal Aid Bureau of the City of Chicago and prepared complaints. Soon I became a real estate broker myself, passing an exam before the Illinois Department of Registration and Education, and sold real estate while taking care of whatever legal business came my way. My first fee, around $25 or so, came from a young business man, Herman G. Jackson, who worked a few blocks away. I handled an eviction suit for him and have been his legal advisor ever since.

In 1942 I went to work for the Office of Price Administration (OPA) as a junior attorney at $2,000 a year. My real estate experience was a help when I was assigned to the Rent Control Division in the Chicago office. Our job was to put the lid on rents and keep it there for the duration of World War II. Also, the federal rent attorney often had to protect people from being unfairly evicted.

A test case in Renters Court, which may have been the first of its kind in wartime America, affected 1,500 black tenants in the Mecca apartment building at Thirty-Fourth and State on the South Side.

The building was owned by the Illinois Institute of Technology. The owners sought to evict the tenants and close the building by claiming that it was a firetrap and unsafe. Apparently they wanted to raze it to expand the school's facilities. Most of the tenants, who had come up from the South to work in war factories, had been in Chicago for less than six months, and housing was extremely scarce. God knows where else they could have gone.

Cases in Renters Court are heard rapidly. It was common for 500 a day to pass through the court. This hearing, although involving 1,500 persons, lasted less than an hour. I pointed out that the school had not yet acquired a permit to raze, which was necessary before the tenants could be evicted, and which, I argued, indicated that Illinois Tech was not ready to tear down the apartment building. Nor had the school been given authority from the government for these evictions. Then I emphasized the critical housing shortage.

When the lawyers had finished, Judge Samuel Heller spoke briefly, noting that many in the Mecca apartments were essential war workers and more than fifty men from families who lived there were in the armed services.

"What do you think it would mean to their morale to know that their parents, wives, and children have been thrown into the streets, with no place to go?"

He denied the motion to evict.

There were at least 100 tenants of the Mecca there. The court was jammed with black humanity. After Judge Heller denied the petition to evict, I heard a deep, deep rumble swell and reverberate through the courtroom until it became an overwhelming and joyous shout.

"A-a-a-*MEN!*"

It was the most spontaneous ovation I have ever heard in a courtroom.

* * *

By the summer of 1943 I had advanced from junior to assistant attorney with the OPA. The raise of $600 now gave me $2,600 per annum; I could expect another raise that would make it $3,000. It was at this point that I heard of an opening in the Cook County Public Defender's Office that paid the munificent salary of $3,600. (In those pre-inflation days this was a desirable starting salary.) But what meant the most, I would have a good chance to gain trial experience in a variety of cases denied me as a government lawyer. I began to work as an assistant public defender in September, 1943, under Benjamin Bachrach, the first public defender of Cook County. Bachrach had been associated with Darrow in the Loeb-Leopold defense in 1924. By the time I became one of his assistants, he was already up in years.

The public defender's office was — and is — in the Cook County Criminal Court Building at Twenty-Sixth and California Streets on the West Side. It is an inconvenient site, and hard to get to for lawyers and witnesses. The only way to get there is by automobile.

The massive, seven-story concrete building was built in 1928, and has not been changed very much since. At first there were about a half-dozen courtrooms. By 1970 there were fifteen: four felony courts and eleven in which indictments were heard. To a person habituated to the courts of television and the movies, those of Cook County would come as a jolt. For one thing, if you don't sit in the front row, you might miss it all. There is rarely any shouting, and the acoustics are terrible. Appearances, in day-to-day proceedings, are usually brief. And so the courts often resemble a mill that is devoid of the kind of drama that enlivens our stages and screens. One observer, WBBM news reporter John D. Calloway, has called the courthouse "a Kafkian nightmare."

The Criminal Court Building has never been air-conditioned and in the summertime it is a hellish place to practice law. When the heat would force us to raise the windows, the noise from the railroad nearby came in stronger than whatever breeze we got. When a train was going by outside, you couldn't hear what anyone was saying inside. It was judicial disaster. There is a story — hearsay, but reliable hearsay — that a judge once issued an injunction against the railroad in an attempt to improve the administration of criminal justice in Cook County.

In this atmosphere, a loud voice is an asset, and I had one. It carried well — but too far, some said — and by speaking deliberately, I learned to vary it for appropriate moments, at times dropping to a well-modulated whisper for proper dramatic effect on a judge or a jury, at other times speaking so low that the assistant state's attorney couldn't possibly hear me.

Our offices were in the northeast corner of the third floor, down a long hallway coming from the corridor where you got off the elevator. We had just that one small corner on one floor of the huge old building. Two large doors were our entrance and over them were the words: *Public Defender of Cook County*.

There were four other assistants besides myself when I first came to that office — Frank Ferlic, Lester Grossman, Joseph Gannon, and John Branion — and we had one secretary for all of us. When I resigned in 1972, almost thirty years later, we had a staff of seventy-five assistants, eight investigators, and nineteen clerical workers. And though we had expanded our offices, by inheriting the space once used by an abolished unit, we were still cramped.

* * *

My first cases as an assistant were "bench" trials, in which the defendant has waived a jury. These are naturally shorter and less complicated. You bypass the tedious selecting of twelve jurors and then appealing to them. The facts and the law both go to the judge; he decides guilt, then sets the penalty.

One of my first bench trials was before a judge who was as new at his job as I was at mine. He had not heard a contested bench trial before. It was a robbery case in which a watch had been taken. But nobody had ever found the watch. When my man was arrested he didn't have it on him.

The state's case was weak. Identification of the defendant was shaky. I put the defendant on the stand in his own defense and he, of course, denied any wrongdoing. In my closing argument I raised the question of reasonable doubt.

"This case is punctuated with doubt!" I shouted. I contended vigorously that the defendant had not been proved guilty beyond a reasonable doubt.

The new judge was very attentive. He followed our arguments scrupulously. When the assistant state's attorney and I had finished, he directed his attention to the defendant.

"Stand up," he said. "I'm going to pronounce the verdict." And then he did:

"I find you not guilty."

The defendant, his burden suddenly lifted, started to walk out of the courtroom.

"Just a minute!" the judge yelled at him. "I found you not guilty, *but give him back his watch!*"

The assistant state's attorney hit the ceiling over that, and I think it was the last not guilty verdict that judge ever gave in a bench trial.

* * *

From the time I entered the office in the forties until the seventies when I was head of the office, there were consistent patterns in our caseload. After Francis T. McCurrie succeeded Bachrach in 1946 I kept records of the ages, nationalities, and types of crimes. Blacks, even then, were the frontrunners. The age was likely to be from the late teens to the middle twenties. The most frequent crime was burglary, followed in order by robbery with a gun or other weapon, plain robbery (strong arm, without a weapon), larceny, rape, and murder. During the fifties we represented between fifty and sixty murder defendants a year — a figure that doubled by the seventies. This, of course, did not include all of the murders committed in Chicago, for some defendants were represented by other lawyers, and some killings went unsolved.

The really unfortunate defendants were the survivors of the husband-and-wife arguments in the black ghetto that had ended in homicide. These killings, usually with a knife, followed a certain pattern. Like that of Hattie Lee White — not her real name.

Mrs. White's husband, Farley, worked regularly, but after work he generally stopped off at a local tavern where he would have quite a few drinks. When he arrived home he would become abusive to his wife. It happened quite often — not every night, but usually on weekends — and she would always remonstrate with him about it.

One evening he arrived home intoxicated once again. She was in the kitchen preparing dinner. The butcher knife was out. He started in on her. This time she had had it. She grabbed the knife and lunged at him. The knife went right through his heart: Farley was dead and she was relieved of her burden.

The testimony of witnesses substantiated Mrs. White's previous beatings as well as the beating she was about to get. They testified to having seen her black eyes, her black and blue spots, and that she had had a couple of her teeth knocked out. The neighbors had not only seen the results of her husband's violence, but had also heard the commotion from the apartment.

I argued that this was a matter of self-defense.

The judge agreed. He found Mrs. White not guilty.

* * *

Other cases were similar. A heated argument between a husband and wife could begin over almost anything. There would be a gun in the house. They would both run for the weapon, and suddenly there would be an explosive shot. The one that got the gun first became the defendant, the other the victim.

These cases didn't even make an honorable mention in the newspapers, since they occurred frequently and in "undesirable" locations. To catch the eye of a newspaperman, a case had to have a human interest angle. The case of one woman I'll call Jo Ann Painter merited three or four paragraphs. Because she was from the hills of Kentucky, and was on trial for biting a guy in a bar, she was considered colorful. The injured party testified that he was minding his own business and sipping his beer when, totally unexpectedly, Miss Painter pounced upon him and bit the top of his ear off.

In her bench trial I brought out that it was a brawl and not the first tavern fight the complainant had been in. According to all the witnesses, the biting had followed an exchange of words between Miss Painter's brother and the complainant. Then the state was unable to prove conclusively that the cut on the ear was caused by teeth. My client had been charged with mayhem, and the common-law definition of mayhem is to injure a person in such a manner that he cannot defend himself. Now this would require the severance of a hand, leg, arm, eye or foot. A man does not defend himself with the top of his ear.

Jo Ann denied the biting, but the judge found her guilty, anyway.

However, the case still was not lost. I hastily conferred with her. She promised the judge "not to do it again," and the judge went along: He let her go on probation. She had her freedom; the guy she bit still had most of his ear. And as far as I know she has never bitten anyone's ear off again.

* * *

Flora Denton, a widow, was accused of embezzling $16,000 from her employer over a three-year period. She handled about $6,000 a month for the real estate firm where she worked as a $125-a-month cashier and bookkeeper. Each month she took out a little for herself.

She admitted it. There was hardly any choice; I pleaded her guilty.

"I took some money," she said, "but I didn't think it was that much. I used it to buy things for my daughter. I'd like to pay it all back, and I'll try to."

I was trying to get probation for her. One man had offered Mrs. Denton a job at $175 a month and was willing to get her daughter a job when she finished high school. I had him repeat these promises to the judge. The mother had stolen the money to provide her daughter with a better education as well as better living conditions for both of them.

"I'll help, Judge," the daughter promised. "I'll graduate from high school next month, and I'll get a job and pay back everything that I can."

Probation, to me, looked like a practical, just way out of the mess. Mrs. Denton's former employer would get his money back, although it clearly would take a long time. Without probation he would get nothing. The defendant would be working toward rectifying her misdeed. How much better than going through the dehumanizing experience of prison, at state expense, while her teen-aged daughter faced a crucial time of life without a mother!

The assistant state's attorney balked. He didn't see it that way. He said she could never pay back $16,000 and urged the judge to sentence her and get it over with. So the judge denied probation and gave her eighteen months in the women's reformatory. The simple, but ultimately more expensive, solution triumphed over the more complicated blueprint for justice that would have been fairer for all concerned.

I still think the judge was wrong in that case.

CHAPTER 3
Judging a Jury

THE ULTIMATE IN EXPERIENCE for the fledgling lawyer is the jury trial. Whatever skills are required for the other aspects of defending a client, they must all be drawn on for the selection of twelve jurors and then for the defense put before them. The defender must learn what to look for in a venireman, and what to suspect. It is a trial-and-error process and he has to learn from his mistakes. After a while the defender develops a special, almost unconscious, sense that guides him and tells him when a juror is particularly good or bad for his client.

In a melting pot like Chicago, he soon acquires general knowledge about members of the various ethnic groups. The nationality of a juror has a lot to do with the kind of verdict he is likely to lean toward. I found that Germans are usually more severe, as are Swedes and Norwegians. This does not mean the individuals of these nationalities will *always* be severe, but the national tendency forewarns the defender. On the other hand, the Irish are more forgiving because at one time or another in history the Irish have been mistreated. Italians, Czechoslovakians and other Slavics, and Hungarians also tend to make good jurors from the defense's point of view. These groups want to know the facts before they will convict. It has to be proved to them. Those of English descent also do well.

Blacks, based on my Cook County experiences, usually do not make good jurors. There are complicated reasons for this. I have experimented with blacks as jurors on many occasions. If you could get an all-black jury, then they would be good jurors, but the state's attorney would usually not permit more than one or two blacks on any given jury. Consequently the one or two black jurors are almost invariably overwhelmed by the white people on the jury, particularly if a white person is on trial. They tend to reason that the whites are judging their own kind, and they accommodate them.

For my clients, always poor, a juror with more education is apt to be too severe. A guy with a grade or high school education, who may be a truck driver, has taken the hard knocks of life. He's an underdog. He's going to be for you as much as he can. Having been poor himself, he has a deeper insight into the defendant's plight than a Ph.D. or an executive who has never worked with his hands.

I also prefer elderly persons, either men or women, on my juries. The older person has seen more of life. He or she has had an opportunity to view the policemen and law enforcement agencies and know how they handle poor people. An older person knows more about the hardships of other people than does the young man or woman of twenty-three who has been sheltered to some extent. More things have happened to the older person, and he or she can draw on this fuller experience in deciding another person's fate.

One caveat stands supreme in the advice I once gave my juniors in the office: Never take anyone who has been an officer in the military. However, if I were the prosecutor, I would get every colonel (especially if a German) I could on the jury. That should insure that the defendant got hanged from the yardarm!

* * *

What are the important things to bring out before a jury? These vary from case to case, but they are the details that you hope will convince all twelve jurors, or at least enough of them, either that the defendant is innocent or that there is reasonable doubt as to his guilt or that extenuating circumstances were involved.

The cases in this chapter illustrate various problems I encountered in jury trials in my learning years. Again, some of the names of those I have defended have been changed in order to protect them.

* * *

Charles Busanski had been accused of robbery.

The complaining witness, Mr. Rakov, said that as he was walking along the street, a car stopped and two men got out and held him up. He identified one of the men as a person he had known for some time. The other man wore a black coat with the collar turned up. Mr. Rakov did not see more than the hair and eyebrows of the second man, but he identified Busanski as being that man.

I cross-examined him about that February night.

"Was it dark?"

"Yes," he admitted, "it was very dark."

The questions flew. How was the robber dressed? Did you see his face? Did he have a hat on? If you didn't see his face, by what do you identify this man in the courtroom? Were any words spoken? How long have you worn glasses? Did you have your glasses on that night?

Then, to make sure the jurors understood the problem of the complaining witness's eyesight, I concluded: "They are rather thick lenses, aren't they, Mr. Rakov?"

Busanski took the stand and denied the charge. I battered him with questions also, which he readily answered, pinpointing his activities on the day of the offense from the time he got off work until he went home in the evening, each response designed to bolster the claim that he wasn't at the scene of the crime and therefore could not have robbed Mr. Rakov.

In closing I summed up the following: The identification was weak. It was a very dark night; there was poor visibility, and the victim had poor eyesight. Admittedly he had not seen the face of the second man. (So how could he be so sure?) All he had seen was a man's dark hair and a black overcoat. Busanski's coat was blue; he said he didn't own a black coat.

I didn't get a not guilty, but I came close enough for Charles Busanski's comfort. There was a hung jury, hopelessly deadlocked eleven-to-one for acquittal. It was as good as an acquittal, though, for the case was never retried.

The holdout juror was a craftsman. A German.

* * *

Identification is nearly always a tricky business. On close examination the witness is rarely as convincing as he at first seems to be. This is not surprising. Our minds play tricks on all of us. Slight impressions are sometimes reinforced by opinion instead of facts. If a witness insists he has positively identified the defendant, the defense starts out behind the eight-ball. (If someone *saw* the defendant committing a crime, then he committed it, didn't he?) In these cases, the state can be expected to go all out for a conviction. But eyewitnesses are just not that reliable, and they can be mistaken no matter how certain they may feel. I've seen it happen over and over, to the point that I became extremely dubious of many such identifications.

Thomas Smith and Percy Cooper were charged with the armed robbery of a cab driver. The cabbie told this story: He picked up two men, whom he later identified as being Smith and Cooper. When they arrived at their destination, Smith pulled a pistol and Cooper said, "This is a stick-up." They took nineteen dollars of his money, seven dollars of the cab company's. It was midnight and dark, but the street lights were on. The holdup men walked away down the street with the money.

Two weeks later, the complainant was hailed by Smith and Cooper in another area of Chicago several miles from the scene of the robbery. He drove them to a bus station on North State Street in the Loop. They went into the station, came out, and hired his cab again. This time he took them to Twelfth and

Wabash. Then he called the police, charging they were the same pair who had held him up a fortnight before.

The state's case, to my mind, was riddled with flaws. I produced alibi witnesses for my clients. No person can be in two places at one time. Furthermore, on the day of the crime Smith had a bandage on his face — which the complainant hadn't mentioned. The state had one witness only, the driver, but he positively identified the two men as the ones who had robbed him.

With a jury, you have to be thorough; spell it all out. Forget to point out one detail and explain its significance to the jury and your client may suffer. I described the robbery scene. "It isn't a retail business district, but a commercial area and not as well lighted. He turned the cab light on. Now from your experience you know how much that light shows. It is made to show a small light over the driver's head. It doesn't light the outside area of the cab. The state wants you to believe it was a floodlight."

I emphasized that the state had only one witness and had not even put on a policeman to prove that the robbery was reported immediately after it allegedly had happened. I pointed out that when the cabbie had picked up Smith and Cooper two weeks after the crime, they were in their own neighborhood and that this was several miles away from the scene of the robbery. While he waited for them outside the bus station that day, he could have called the police if he had thought them to be robbers. Why hadn't he?

"He was in the heart of the Loop. Across the street from the Chicago Theatre. Yet he tells us he couldn't find a policeman! The question is, did he think these men were robbers at that time? He took them in his cab again and drove them to Twelfth and Wabash. Would a reasonable man put two men he thought robbed him two weeks before behind him in his cab and drive them several miles through the Loop down darker streets to Twelfth and Wabash? As he drove them, didn't he pass police and squad cars? If he traveled State Street to Twelfth Street, he passed one of the largest police stations in the world, at Eleventh and State. When did he decide they were his robbers of two weeks before? I don't believe he would have placed himself as a potential victim if he was sure these were the men. He wasn't sure then and he isn't now.''

Another not guilty.

* * *

In another trial, the defendant's race played a major part in his identification. The charge was assault. An Indian, Joe Goody, was accused of spinning the complainant around in the washroom of a bar and hitting him while another man grabbed five dollars from him. The money-grabber was then grabbed by the bartender, and had been convicted by the time Goody came to trial. The complainant later had lost his eye, so it was a serious charge: Robbery and mayhem.

The complainant identified Goody as being his assailant, but there was more to it than that. The complainant had been drinking in other bars, apparently, and he disagreed with the bartender on several important points.

''One of them is dead wrong as to what took place here,'' I insisted.

There were forty other persons in the bar and it had happened in a split second: I doubted that the victim knew who had hit him. Then a police officer testified he had seen Goody many times during a period when he wasn't in Chicago but on the boats! And it was months after the incident took place that he was picked up, even though he lived only a short distance away.

''Ladies and gentlemen,'' I told the jury in examining the bartender's testimony, ''all he knows is that while a lot of people were in his place drinking and entertaining each other, a man was seriously injured and an Indian was in there at the time, so he is identifying this defendant. Well, there are a lot of Indians in that neighborhood as well as black and white people and they all frequent this tavern as well as the other taverns in that block.''

Somebody had to show this to the jury. The state's attorney

wasn't going to. Goody was found not guilty of robbery but guilty of mayhem and sentenced to one-to-three years.

* * *

The defendant does not have to prove he is innocent. Under our laws, the state must prove, beyond a reasonable doubt, that he is guilty. So he does not have to present a defense at all. But generally he will have a defense, and certainly his lawyer is derelict in his duty if he does not insist that the state *prove* guilt conclusively before a man is deprived of his liberty. Throughout a defense, logic is just as important to a lawyer as a hammer is to a carpenter.

All these factors figured in the trial of George Stumer, a merchant seaman accused of hitting a man in the eye, taking his wallet containing twenty-eight dollars and his cigarette lighter. Several days later the complainant had received back his chauffeur's license and other papers in the mail. These were not, however, introduced as evidence at the trial.

Twenty-four days after the strong-arm robbery, the complainant saw Stumer and called the police. He said Stumer was the same man who had held him up.

By his own admission the complainant had had five bottles and four glasses of beer on the night of the crime. If he admitted this, he had had more. He had not been sober. The crime took place on a dark street on a dark night and lasted one minute. How sure of the identification could he be? And was he sober on the night he had first identified Stumer?

The billfold that was found on Stumer at the time of his arrest was, perhaps, the crucial focus of the entire matter. The complaining witness said it was his. He identified it as his because it had a pin mark where he had attached his chauffeur's license.

"The pin mark is there," I said in closing, "but, ladies and gentlemen, look closely at those marks, and decide if they are fresh marks or marks made six or seven months ago when he put his 1945 license in. Where is the chauffeur's license to prove the pin marks on the license match the marks on the wallet? It isn't too much to ask. The complaining witness says he has it, but it was not introduced in evidence. The state is again withholding evidence that would not fit into their case.''

Stumer said the wallet was his, that he had bought it three and a half years before in Detroit and had paid $3.50 for it. On the stand he had seemed to know more about the wallet than the complaining witness. ''Look at the wallet,'' I said. ''Three and a half years seems reasonable for the age of the wallet and it is a good enough leather to warrant a price of $3.50 when new.'' A union official to whom Stumer had paid dues had testified as a character witness for the defendant and as one with no interest in the case. He had known Stumer for three years and had seen him with a wallet similar to the one in dispute.

''This whole case seems to hang on who owns the wallet. Has the complaining witness brought anyone in to verify the fact that they have seen him with a similar wallet?''

Other things were in Stumer's favor. He not only had repeatedly denied committing the crime, but, he said, he was twenty miles away in South Chicago at the time. That night he had finished a job and had $385. He didn't need to hold anybody up. The next day he had shipped on another job. He worked for his money.

And one more thing: ''Ladies and gentlemen, the first thing and the outstanding thing about the defendant's appearance is his missing left ear. Never once did the complaining witness identify the defendant by that mark. In felony court the judge and prosecutor asked him about this, and he said he didn't know of it.''

The jury found Stumer guilty and the judge gave him two to four years. It was a light sentence — indicating the judge did not think much of the case against Stumer.

* * *

Although I had emphasized the brevity of the time element in the Stumer case, a few years later I learned my lesson on time. My client was accused of robbery. During cross-examination the complaining witness stated that he only saw his robber for one minute but he was positive it was the defendant. In my closing argument I made much ado about the time factor. How could anyone really identify a person whom he had seen for only one minute — just a moment in his life?

Jim Brown was the assistant state's attorney opposing me and he had the last say.

"Ladies and gentlemen," he began, "Mr. Getty has played down the fact of identification. He has told you that no one can identify a person if he has only seen him for one minute. Well, I'm just going to show to you just how long one minute is. I am going to check my wrist watch right now — there it is — and I am going to tell you when one minute ends. That will tell you how long one minute is."

Well! There was an unusual quietness in the courtroom. Jim Brown walked all over the courtroom and back to the door and down to the judge's bench, and I have never, before or since, experienced such a long, unending minute. In that setting and under these circumstances, it seemed to be an eternity.

After that, I never again made light of one minute — or of one moment.

* * *

I also learned another lesson about time in my apprentice years. Believing that juries liked long speeches, I energetically supplied them with just that. But in the process of one such closing argument in Judge William Lindsay's court, a juror fell asleep.

Judge Lindsay was an elderly man who wore a hearing aid, which by then he had turned off. Finally, I managed to get the judge's attention, and he turned his hearing aid back on.

I told him the juror was asleep and requested that he wake him up.

"Hell, young man," said Judge Lindsay, "you put him to sleep. *You* wake him up!"

I dropped a book on the floor. *Whaap!* That did it.

* * *

A public defender has to scrutinize any discrepancies in the prosecution's case. Particularly if state's witnesses disagree as to what happened. It is the defender's duty to clarify every single aspect of a case that might be to his client's benefit.

This may have been all that kept Albert Ferguson from going to the pen for larceny. Ferguson had once served two years in prison, and the prosecutors always go out after a man with a record. Too often a jury is prejudiced by a man's prior conviction. So there was already one strike against Ferguson when he was tried in connection with an incident that happened at a pawnshop in the heart of the Loop. What actually happened there was subject to a three-way difference of opinion.

The shop was a father-and-son business. The son testified that he walked behind a display case to show defendant Ferguson a watch. The father was at the end of the counter. The watch wasn't what Ferguson wanted. The son went to the show window to get another watch. He closed the sliding door of the display counter. He was in the window forty seconds when his father shouted, "Stop, thief!" The son then swung around and dove for the gun they kept in the office.

As the state's presentation unwound, there were discrepancies. The father said he was in the shop's grilled cage, not at the end of the counter as the son had said. The father said his son never opened the case but went directly to the shop window, which refuted what the son had said. The father said he told defendant Ferguson, "You look like the one who stole a tray of jewelry a year ago." The son did not remember this being said. Both disagreed as to whether Ferguson was searched or not.

They agreed on three things only: the time, the fact that the defendant reached over the counter and had his hand on a watch, and that the sliding case door on the showcase was closed. In addition to this, a police officer who had appeared shortly afterward said he had never seen a watchcase out anywhere in the shop.

From the first Ferguson denied taking or ever having the

watch. He testified that in felony court he was offered a ninety-day sentence if he would plead guilty. He refused and demanded a jury trial. He was indicted. By the time of his trial he had been in the county jail for sixty days. He was too poor to make bond.

"Who opened the sliding door?" I asked the jury. "Nowhere in the testimony is there any mention of the door being opened. Both father and son have the case door closed. The son says, 'I closed the door when I went to the show window.' The father says, 'The son never opened the case door.' This is where the state's case falls. They are having the defendant put his hand through a sliding door without opening it. That's an impossibility! That's as clear-cut as the Chicago skyline on a sunny day. No matter what hocus-pocus the state's attorney puts on he is not going to get that door open.

"These men are businessmen in the heart of the Loop. They know they can't pull guns on customers and be mistaken. It would leave them open to a civil suit." I suggested to the jury that when the father realized that it was not the same man as the year before, he had to accuse him of stealing the watch in order to justify producing the guns. With all the state's witnesses, their police force and experts, they could have proven if the defendant was guilty beyond a doubt. What is agreed by the two witnesses is that the defendant had his hand on a watchcase. The police have a crime detection lab. The case could have been analyzed for fingerprints. The state didn't do this.

"The state must prove him guilty beyond all reasonable doubt. The issue is, did this man take and carry away a watch? Not, does this man have a record or not? Let's not guess this man into the pen!"

Some of the jurors were nodding their heads very slowly, in deep thought, as I drove home the facts from the viewpoint of the defense — a sure sign that you have made your point.

In a very short time the jury returned a verdict of not guilty.

* * *

What looks like an open and shut case to the police may not always be that. In one larceny trial, the defendant was accused of stealing a watch worth $71.50 from the counter of a jewelry store. When his statement to the police was introduced, he claimed he had been coerced to make it. He had signed it with his mark, or X, because he had grown up on a plantation down South and had had no schooling. The officers, denying they had used coercion, said he had read it first before putting his mark on the statement. Well, there was just one thing wrong with that testimony. The defendant, Clyde Lowry, couldn't read.

The judge then took charge. He directed the jury to find the defendant not guilty.

* * *

In one of my early jury trials, I defended seventeen-year-old Chester Britt, charged with automobile larceny. Despite his youth, Chester was being tried under the Illinois habitual criminal act. If convicted as a habitual criminal, a defendant received an automatic life sentence in prison. It was a dastardly law. Because of it many prosecutors would throw in the habitual criminal count just to force a guilty plea, but some ex-cons would roll the dice anyway — and take that jury trial. The act, fortunately, was abolished in Illinois in 1962. Chester already had a police record, so he was fair game under that law.

On the surface, Chester's guilt seemed obvious. He had been found in a 1939 maroon Buick that had been reported stolen. The owner spotted the car at 7 A.M. and called the police. The car was five blocks away from its garage. The doors were locked and the windows up. The owner didn't see anyone inside the first time. The police didn't come. Later that day, around noon, the owner went back to the car. Now he noticed the defendant, Chester Britt, sleeping in the car. He called the police again. They came and arrested Chester.

"I thought the car belonged to my friend. I got in the car about four o'clock and went to sleep. I didn't take the car," said Chester from the witness stand.

In closing, I dwelt on the holes in the state's case.

"The police find a seventeen-year-old boy asleep on the front seat of a car at about twelve o'clock noon and indict him for larceny of an auto, and that's not all — they say this young lad is a hardened habitual criminal. On this evidence the state asks you to put this boy who is not old enough to register for the draft away for his natural life.

"Now, let's see what the defendant tells us. He says that he was working as a busboy for the past four months, that his salary was between fifty and sixty dollars a week with his tips. A boy making that much money doesn't have to steal. Prior to going to the hotel, he worked for a wholesale company for four years. This boy has been on his own since he was twelve years old. He told you he sent money to his mother in Tennessee. He came north so he could have more advantages and advance himself. He is an industrious young fellow.

"August 22 was his day off. He went to a show and at about twelve o'clock he went to a party he was invited to. It had been the day of the Elks parade. Friends from the South were at the party. He drank some beer. He became groggy. A friend told him to get into his car and he would soon be down and join him. His friend had a maroon-colored Buick. He saw a maroon-colored Buick — the only car there at that time of the morning. It was open and he got into the car and went to sleep. He slept until high noon when the police woke him up. The first thing he said was: 'I thought the car was my friend's. I didn't take the car.'

"So, the state says this boy is guilty because he was found sleeping in that automobile. The state has made no further investigation. They have made no investigation in the area from which the car was taken. They have made no attempt to locate the person who *did* take this car. The state's attorney told us their attitude. He said to the defendant, 'You were in trouble before this time. We will put you away.' The fact that this boy was guilty before, in another case, has no bearing on whether he is guilty now."

The jury refused to sign the verdict of guilty as a habitual criminal but found him guilty of larceny of an automobile. The judge had some doubt; he sentenced him to one-to-three years. Without a public defender to point up the weaknesses in the prosecution's case, Chester, at seventeen, might have faced a lifetime in jail.

* * *

The cases followed, one after the other, in a haphazard order that left no way to anticipate what the next case would be like or what kind of client I would get. But for every case I pledged to do the best I could for the client, whoever he was, whatever he was accused of doing.

In the late forties I once ran up a string of fourteen straight not guilty verdicts in jury trials.

And along the way, I learned to know, and to know about, the various judges. We have had them all in Cook County: the fair and the hanging types, the competent and the incompetent, the lenient and the severe. Now there are 136 circuit court judges and 200 associate circuit court judges in the county. If a judge were on the bench for any length of time he most likely passed through the Criminal Court Building or at least sat on misdemeanor cases in the City of Chicago or the suburbs. A public defender has to become acquainted with the backgrounds of these judges, their ability with the law, their fairness and unfairness, and all those little idiosyncrasies that they, like the rest of us, have. Over a period of years a lawyer obviously has a far better opportunity to know the judges than he does the jurors.

One of the toughest judges I ever tried a case before was Judge Elmer Schnackenberg. He was severe. He handed down heavy sentences. He was of German descent with an austere, pompous manner. He was not a friendly man; in fact, he was actively *un*friendly. Young lawyers justifiably feared him because he used the contempt of court bit quite freely.

Schnackenberg was tall, stately, majestic — all the outward characteristics you would expect in a movie portrayal of a dignified Prussian jurist. He was a Republican who had come up through the regular GOP ranks and had been a state legislator. He had succeeded in being slated for the bench through one of those coalition deals whereby the Democratic powers agreed to elect a couple of Republicans to sprinkle among the tide of Democrats. In his later life during the Eisenhower administration, after having spent years on the Cook County bench, Schnackenberg rose to the Federal Appeals Court that covered the Northern District of Illinois, Wisconsin, Indiana, and Minnesota.

For reasons I'm not certain of, I was not afraid of Schnackenberg. I knew what it took to get along with him. Maybe this provided me with a feeling of security and confidence while trying a case in his court. I knew I could handle him. There was only one way to handle him, however: You did things his way. You had no choice. You had to be ready for trial when the day came. Asking for a continuance to a later day, no matter how valid the reason might be, would not make him happy. He let it be known that when he set a case it went to trial — and it did. If the public defender's office had stipulated we would be ready for trial by a certain date, then the case went to trial even if the particular assistant assigned to it was sick in the hospital. A replacement would then hurriedly be sent to his court.

Despite Schnackenberg's toughness, one of my most interesting defenses occurred in his court early in my career.

Two young men were charged with robbery. It was alleged that they had slugged and robbed Philip Stephens of eighteen dollars and his watch as he walked down a street near his home one night. Three hours later Jimmy Lester and Nick Hadley were arrested near the scene. The watch was found on Hadley. Stephens positively identified Lester and Hadley. He said it was his watch that had been found on Hadley. As an assistant public defender I was assigned to the case. It looked like an airtight one for the state's attorney.

Then a rare thing happened. A young man we'll call John Northley came to see me in the public defender's office. He was a friend of Hadley, he said, and he made some intriguing revelations. I listened. Then I sent him to see the state's attorney.

Nothing happened.

Three weeks later the case came to trial before a jury in Judge Schnackenberg's court. The assistant state's attorney confidently presented the evidence for the prosecution. The watch, recovered from Hadley, was introduced and identified. The victim formally identified the defendants as being the ones who had slugged and robbed him.

The state rested. It was the defense's turn. I called John Northley to the stand.

"Did you ever see me before?" I asked him.

"Yes," he said.

"Where?"

"I came to your office."

"Why?"

"Because I had a guilty conscience."

"Why did you have a guilty conscience?"

"Because I committed this crime."

I had him describe his version of the crime. He said he and a friend named Ralph Brown had seen Stephens get into a street fight on the night of the crime. After the fight they approached him and offered to take him to the hospital. But instead, they rolled him for his money and his watch. Northley then sold the watch to Hadley, who he said was a friend of many years. Later, when he learned his friend had been arrested and charged with robbery and was possibly headed for the pen his conscience stirred him. He decided to confess. He didn't want his friend to go to jail for a crime he did not commit. He knew I was defending Lester and Hadley, so he went to the public defender's office and told me the whole story.

"Did I send you any place?" I asked.

"Yes," he said.

"Where did I send you?"

"To the state's attorney's office."

I asked him whom he had talked to there. He told me the name of the lawyer.

"What, if anything, did you say to him?"

"I told him the same thing I had told you."

But his confession had been brushed off, and so he had returned to me and had agreed to make his confession in open court from the witness stand.

William Brumlik was prosecuting the case that day and, seeing his previously airtight case suddenly ballooned with air, he began to energetically cross-examine Northley. He tried to prove Northley was trying to take the rap for his friend. But he couldn't shake his story.

The only question was, would the jurors believe Northley?

They did: Lester and Hadley were acquitted.

Judge Schnackenberg was incensed, and he didn't bother to conceal or curb his feelings. "Your verdict is a disgrace to the people of Cook County!" he thundered at the jurors. He left no doubt as to what *his* verdict would have been had we had a bench trial instead.

The case was not quite over. Lester and Hadley were free, cleared of the charge, but there was still Northley. He had made a judicial confession, under oath and in open court before some of the most reliable witnesses in all Cook County. It had been recorded verbatim by the official court reporter. Judge, jury, lawyers, news reporters, and the usual courtroom audience; they had all heard it. Wasn't that enough for an automatic conviction?

Not quite. Northley was taken into custody and held for two days, then brought into Felony Court. By this time the prosecutors were painfully aware of having no case against him. The eyewitness had already identified Lester and Hadley. He couldn't change his story now. He couldn't suddenly say, well, after all, one of them was Northley. The police had no evidence to connect Northley with the crime. There was only his open court confession, and a confession without some other substantiating evidence is not sufficient. The police had none. And, now that his friend was off the hook, Northley had a rapidly lessening interest in solving the crime. So the robbery accusation was dropped, and Northley was free too.

Judge Schnackenberg, Brumlik, and the newspapers interpreted the judicial confession as a conspiracy between Northley and the two men on trial, and made a big thing of it.

But I never agreed that there was any collaboration. Things just don't happen that way.

CHAPTER 4
The Strangled Child

ANY LAWYER in the public defender's office of a big city like Chicago will get all the trial experience he wants, eventually handling murder, rape, theft, and burglary cases, all the serious crimes that are committed anywhere in the world. And in the early days, the experience was not only in the courtroom; our office didn't have its own investigators then, so I got into the habit of interviewing witnesses and studying the scene of the crime. It all paid off. I might not save a client from the penitentiary, or even from a life sentence, but I gained valuable experience that could save a future client's life, whittle down a term of years, or even win a not guilty in a really tough case.

Some of the worst cases that reach the public defender's office, involving the most terrible crimes, happen in the hot summer months, usually July or August. There are always rising public feelings against your client — and the prosecutors bring the case right on to trial. The state's attorney and the public defender, as public servants, are expected to prosecute and defend without delays. You can't say, as might a lawyer in private practice, that because of the press of other matters you need a postponement. The judge won't hear of it. (Today, undue publicity would be grounds for a delay until a calmer atmosphere would prevail. The

U.S. Supreme Court established this principle in several decisions during the 1960s, specifically in the Sheppard case.)

One case of this kind began on a July night, when three-year-old Frankie Hillfern was taken from his bedroom as he was sleeping. His mother was working the late shift in a factory, and his father had put him to bed at 8:30 P.M. A few hours later when the father checked the little boy's room, the bed was empty. The boy's clothing was scattered about the room. Frantically, the father began looking for his son. He notified his neighbors, with whom he earlier had been talking. About eleven that night he went to the neighborhood tavern, a gathering place for residents there, and spread the news that his child was missing. They all went to his home and a search got under way. After four and a half hours, they gave up for the night without having found a trace of the boy.

Early the next afternoon the police arrested Stephen Wola, a twenty-seven-year-old factory worker from the neighborhood, as a suspect in the child's disappearance. They took him to the Marquette District Police Station. Police Lieutenant John Scherping talked to Wola for about fifteen or twenty minutes. Then Wola told him where to find the child. He didn't want to go to the scene with them. He didn't want to look. He wasn't sure what he had done.

The nude body of the little boy was found under the porch of the house where Wola had directed them; he had been left lying on his stomach with his legs spread apart. The boy was dead and had been dead for a long time. Strangled.

By ten o'clock that night, a little over eight hours after Wola's arrest, they had his formal confession, and he was charged with the kidnap-murder.

I was first assistant to Public Defender Francis T. McCurrie by then. Like everybody else in Chicago, we read about the crime in the newspapers the next day, and we wondered if our office would wind up with the case. Wola was brought before the nearest magistrate and after the state had made a brief statement of his involvement in the kidnapping and murder he was held to the grand jury. Under the law at that time he was not required to have counsel until he had been indicted; since he couldn't afford a lawyer he just sat there in the county jail waiting.

The case was rushed along. The grand jury heard the police testimony and that of a few witnesses, and Wola was formally indicted for the murder of the little boy. He then appeared before Chief Justice Harold G. Ward of the Criminal Court and was arraigned. Wola was indigent, so the public defender was appointed to represent him.

Although I did most of the trial work, McCurrie sat in on the case with me. Before he succeeded Bachrach, he had spent thirteen years in the state's attorney's office, and had become one of the better trial lawyers there. He and Chicago's future mayor, Richard J. Daley, had gone to school together at De la Salle High School on the South Side and had been friends in their youth.

McCurrie was Irish but without the stereotyped Irish geniality. He was an intent, growling kind of man with a bad stomach who had not been an overly friendly person. But after he came to the public defender's office, and particularly after an operation that removed his ulcers, his personality changed. He became more friendly. He seemed to enjoy life more. He stuck mainly to administration of the office and was not in the courtroom much, but it was clear that he liked being for the underdog and for the underdog's protection — and that's who we had to represent, underdogs.

After indictment, I met Stephen Wola for the first time. This was before the Supreme Court rulings that protect a defendant's rights before he reaches indictment, and much damage had already been done his cause. He had already signed a confession without consulting with counsel, and the crime had become an atrocity in most Chicagoans' minds.

Gaunt and hollow-eyed and dressed in denim jail garb when I talked to him, my client was a sad sort of individual. He had grown up in a Polish section of Chicago where he had gone up to about the fourth grade and, thus, had virtually no education. He was a rather slender man and wore his hair in a crew cut. Although he did work as a factory hand, his was little more than a hand-to-mouth existence. The night before his arrest he had slept on a lawn about two blocks from the Criminal Court Building, beside a parkway that runs along California Avenue.

* * *

I began the pre-trial investigation by looking for the address on Luther Street in Chicago where the Hillfern boy had been kidnapped, but I had never heard of Luther Street. I thought I knew the streets of Chicago as well as anybody, including cab drivers, but I didn't know where Luther Street was. Then I found out, to my surprise, that it was only a few blocks from my office in the Criminal Court Building — a short street just two blocks long.

There was a tavern in the block that was the center of action for the street. Everyone who lived on Luther Street congregated at the tavern, and these people were all up in arms over the murder. Genial as I tried to be, I didn't find the neighbors very friendly or cooperative. Luther Street was like a little village, or perhaps an island, in the teeming city of Chicago.

The call I made on the Luther Street tavern helped. During that visit I was able to establish that Wola had been in the tavern on the day of the crime and that he had been drinking. I wasn't able to find out just how much Wola had drunk, but I did learn that booze was involved and that Wola was an alcoholic.

At the tavern I talked to Stanley Romasiewicz who had been in the saloon about eight-thirty that evening and had talked with Wola. In fact, Romasiewicz remembered that they had talked about a sewing machine, and that they had been together until about ten-thirty. I confirmed that Wola had been in the tavern at about eight-thirty, had had a bottle, and that both Wola and Romasiewicz had later gone outside the tavern. As I probed about among the citizens of Luther Street, I got the impression that Wola had been drinking outside, too.

Another thing I did was to have Wola examined by a psychiatrist. Because Wola understood the nature of the charges against him and he knew how to cooperate with counsel, there was no question of pleading not guilty by reason of insanity. But the psychiatrist was able to determine that Wola was a chronic alcoholic: he was abnormal, at least in that respect. After one drink, he might even have hallucinations. He might also have delirium tremens or irresistible impulses and loss of judgment. I also learned there was no permanent cure.

I read up on chronic alcoholism in medical books so that when the psychiatrist took the witness stand, I would be able to discuss the matter with him intelligently.

* * *

Away from Luther Street in the rest of Cook County the feeling was also running high. Unfortunately for Wola, his crime had come close on the heels of another child murder the preceding September. William Heirens, a seventeen-year-old University of Chicago student, had been sentenced in the Suzanne Degnan murder, in which a six-year-old girl was kidnapped, killed, dismembered, and parts of her body hidden in sewers. Heirens had pleaded guilty to that and two other murders and to a long string of burglaries. Wola was in the same jail Heirens had been in, and the Chicago newspapers gave front page headlines to the case. With this publicity, nobody had to draw me a picture explaining how rough it was going to be.

What do you do in a case like Wola's? He had admitted that he had caused the child's death. No doubt he would have settled for a prison term. Yet a plea of guilty with a negotiated sentence, such as Heirens had got, was out of the question. The state was going to demand the death penalty. But should we take a jury or a bench trial? Clarence Darrow had waived a jury in the Loeb-Leopold case, knowing he couldn't get an unprejudiced jury in Chicago and counting on the seasoned, objective legal mind of Judge John R. Caverly, chief justice of the Cook County Criminal Courts, to save his clients from the electric chair; the result, life imprisonment for them, proved the wisdom of his strategy. But I had seen another side of this. Many times a judge in a really hot case would say, "Take a jury trial. I'll give you some breaks, but take a jury trial." This meant he didn't want to stick his neck out when the public's indignation was high. In justice to your client, you couldn't disregard that kind of advice.

The judge who would hear the Wola case was Chief Justice Harold G. Ward, who had presided at the Heirens case several months earlier. A judge is appointed chief justice of the criminal courts for a one-year term; Ward held it for three terms. He was a constant worker, giving the impression he wanted to break his predecessor's record for annual volume of cases even if he had to process the cases then and there, disposing of them without delay. A former legislator who stood about five-nine and had sparse, greying hair and a little mustache, he arrived at the courthouse about eight-thirty every morning with a lunch pail, ready to go to work. He wouldn't take the time to go out to lunch in a restaurant, but ate in his chambers.

Though he had handed out life sentences for rape, he was not always excessive in his penalties. He couldn't be. In order to break a record for the number of cases handled, he had to get lawyers and defendants alike to change pleas from not guilty to guilty, and then give the defendant a light sentence; otherwise, the defendant would insist on a trial. Some sentences were very light indeed, but the cases moved along splendidly.

After Ward left the chief justice's position, some of the light deals came back to haunt him. Many defendants who should have got ten-to-twenty years but had pleaded guilty to a one-to-three year sentence were soon back out on the street, burglarizing, robbing, or killing, and when they were arrested again, the earlier light sentences were headlined in the newspapers.

In the Wola case, Judge Ward didn't have to call me aside and advise, "Take a jury." The message was clear enough without words because of the feeling in the community. I felt that if I waived the jury and asked for a bench trial, the judge would have given Wola the electric chair. Wola had confessed; there appeared no doubt that he had caused the little boy's death. So I thought we would have a better chance with twelve jurors, sworn to try the issues.

This meant we had to impanel a jury at a time when the initial notoriety of the crime was still with us. It was anything but a calm atmosphere conducive to discovering the truth in a fair and impartial manner. But there wasn't any way to delay.

It was clear at the outset that if we went before twelve persons in the city of Chicago and came out with anything less than the death penalty, it would be a major accomplishment. Even where there is a public defender system, the indigent defendant starts out behind because the resources of the state's attorney's office are so much greater. Sometimes two or three lawyers were assigned to a particular case and the lawyers had an assistant. And they had policemen for investigators.

In the Wola case, as in other big cases, the defense faced not one prosecutor, but a team. This time the team was composed of Edmund H. Grant and Edward Healy. They were major league opposition, for they both knew the law and had the trial experience and top records to prove it.

Edward Healy had been in the state's attorney's office about twelve years when I first tried cases against him. A short, stocky, jovial man, he had a quick Irish wit that went right along with a quick Irish temper. He was a hardworking, but fair, prosecutor and was also a hardworking politician at the ward level on the Near Northwest Side. In the sixties he was elected to the bench and became one of our best-qualified judges.

"Bud" Grant was about the same age as Healy and about the same size, except that he was slender. A South Sider, he was also hardworking. He had been in the state's attorney's office about fifteen years.

* * *

On August 26, a Tuesday and less than a month after the crime, we began selecting a jury in Judge Ward's court. The courtroom was jammed to the doors, as crowded as any trial I'd ever had. Many were from the "village" of Luther Street where the killing had taken place. For them the court was within walking distance.

Before the case was called, Judge Ward conferred briefly with opposing counsel. In a capital case, he pointed out, the jury must be locked up between court sessions unless the defense waives.

The long Labor Day weekend loomed ahead of us. This meant the possibility of the jurors' being locked up during the three-day holiday. Did the defense care to waive? The defense refused. It was too serious a case to permit the jurors to separate and return to their homes while the trial was in progress. If they left the courtroom each day and returned to their neighborhoods, they would be exposed over and over to the lynch-mob sentiment that seemed to prevail over the city. It was only fair that they be kept apart from the inflamed community.

It's imperative for the defense that the jury be locked up, but you don't dare tell the prospective jurors that they are going to be locked up. Neither side would tell them because they might then blame the side that told them. And you can't tell them while you're picking them or they might not want to serve. It's a delicate thing, but the possibility of being locked up usually doesn't hit the jurors until it is too late. Then it comes as a great shock to some of them as they realize they will be away from their families perhaps two or three weeks or more in a long trial. And it is not like life at the Waldorf. The jurors are left to their own company when out of the courtroom. They divide the men and women into rooms, where they are given cots to sleep on. Deputy sheriffs call their families for them to deliver personal requests and all their meals are brought in. They are not permitted to call home or to make any other contact with the outside world they have so abruptly left. Newspapers, radio and television are all verboten.

It's hard to say how being locked up will affect jurors. It depends on what kind of individuals they are. You never know for sure. It could impress upon them what it's like to be shut up in a penitentiary. And this especially might have been true in the Wola case. At that time it was the law that if the jurors made a finding of guilty in a murder case, they also set the penalty.

It was clear from the beginning, if anyone still had any doubts, that the state was going all out for the death penalty. They wanted to burn Wola in the worst way, and they needed twelve jurors to sign a death penalty verdict. Bud Grant carefully asked the jurors about the death penalty, always the indisputable sign that the prosecution was going to do all in its power to send your man to the electric chair.

We went through forty-five men and women to get our jury, but we did it quickly. There were eight women and four men — all willing to inflict the death penalty if, in their opinion, the facts warranted it. That meant the deck was stacked against the defendant once again.

The jurors were middle-aged or older except for a thirty-two-year-old woman and a man who was twenty-nine. The women generally were middle-aged and housewives. There were a few elderly men and women, whom I was happy to have on the jury. If not ideal, the jury was as good as I could expect under the circumstances.

The trial proper got under way the next morning. Wola was led into the courtroom dressed in the regulation jail uniform of blue denim shirt and khaki pants. The clothes he had been wearing were taken to the crime lab for analysis after his arrest, and he had no others. Because he appeared dressed in the fashion of the Cook County Jail it was hard for the jurors not to get an impression of "jailbird" when they saw him. He took a seat at the defense table with McCurrie and me and stared straight ahead throughout the proceedings. Extra bailiffs had been brought in to handle the crowd. Wola's life had been threatened when he was first arrested and the court didn't want to take any chances.

In my opening statement I brought in the fact that other, worse crimes had been committed in Cook County and their perpetrators had not gone to the chair.

"Heirens is down in the penitentiary for life for cutting a body up. Loeb and Leopold got life and you know what they did."

The judge broke in. "Don't say that again."

"I won't, your honor," I promised.

"It's not part of the evidence."

"I know," I agreed, "but it's part of this community."

The prosecution moved swiftly and effectively through its presentation of evidence. On that first day Grant brought eight witnesses to the court.

The first witness was Carl Hillfern, the stocky father of the three-year-old victim. By the time he took the stand the sun was already high and it was very hot in the courtroom.

Hillfern, struggling to control his emotions, told how he had first missed his son the night of July 30 and how he had then looked under the bed and in the other rooms, even the attic. Then seeing the boy's clothes were still in the bedroom his alarm grew. "He never went out without clothes, and he was able to dress himself," the father explained. He told of the search and the subsequent finding of the body under a porch on West Twenty-Sixth Street after Wola's arrest. It was a tense moment in the trial, and the little boy's mother, who was not called as a witness, broke into tears in the audience.

McCurrie cross-examined Hillfern, who said he knew Wola, but only by sight, although he "might have had a drink with him about a year ago." He had never argued with the defendant. No ransom note had been left. Nothing was taken.

Each of the neighbors who testified told of seeing Wola loitering near the Hillfern home on West Luther Street and of later joining in the search for the child after it was discovered that he was missing. On cross-examination I kept concentrating on how much Wola had drunk beginning that afternoon, trying to prove he was so intoxicated at the time he strangled the child that he was incapable of forming an intent, which must be present for the defendant to be found guilty of murder. This was not easy to do. One witness said that Wola had had a bottle of beer about five o'clock in the tavern, another bottle at eight-thirty with Romasiewicz, and that while outside the tavern he had helped drink three or four quarts. The bartender told of cashing a five-dollar paycheck for Wola and returning $4.85 after taking change out for a bottle of beer. Stanley Romasiewicz, repeating what he had told me that day on Luther Street, testified to seeing Wola, talking for some length about a sewing machine, and staying with him, inside and outside of the tavern, until ten-thirty. This testimony boosted Wola's alcoholic consumption.

The other witnesses helped piece together the state's story. A fourteen-year-old high school student testified that she heard her dog barking in the house after she had gone to bed. She heard the shuffle of feet, looked out her window, but saw nothing. Then she heard "a soft human sound." Again she saw nothing. The next day the boy's body was found behind the house.

Over my objections, because I considered them prejudicial, the state introduced into evidence photographs of the little boy's body. The pictures showed the body naked with legs spread apart, hinting of a possible sex crime, even though there had been no evidence of such. Because the case came close on the heels of the Heirens trial, many citizens seemed to believe this was a sex crime, too, and at least one newspaper had already referred to Wola as a "psychopathic sex offender."

Then the state introduced Wola's confession. We immediately objected and the jury was excused from the courtroom while we argued the admissibility. Then we put Wola on the stand. He testified that the police captain had beaten him to force him to confess. Of course, three policemen followed him to the stand to testify that no one had struck or threatened him. Judge Ward overruled the defense objection, and the jury was recalled.

Wola's confession was read to the jury. This was the first time we had heard it. In those years, unlike today, the defendant was not entitled to a copy of the statement even after he had signed it. But at least part of it was helpful; he never stated that he had committed any unnatural sex acts, and this seemed to be what the prosecution was trying to suggest.

He told of taking the little boy from his bed and the crucial portion read: "I just sat and hugged him ten minutes. I held him in my lap. I told him I liked him so much I could choke him and I did choke him."

His description of the fatal act made me think of the strong-backed, dull-witted Lenny in John Steinbeck's novel, *Of Mice and Men*. Lenny liked to keep mice for pets and stroke their soft, velvety fur. But as he told his sidekick, "I'd pet 'em, and pretty soon they bit my fingers and I pinched their heads a little and then they was dead — because they was so little." Lenny killed the mice, then a pup while petting it, and then a young woman.

In a case like the Wola trial you keep going after the regular courtroom hours, if the judge is willing, and Judge Ward was. He held court that night and the state called Dr. Jerry Kearns, the coroner's pathologist who had examined the child's body. For the first time in the trial, Wola sat forward in his chair and listened intently as if he himself didn't know what he had done and would only believe an expert. I had previously talked with Dr. Kearns and knew pretty much what he would testify to.

Dr. Kearns described the bruises and scratches he had found on the child's head, face, and neck. There was a bruise on the scalp, four scratch marks on the left side of the face, one scratch at the nose, a bruise over the cheekbone, three scratch marks on the neck. The tongue bore teeth marks. The scalp tissue revealed hemorrhage. The organs of the neck showed hemorrhage. There was congestion in the passages of the nose.

On cross-examination I asked Dr. Kearns if he had found any evidence that any sexual act had been committed and he said there was none. I was also able to bring out that strangulation causes a convulsion that triggers the biting of the tongue. This was necessary in order to dispel absolutely from the jurors' minds that there was any evidence whatsoever of any sexual or unnatural act. Establishing this was crucial to our strategy.

The state called one more witness. Lieutenant John Scherping of the detective bureau had taken Wola's confession following the arrest. On cross-examination I went into Wola's drinking. Scherping said Wola had shown no evidence of intoxication. This interview, of course, had been many hours after the crime, so we got around to the amount of alcohol Wola had told Scherping he had drunk. It amounted to four shots of whiskey, ten bottles of beer, and one fifth of wine.

With Scherping's testimony the state rested its case.

The state, in the persons of Grant and Healy, had gone all out to present as tight a case as it could. At one point in the trial the pair had even got into a heated argument about how the case should best be presented. They were back in chambers during a recess and I happened to be present. From what I saw of it, Grant had apparently asked one of the witnesses a question that Healy considered a tactical mistake. This started the stew going. Within a few minutes Healy became so upset and excited that I was afraid he would physically throw Grant out of the window of the Criminal Court Building. This kind of action was extremely rare, for they were excellent prosecutors and worked well as a team, but in this trial their emotions had become overwrought as they gave it everything they had. This friction did not make me unhappy. Any disagreement among the opposition could only be helpful to our side.

* * *

We began our defense of Wola the next morning.

The defense of this kind of man poses special problems. None of his friends, if he had any, was in the courtroom. He had no money or influence. He was a loner, a sad sort of person; certainly he was someone to be pitied, someone who needed psychiatric attention. In brief, he was someone who should not be held totally responsible for what he had done. What enlightened person in the middle of the twentieth century in one of the world's great urban centers would have held Steinbeck's Lenny totally responsible? Few, if any. But Lenny was an imaginary character out of a book. Wola was a flesh-and-blood, breathing man. And the community was whipped to a fever pitch.

Our strategy was to show, through his family and others who would testify, what a hard life he had had, and particularly how his stepfather had reacted to him. The psychiatrist had said he showed no signs of mental disease, but he had taken severe beatings as a child and once had been hit accidentally in the head with an ax. I had witnesses who would testify to this.

The first defense witness was a sister of Wola who testified that her parents had separated when she and her brother were children. She and Stephen had been placed in an orphanage later. Did her brother drink? Yes, since he was eighteen years old. A cousin testified that she had seen Wola drunk four times during the previous year. Other witnesses whom I had to subpoena produced similar observations. They left no doubt that he was frequently drunk.

At this point we produced what was to many people a surprise. We called Dr. William H. Haines, head of the Criminal Court Behavior Clinic, as a defense witness, although he had already given an opinion that Wola was sane.

Dr. Haines gave the jury a clearer picture of the defendant's personality. Wola, he testified, had an IQ of 72, which was considered "a borderline intelligence." He was not a sexual psychopath — (a statement that couldn't be made too often in this case!) — he was a "chronic alcoholic."

"What is a chronic alcoholic, Doctor?"

"A chronic alcoholic is a person addicted to the constant use of alcohol and unable to stop using it of his free will," he said.

"And this describes the defendant, Stephen Wola?"

"Yes, it does."

Then we got down to details. Was alcoholism normal? No, it was not. Then would you say it was abnormal? Could an alcoholic have hallucinations, delirium? Melancholia? Irresistible impulses? Loss of judgment? Yes, he could.

Eventually I was able to establish through Haines' testimony that alcoholism could cause madness, and that a paternal instinct in the defendant, coupled with a mentally sick mind, could have brought on the hugging and the squeezing of the little boy.

Then I called Stephen Wola as a witness. I had to put him on the stand and hope for the best from the jury. There's nothing so sympathetic as a man coming in and confessing; when his life is in their hands jurors almost *can't* give the death penalty. But first it had to be demonstrated to them, in Wola's own words, what life had been like for him, and why he had ended up in that courtroom, facing death at their hands.

He was a pathetic person in the blue denim shirt and faded trousers they had given him in the jail. In a sometimes weary, singsong voice, with a heavy Polish accent, he testified that his parents had been divorced and he had been placed in an orphanage when he was seven. His mother remarried, after which he was given a home again, but his stepfather drank a lot and he himself started drinking when he was seventeen. On one occasion, he said, his stepfather had hit him on the head with an ax.

"I drank almost every day," he said.

How had he supported himself?

"I had jobs here and there, but I never had steady work. The longest job I had was three weeks."

He had a dishonorable discharge after a year and a half of Army service. Although he had been sent to a psychiatrist, he had continued to drink while in the service. At one time, he said, he had bought moonshine liquor for five cents a glass in the house where the little boy had been kidnapped before the Hillferns had occupied it.

"Do you hear voices?" I asked as we discussed what drinking did to him.

"Yes, once in a while," he said.

When he drank a great deal, he said, he would hear strange voices and then his mind would go blank.

And there was other vital background material that he could supply.

"Do you like little children?" I asked.

"Yes, I love them very much!" he said, and then began sobbing as he lowered his head.

I asked him to recount the events of the night of the slaying. He told of being drunk on beer, wine, and whiskey as he walked home toward Western Avenue.

"Everything went dark in front of me," he said, and as if reliving it, he buried his face in his hands and began crying. After he had wiped his eyes with a dirty handkerchief, he went on. "There was something on my mind. I tried to fight it off, but I couldn't. I didn't go home. I just walked.

"I was afraid, afraid, afraid. Something blurred in my eyes. I didn't know what it was. I tried to walk it off. Everything was twisted in my mind. I could not help it. Everything was ripping me apart. I was afraid. I didn't know what it was and I started walking down an alley.

"I came to the alley and I had a feeling I wanted to hold something, anything. What it was I couldn't remember. I saw a bluish light in a house and walked in. I wanted to hold something. I went in and saw this thing on the bed. I picked it up and held it. Then I knew it was a little boy. I picked up the little boy off the bed and ran out the door. I was scared. I hugged him and something, I don't know what, tried to tear me apart. I heard voices. It was like everything was tearing me apart. Then I put him under the steps."

He ran across the street to a park. He woke up the next morning on the grass. "There was a bad taste in my mouth. I had been trying to eat grass." He didn't remember at first what had happened.

"I don't know why I did it!" he screamed and broke down into sobbing before the tense courtroom.

After he had regained his composure, for the third time I asked, "Did you know you had killed him?"

"No, sir."

"Did you know what you had done?"

"No, I never realized what I had done until around noontime the next day."

When the police arrested him the following day, he testified, "My mind was in a cloud."

I asked, "Did the police strike you?"

"Yes, they did."

Later, he said his mind cleared and he gave a statement to Lieutenant Scherping.

Grant cross-examined Wola, eliciting from him that he did not know why he had seized the Hillfern boy by the windpipe and had struck him on the head. But he admitted he had been able to direct the police to the alley stairway where the body was found.

That was it. With Wola's testimony the defense rested.

* * *

In this case the lawyers on both sides agreed not to have time limits for our closing arguments. It was an important enough case to allow each as much time as he needed. I closed for the defense. It was two in the afternoon when I began speaking. The courtroom was packed. All the population of Luther Street, young and old, must have been there. The crowd overflowed into the hall outside.

My only goal was to save Wola's life. So I first dwelled on reasons why they shouldn't take his life. Death, after all, was just one of the penalties provided by Illinois law. Then I moved toward the evidence that had been heard.

"The state has presented a lot of witnesses, witnesses that have known the defendant all his life or a great portion of his life from that little block which is known as Luther Street, a street only two blocks in length, a setting in itself. Those people say that they have known Stephen for a long time. Some of the defense witnesses were even with him on the night of July 30th. The defense witnesses have kind of held back as to how much he drank, and there is a reason why, ladies and gentlemen. They are from Luther Street. A vicious crime has taken place in their block and it is natural that there is feeling against this man. I do not blame them if they are trying to, well, just place up a shield as to how much he was drinking with them and as to how much they saw him drink. You can't blame them for that, but you have a right to draw on your own experiences and your own knowledge of human nature.

"But we brought witnesses in from that same block under subpoena, you may say these were witnesses that did not even want to be here, and the state tried to cross them up and recross them, and these people said they have known Wola for years and he was drunk all the time. One man even said he saw him intoxicated one hundred times!"

I discussed Dr. Haines' testimony and what chronic alcoholism meant, then reviewed Wola's early life and showed how his mind could have been affected by drinking.

"I am not asking you to find this young man not guilty of the crime as charged. We are trying to aid you in making a decision.

That is our only objective in our defense of this boy: to try to give some explanation of this terrible crime, to show how it could happen in the city of Chicago.

''Did this boy have all of his faculties? Was there something forcing him? Did he know what he was doing at the time he walked into the home of the Hillferns and took the little child from the bed? Did he have the malice aforethought that they say he had in this indictment? Could he have? A boy suffering with such a mental disorder as that? He cried on the stand and he said, 'Things were black and I did not know what I was doing. I love little children and I took this little boy from his bed, and I don't know why I did it, and I don't know what I did.' You must decide the fate of this type of boy.

''I am not trying to look for sympathy for this boy, but we are trying to analyze the cold facts. The state says, 'We want you to kill him.' The state through Mr. Healy and Mr. Grant says, 'Kill him.' They think you are a machine and not human beings. They want you to say, 'Let us kill him; give us the authority to pull the switch on this boy,' even though there is something wrong with his mind, even though they know he was drinking liquor and beer and there is no telling what amount you have to drink — a man that has been suffering with that disease — and what effect it would have upon him.

''The state cannot show a reason for this crime. In other words, there is no motive. The state is weaving little things in, trying to show a sex motive. Well, now, there is no sex motive and if they had concrete evidence of it, it would have been presented here. But they have shown you pictures of how this little boy was lying, attempting to create a prejudice in your mind. And you have heard how this little scheme to try to establish a sex motive was worked. They took away the defendant's clothing and never gave it back to him. He had to put on the clothing they hand out in the county jail. But nothing was on the clothing that they took away. You heard Dr. Kearns, who examined the boy's body. There was no sex angle; no sex act had been committed. But they are trying to weave it in, creating a prejudice. Why, there is enough prejudice against this young man already without that.

"There is no ransom; there is no burglary; there is no answer as to why it was done. The defendant can't tell you. His mind was blanked out. He did not know what he was doing.

"Well, now, if there is no motive in a crime, no matter how dastardly it is, that takes it out of the class of deep guilt. You have heard of other crimes in other states and in this state where there were motives. Maybe those people went to the electric chair and maybe they didn't. And you don't have to go far back, ladies and gentlemen, in this very city where crime has been committed and there have been motives that were more dastardly than this. Did these criminals go to the electric chair or did they get life imprisonment?

"There are a lot of reasons against giving the death penalty in this case. You must know by this time that that is what we are fighting against. We do not feel it is right; some of the reasons are the mental condition that must have existed in this man, the drinks he had the night it happened, the drinks he has had all his life. These are sound reasons against giving the death penalty.

"Another reason is, ladies and gentlemen, surely we are in an advanced society, we are progressing and not going backwards, and we do not take an eye for an eye and a tooth for a tooth like the Philistines while teaching love and affection. Our society has advanced far enough that we have medical science to take care of men. And, my God, why didn't medical science take care of this boy before this happened?

"I feel sorry for the Hillferns. It is too bad. But I also, maybe because I am defending this boy, have a deep sorrow for him; for his predicament in the society he was kicked around in, in a society that lets minors drink moonshine, in a society that lets a human being become a chronic alcoholic.

"Ladies and gentlemen, if you give this boy the electric chair, are you ever going to be sure that you did the right thing? Are you going to think about it when you are alone, when there is no one around, when some tragedy hits you? Are you going to think,

'Did I do the right thing?' You are never going to do that. Because you are taking life, you will never be sure.

"When you leave here after the verdict is reached and your loved ones at home ask you about it, are you going to tell them, 'The rest of them overpowered me and I said they could electrocute him, but I wasn't sure, I was in doubt'? Are you going to give that slim excuse? Ladies and gentlemen, *be sure* when you return a verdict in this case.

"Our religions teach us to be merciful, to have love and affection. And there is going to come a time when we are going to be judged by a Supreme Judge, and you may be asked, 'Did you judge others with mercy?' For it is written that those who do not judge with mercy will not be judged with mercy. By electrocuting this boy you are not going to cure the ills of this state or of this nation.

"We are trying to show you, ladies and gentlemen, why this should not be done. That is what we are fighting for. And the state's attorneys are hollering for death because they are sent up here to holler for it, but you are the supreme judge and you only have to square with your own conscience and Almighty God. And they are asking you to electrocute this boy. Well, ladies and gentlemen, if he is to be sent to the electric chair you are the ones that have to do it. And when this boy walks down that aisle to the electric chair and there is the smell of burning flesh, and there is the twitching of the muscles of the body, where are you going to be that night? Are you going to have Grant and Healy consoling you and telling you, 'You did the right thing'? Are you ever going to be sure you did the right thing? Ladies and gentlemen, you will never be sure. You will never be sure because of the many circumstances in this case, because of the condition of this man's mind. There was no malice aforethought here. He did not plan this. There was no motive. It is something that he can't even explain.

"I have tried to help you in this case. I know it is a terrible responsibility, ladies and gentlemen. All I asked of you when I selected you as jurors was that you do the right thing and the decent thing. I know you are going to do that. Thank you."

Bud Grant closed for the state. From the beginning he adamantly and vehemently asked for the death penalty, citing the cruelty of the defendant, how in stealth he went into the home and to the manger of a three-year-old boy, took him from his very bed, and then like an animal killed him. It was a "ferocious and fiendish crime" and because of it, Wola had forfeited his right to live. Then he wound up with this thundering denunciation of the defendant:

"There is only one way that sex crimes are going to be stopped in Chicago, and that is by the imposition of the death penalty!"

The trial had begun on a Tuesday. Now it was Thursday afternoon and Judge Ward was charging the jury. At seven that evening, Wola's fate was in the hands of those eight women and four men.

That night as the wait began entire families from Luther Street came in to hear the verdict. The crowd spilled over into the hallway. It was the tensest time of the trial.

The jurors deliberated slightly more than two hours; they reached a verdict at 9:10 P.M. Judge Ward, who had delayed his own dinner, returned to the courtroom. At 9:25 the verdict was read.

Guilty.

There was a rising murmur from the crowd. Many of them were standing. Others were in the hallway. A bailiff called for silence.

Then the foreman announced the punishment to a hushed audience: Imprisonment in the state penitentiary for life.

Under Illinois law this meant he would be able to apply for parole after serving twenty years. It was a victory.

The crime had been committed on July 30. The trial had lasted three days. Now it was August 28, less than thirty days after the act. An accused person in the United States is entitled to a speedy trial. In cases like Wola's the defendant got one whether he wanted it or not.

CHAPTER 5
Old Pros

ORDINARILY, Bear Collins and Tommy Holden wouldn't have added to the public defender's caseload. But each, in his own way, was down on his luck.

Nolan "Bear" Collins, as I will call him, had once been associated with the Bugs Moran gang in Chicago, which would have been sufficient for many people to classify him as a professional criminal. Some of Bugs Moran's boys had been on the losing end of the St. Valentine's Day massacre in 1929. That was all before Bugs went to the pen for an out-of-state job. When I represented Bear he was forty-seven and there was no Moran gang; Bugs had been sentenced to prison.

Bear was accused of engaging in a little tavern holdup at Clark and Lake Streets, downtown in the Loop area. It wasn't much of a tavern, but the state claimed $2,300 had been taken on that Sunday morning in question. Bear had been captured six months after the holdup, identified by an eyewitness, and brought to trial.

Although Bear was the only one arrested and tried for the holdup, there were supposed to have been two men on the robbery. The state's story was that two men — one short man, and the other identified as Bear — had entered the tavern with guns drawn on this particular Sunday morning. A porter was cleaning up and minding the store until the owner came in, and the bandits ran him into the men's lavatory for safekeeping. He was the eyewitness.

There was money in the till of the cash register and it was assumed that the pair knew it and made the score. The investigating policemen testified that the witness who had been herded into the men's lavatory told them that and the money was taken and then the men left. The porter positively identified Bear as being one of the men, six months later in a lineup at the police station.

Just before the eyewitness was about to take the stand, Bear touched me on the arm.

"When he comes on, press him," he whispered. "I never told you this before, but now you press him, because there were two other men there."

The police had said there was only one witness and had stated that the porter told them he was the only one present. Why had he said he was the only one? Was he shielding someone?

The witness took the stand. He described the holdup, how two men with guns entered and drove him into the washroom. He said they told him to stay there or they would shoot him. He didn't know how much money had been taken, but the owner had told him the sum was $2,300.

I cross-examined him.

"Did you tell the police you were the only one there?"

"Yes," he said, "I told the police I was the only one."

"Well, as a matter of fact, wasn't there another person herded into the washroom with you?"

"Yes," he said after a slight hesitation, "there was."

"Why didn't you tell the police this?"

"Well, they didn't ask me and I didn't tell them."

"Do you know what happened to the other person?"

"No, I don't know."

I kept digging, based on the earlier prompting from Bear. I asked the witness if there weren't a second man in addition to the one he had admitted had been on the scene at the time. Again he admitted that there was still another man. This brought up two additional witnesses who could have identified the bandits — not one of whom had been previously mentioned by the witness or the police and neither of whom the state had called to testify.

Suddenly the trial was going Bear's way. Obviously he had known this information, but he hadn't said anything to me until he saw what the police did. Now the cross-examination had cast doubt in the jurors' minds. If the porter was covering up for himself or someone else, I could see them thinking, then maybe some of the other things he said were not quite right either.

Then Bear got on the stand and said he had not been at the tavern when the stickup took place and was not, in fact, even in Chicago. He said he was in Milwaukee, that day. But obviously, he knew a number of significant things that had happened at Clark and Lake, however he had come by that information.

On the stand he made a proper impression. He was a pro. He knew the ropes and recognized the value of certain information and knew what to do with it.

The jury deliberated for ten minutes. The state's case was so weakened by the unexpected turn of events that the jurors' minds were filled with doubt. They found him not guilty.

Bear walked out of the courtroom a free man and I never saw him again.

* * *

Thomas J. Holden had much bigger troubles: he was on trial for murder. For another defendant the case might have been classified as a fatal family squabble. But for Holden it became a headline story flavored with "gangsterism."

Tommy "Red" Holden had a colorful past. He was one of the last of the old-time gangsters. Chicago born, from the city's West Side, Holden had taken the lead role in the last of the mail train robberies when he and others held up a Grand Trunk train in 1926 at Evergreen Park, a suburb of Chicago. The haul was better than $135,000. It made his reputation, gaining him publicity that sometimes equaled that of Al Capone and other gangsters.

Two years later a federal agent arrested him. He was convicted and sent to Leavenworth. But in 1930 he and his cellmate made a successful break out of Leavenworth and remained at large for more than two years. Then the FBI caught him and he was sent to Alcatraz, "The Rock," out in San Francisco Bay. He served fifteen years this time.

Holden was a small, frail-looking man, but he was as tough as he was little. At one time a police magazine article had billed him as one guy who could run Al Capone out of Chicago.

In all he did seventeen years after being convicted of the mail train robbery.

He was released from prison in 1947 at the age of fifty-one. He returned to Chicago, married, and lived quietly with his wife Lillian. Then one night in 1949 he and his wife joined a little drinking party in a tavern. (Holden apparently didn't drink much.) There was an argument. Holden abruptly left the tavern, went back to his apartment, and went to bed.

Tempers had flared in the argument, which had involved his wife, her brother Raymond Griffin, and her half-brother John Archer, Jr. Afterwards, they all went after Holden, following him to the apartment.

A few minutes later the dispute was over. His wife and her brothers entered Holden's bedroom and Holden fired four shots: Lillian Holden, Ray Griffin, and John Archer all lay dead.

Holden fled the scene and soon afterward the city. He remained at large for two years, during which time he headed the FBI's Ten Most Wanted list two years in a row, winning out over several thousand other fugitives. On one occasion he was considered "a menace to every man, woman, and child in America." His reputation had grown.

He was finally picked up in Beaverton, Oregon, where he was working as a plasterer under an assumed name. A fellow worker on the construction job recognized him from a "wanted" circular. He was returned to Chicago and tried for the murder of John Archer, Jr. I shared Holden's defense with Art McGloon, another assistant public defender. Art was later to become a state senator from the West Side and later the minority leader in the legislature. In the seventies he was appointed to the Illinois Appellate Court. We pleaded Holden not guilty and thought there was a valid pleading of self-defense for his acts. Certainly there were extenuating circumstances.

The jury trial, before eight women and four men, was held in Judge Abraham Lincoln Marovitz's court. Marovitz was one of the best. I had known him when he was a defense lawyer in private practice. Before that he had spent some time in the state's attorney's office. He was well-connected in Democratic politics and was a close friend of Richard J. Daley.

Marovitz grew up in the Jewish ghetto on the West Side. He had come up the hard way and he never forgot to show compassion for others. He was a man who wanted to use his judicial powers to do good for others who were in trouble and might be encouraged to do better in life. On many occasions I had heard him mention that if it weren't for the grace of God and for his mother he would probably have been in the same situation himself. So he was a sympathetic man, particularly with the underdog. If anyone was convicted of a crime, he would place that person on probation if it could be done. Once on probation Marovitz didn't forget the person. He had him also report to him personally. He gave advice to some probationers if they sought it or if he thought they needed it.

He was a distinguished looking man, slight of stature, and a dapper dresser who always wore immaculately-tailored clothes. A great family man, he lived with his mother, a major influence in his life, and took care of her until she died.

When Marovitz was assigned to the Criminal Court he requested that I be assigned to his courtroom exclusively. He knew me and had confidence in me, and he wanted the indigent in his courtroom represented well.

* * *

The problem for Holden was in the testimony from the witness stand — the major witness's and his own. The sixty-four-year-old mother of all three of the victims testified that she saw Holden shoot her son, John Archer. What proved damning to Holden was that she said she saw no evidence of a struggle in the room where the shooting took place. That made the killing seem somewhat colder than Holden contended it was.

Holden had quite a different story. He said that he had walked away from the argument, but that they had come after him right into his own home. He denied that his mother-in-law was in the room at the time. He said he was the only one still living who was there and knew what had really happened when the shooting took place. To bring this out I had to put Holden on the stand, and once he was on the stand, the state could bring in his past criminal record during cross-examination. That's just what occurred. The state dragged in his long history of gangsterism, despite his already having paid for it with long years of his life. It became impossible for the jury not to let those facts color their thinking, impossible not to look upon him as a "gangster." Yet if he *had* killed in self-defense — and we had a stong case for it — why should it matter whether he was an ex-convict or a clean-cut working man who had never even had a traffic ticket? But as long as the prosecutor is allowed to bring out the witness's former record as a means of attacking his credibility, the jury will always weigh the prior fact of what the accused did years ago — in Holden's case, over twenty years earlier.

The jury found him guilty of murder and gave him twenty-five years in the penitentiary. The jurors realized that Holden was now up in years and not in the best of health, and that there was still an element of self-defense in the case. For these reasons he was never tried for the killing of his wife or of her brother Raymond.

A few years after his conviction, Tommy Holden, the last of the big-time train robbers, died in prison.

But Tommy Holden and Bear Collins had proved one thing — that as far as the public defender's office is concerned, a professional criminal is just like any other client.

Which is to say, he's broke, and in a jam.

CHAPTER 6

Execution, Gangland Style

JUDGING BY SOME CHICAGO NEWSPAPER REPORTS, time began on February 14, 1929.

That's the date of the St. Valentine's Day massacre of seven gangsters on the city's North Side, and certainly it is a landmark of violence. Since then, almost every multiple killing has been compared to it. In a city that has nurtured Johnny Torrio, Dion O'Banion, and Al Capone, this comes as no surprise. With the right case, the press can have a field day. And if you're a public defender in that case, you've got your work cut out for you.

That was the way it was in the Huskens trial. One Chicago paper said the crime had ". . . made a record for savage murder that had not been reached since the St. Valentine's Day massacre." Strong words.

Here is how it started:

On a freezing-cold, snow-draped December night (it dipped to 10 below zero), three men walked into a garage operated by George Skorios and Peter Murzikias. The trio consisted of Jack Ryan, an ex-convict in his forties, and two teen-age youths later described as "minor police characters," Robert Gardona and Alvin Huskens. The scene was on the near-South Side, between the Union Stock Yards and White Sox Park. From the garage you could walk to either of these famed Chicago sites in a matter of minutes.

The police's story was that Ryan, Gardona, and Huskens entered the garage looking for Skorios, because Ryan and Huskens had suspected Skorios had turned them in as robbery suspects. Gardona, according to this version, went along because Ryan and Huskens were his pals.

When they entered the garage, Skorios wasn't there. So they pulled guns on the four men who were there: Andrew Litral, twenty-two; Max Steuben, twenty-nine; Peter Murzikias, twenty-eight, and John Driffield, sixteen. These four were held prisoners.

When Skorios, thirty-three, returned, there was a fight outside and then Ryan shot him in the head, killing him. Police said Gardona also may have shot him, but Gardona denied it.

The dispute with Skorios had been settled. And though Ryan and his two friends had nothing against the four prisoners, they were now witnesses to a murder. So the Ryan trio herded Driffield, Steuben, Litral, and Murzikias into a car. All four were ordered into the back floorboard, where they lay stacked on top of each other. Then they were taken for a ride, gangland style.

Huskens, behind the wheel, drove fast until they reached Brookfield, a South Side suburb almost due west from the garage; Brookfield is just west of Cicero, the suburb that Al Capone made famous.

Then, the police version continued, Ryan shot Murzikias, pulled him out of the car, and dumped him in a snow-filled ditch. A little farther along, Gardona shot Driffield and he too was thrown into a ditch and left for dead. Two miles away, Litral was killed and his body dumped. The trio reached McCook, another suburb directly south of Brookfield, before Steuben was killed. Then they drove back to Chicago.

There was just one deviation from the pattern of the usual gang-style killings: Murzikias and Driffield not only lived, they later testified in court. That night Murzikias, seriously wounded, crawled on his knees through snow-covered fields. When he reached a telephone he called to warn his family: "Ryan's gone crazy. He killed George and shot me and he may come after you."

On the basis of Murzikias' call, police quickly identified Ryan's companions. They arrested Huskens first at a hotel close to Jackson Park and he told them where to find Ryan and Gardona on South Winchester Avenue. Gardona escaped through a window; he reached the roof, then jumped from roof to roof until he got down and away.

Ryan, meanwhile, was hiding in a bedroom. When Police Sergeant Frank Pape located his hiding place, Ryan, who was armed, tried to escape, and Pape unloaded his revolver into Ryan, destroying him on the spot.

Gardona gave himself up a few days later.

In custody now, Huskens allegedly told police that Gardona had shot Litral but that he himself had fired only one shot and that into the air. In his story, Huskens called Ryan a "mad dog." Irony of ironies, the label was taken up by the newspapers — and applied to him and Gardona as well.

In due time, Huskens and Gardona were brought to trial for the murder of George Skorios. Each had a well-known lawyer for counsel as they were tried. They were convicted and each sentenced to 199 years in the penitentiary.

The state's attorney was not satisfied. The Case of the Mad Dog Killers was a headline case. Although Ryan's bunch was not an established underworld element as we know it today, he was possibly developing a gang and might have done so if these killings and arrests had not happened. The state wanted to send Huskens and Gardona to the electric chair. So they brought them to trial again, this time for the death of Andrew Litral.

Everybody — defendants, lawyers, the entire city of Chicago — knew what the stakes were in the second trial. State's Attorney John Boyle said publicly that if his prosecutors didn't win the death penalty in the Litral case, they would try again in the death of Max Steuben.

The time was in the late forties and the opponents of capital punishment were few, compared to today.

* * *

As assistant public defender, I was appointed to defend Huskens in the second trial because by then he was out of funds.

For the second trial Gardona had the well-known Charles A. Bellows as his attorney. Charlie Bellows had a strong reputation in criminal cases and was a veteran of the Cook County Criminal Court Building.

Bellows and I were not a defense team in the strictest sense: the main objective for each of us was to save his particular client's life. Bellows had nothing to do with Huskens' defense (in fact, he had attempted unsuccessfully to sever the two defendants, so there would be separate trials), and I had nothing to do with Gardona's. But it was a joint trial and we were arrayed together against the prosecution.

The state's attorney's office sent in one of its top prosecution teams, Alexander J. Napoli and Edward F. Healy. I had tried the Wola case against Healy and Grant, and I had tried several jury trials against the team of Napoli and Richard Austin, who were among the best anywhere. I didn't win many jury trials against them because if they felt they didn't have a strong case they would call for a dismissal of the charges or indictment. Later, when Napoli and Austin became judges, this same quality spilled over into their bench role and they became excellent judges; they were fair and impartial, and they knew the law. Judge Austin was to be an unsuccessful Democratic candidate for Governor, and Napoli was rated one of the top federal judges by a group of lawyers practicing in the federal courts.

In the Huskens-Gardona trial, as in all of his others, Napoli, a dark-complexioned, dark-haired man, was always the calm center of any storm. A good orator, he never became excited or overly heated as lawyers sometimes do in the midst of battle. He knew when to quietly and effectively bore into a witness, and he would lay the facts out cold before a jury or a judge without much emotion at all.

Selecting the jury was exhausting work for both sides. By then the papers had already habitually referred to the defendants as "Mad Dog Killers," which increased the defense's burden to find unprejudiced jurors. For its part, the state was qualifying the jury for the death penalty to make sure that the panel wouldn't hesitate to burn the defendants if convinced they were guilty.

We began on a Thursday in the first week of the new year. It took seven days to get a jury. We examined, in all, 179 veniremen. The defense exhausted its peremptory challenges; at the end we had to accept one man who admitted knowing fifty policemen.

John A. Sbarbaro was a fast, hard-working judge. He wanted trials held efficiently and without any waste of time. He was habitually in his chambers at seven in the morning and if you wanted an early trial, he would hold it at seven in the morning.

His favorite expression, which he was almost constantly using, was "What's next?" Or, if he had just wound up a minor case, he would immediately ask, "Do we have another case?" In Judge Sbarbaro's courtroom one case readily blended into another; an imperceptive visitor might miss the words of transition and become confused as to which case he was hearing.

When a witness got through testifying, Judge Sbarbaro would say, "Okay, what's next?" The next witness had to be ready. A lawyer never knows how long it will take for a witness to testify. You might assume that three to four witnesses would fill up a whole day, but if things moved quickly, there might be time for ten. With a judge like Sbarbaro you couldn't afford to guess and be wrong. In his court where the word *leisure* was unpronounceable, you had to corral all of your witnesses and keep them there waiting.

That's tough to do in any court. Witnesses get restive. If they won't stay, you have to get a bench warrant and hold them in custody which you don't like to do in a criminal case. You need to keep the witnesses' good will for the sake of your client.

In the Huskens-Gardona trial, all the lawyers knew Judge Sbarbaro and his ways. We took extra effort to prevent anything that might slow down the trial. We worked from nine in the morning until twelve o'clock at night presenting the case. The jury was locked up, as was required for capital cases, and Judge Sbarbaro didn't want the jurors sitting idle over in their county jail jury quarters when he could dispose of the case and send them home. That's the way he operated.

* * *

The trial, as always, began with the opposing lawyer's opening statements. The prosecutors can't argue the evidence at this point, but they do summarize what they expect the evidence will show. Then the defense has an opportunity to alert the jurors to the defense's viewpoint of the evidence. This is usually the first time the jurors have been in a courtroom and the opening session provides them an idea of what this spontaneous drama is going to be about.

Healy, of course, demanded the death penalty.

The first major prosecution witness was Peter Murzikias who testified that he had sold a 1938 Ford to Ryan for $650 which included accessories and additional work he wanted done on it. He had received $225; Ryan was to have paid the balance on the date the car was ready to go.

At three o'clock on the afternoon of the shootings, he had seen Jack Ryan at a restaurant in the block. Ryan asked him how the car was coming along. Although Skorios had had a fight with Ryan two weeks before, there had been no unpleasantries that afternoon between Murzikias and Ryan.

That evening, the witness continued, he was at the garage, along with Skorios, Andrew Litral, and Max Steuben. Steuben was helping Skorios work on a car; Litral was a customer. Steuben went after sandwiches, later returned. After he left, John Driffield came in. Then Skorios went after some parts.

Soon afterward, Ryan and Gardona walked in. Gardona asked, "Where is George?" Murzikias said he had gone to get parts. A few minutes later the phone rang and Ryan commanded, "Don't talk in Greek." Murzikias answered the phone. Skorios was on the other end and said he couldn't get the parts. Ryan had a gun out and listened in on the conversation, then hung up the receiver. Ryan told the three men, "Go to the center of the garage." Gardona was at the exit with his hand in his coat.

"Why aren't you working on my car?" Ryan asked. He still had his gun out. Murzikias explained they had had to stop to put bolts on Litral's car. Ryan walked out of the garage. Gardona, a gun in his hand, told them, "Stand where you are. Get your hands out of your pockets." Gardona's gun looked like a .38.

Healy asked, "Does this appear to be the gun?" He showed him one.

"Yes. That is the gun," said the witness.

Then Murzikias continued his story. The four captives in the garage were ordered to line up and file out after Huskens. They walked thirty feet to the alley and then to a waiting car. Huskens ordered them to get inside and sit on the floor. Murzikias heard a car and recognized it as his own which Skorios had driven off.

Murzikias heard voices and could see the figures of Skorios, Ryan, and Gardona. He heard scuffling. Murzikias told Huskens he shouldn't be mixed up in this. Huskens told him they were just going to beat up Skorios. Then Huskens said, "Don't move or you'll get shot," and he left the car.

Then Murzikias heard a shot. Huskens only had one gun when he came back to the car. Murzikias heard Skorios call for help. There was another shot.

Ryan and Gardona came to the car with blood on their faces. Ryan said, "You are a good boy, Bobby," to Gardona. Huskens started backing up the car.

Ryan had a .45 automatic. As they drove over a bridge on Thirty-Ninth Street, he pointed it and clicked the trigger. Murzikias pleaded with him not to shoot.

"I'm not going to shoot," he quoted Ryan as saying.

Then Ryan shot and Murzikias dropped with a bullet in his neck.

"Is he done for?" Huskens asked.

"There goes two Greeks," Ryan answered.

Murzikias didn't want to breathe and let them know he wasn't dead. He would swallow and breathe just a little, to conceal that he was alive. Up front Ryan and Huskens discussed what to do with his body. Ryan first suggested throwing him in a nearby canal, then wanted to leave the body on a train track, but was overruled. When they reached a quarry in suburban Brookfield, Ryan ordered the car pulled over and he held the seat back while Huskens put his hands under Murzikias' arms and dragged him for about twenty-five feet. After they dropped him into the quarry, Murzikias rolled a few times and then lay still, his head facing the car. As Huskens walked to the car, he heard what sounded like a shot. Then he saw Huskens dragging someone else. He felt a body hit him.

"Then what happened?" asked the prosecutor.

"Whoever was shot was still kicking, because I heard Ryan holler out from the car. He says, 'Shoot that punk, he is still kicking!' So then I heard a shot fired, and I saw Huskens walking back toward the car."

That other shooting victim with him was John Driffield. After the car had pulled away, both were able to get up and make their way through the snow to a small house across the highway. Driffield was holding his chest where he was shot, and Murzikias pulled him along, covering two blocks as he bled. Murzikias' finger went a half-inch into his own neck wound and he put a handkerchief into the hole to slow the bleeding. At the house he called the Berwyn police; then he called his family.

Peter Murzikias and John Driffield were taken to MacNeal Memorial Hospital. After seven days in the hospital they were both laid up for three and a half months at home. MacNeal was a good hospital to go to for the kind of wounds they had; they were in good hands. The hospital was in Berwyn, a Chicago suburb right next door to Cicero, the old haunt of Al Capone and his associates, and the staff had lots of experience with gunshot wounds.

That was Peter Murzikias' story. When his direct testimony was over, Bellows cross-examined him first. Bellows asked about the fight between Ryan and Skorios that had led up to the shootings. The fight took place a few weeks before the December murders at seven or eight in the evening. Murzikias had seen the whole thing. Skorios knocked Ryan down and Steuben had to pull Skorios off Ryan. Both of them had been drinking. Then a fight broke out between Steuben and Skorios. In the process Murzikias took a gun from Steuben. It was loaded. Afterward, when they had drunk some more at a tavern, Skorios and Steuben went after Ryan again — but Ryan had a gun and held them off. During the following two weeks Ryan had been to the garage often, but there had been no further difficulties until the fatal night.

I had some questions of my own. Huskens, I established through Murzikias' testimony, was not present at that earlier fight. Two weeks later, when the trio held them hostage in the garage, Murzikias stated that Huskens had not threatened him and had once let Driffield answer a telephone while they were being guarded. I brought out that Huskens had told him twice that it was going to be a fight and that no one would get hurt.

At one stage of my cross-examination, Healy leaped in with an objection.

I told him, "Now, Healy, there is no use becoming excited!"

Bellows joined in, "He sits there and laughs at every question."

Healy responded, "I don't crack one of those counterfeit smiles like you do."

The irritation between Bellows and Healy was to be a continuing characteristic of the trial. Charlie Bellows was as energetic an advocate that ever went into a courtroom. He handled the toughest of cases, but he had seen more than one prosecutor fumble the case; if his opposing attorney lost his temper, it was a gain for the defendant. Bellows had earned a reputation as one of the top criminal attorneys in the state, and he remains at the top.

In this early exchange, the judge intervened, as he was to do over and over. He was impatient to get on with the trial.

* * *

I continued my cross-examination of Peter Murzikias.

"When you were out in the country and the car stopped and Ryan shot you," I asked, "didn't Ryan tell Huskens to take you out of the car?"

"Yes, he did," said Murzikias.

"Huskens never shot you, did he?"

"No, he didn't."

"While you were lying there in that field and while Huskens was walking back to the car, you heard another shot?"

"Yes, I did."

"Huskens didn't fire that shot, did he?"

"No, he didn't."

This became my strategy for the remainder of the trial: to demonstrate in every way possible that the gun had been in another's hands, not in the hand of Huskens, when a fatal shot was fired. Through Murzikias we had established that Huskens had neither shot him nor Driffield. This was important, because by the time Litral was shot, there were only two other witnesses destined to survive that nightmare ride — Huskens and Gardona. Both Huskens and Gardona denied shooting Litral; if I could prove Huskens had not shot any of the other men, his denial in the Litral killing would gain strength.

The second survivor, John Driffield, took the stand. He reported Gardona's hitting Litral with a cocked gun while Huskens was guarding them. Later in the car, he had asked Huskens to let them go and Huskens had said he couldn't do that. He had looked out the back window and had seen Skorios on the ground with Gardona standing over him. Then he saw Huskens go back and stamp Skorios' head. When Gardona and Ryan got back into the car, Ryan was clicking a gun. Gardona told Murzikias, "See what your partner did? You will pay for it." Soon afterward, Ryan shot Murzikias and Murzikias slumped. When they reached the quarry, Huskens dragged Murzikias out of the car; then Gardona shot Driffield about an inch above the heart. Huskens dragged him out of the car, but Driffield never lost consciousness. He heard Ryan shout, "Shoot that punk, he is still kicking." He said his left index finger was then hit when Huskens fired.

On cross-examination I brought out that Ryan had ordered Huskens to drag Murzikias and Driffield out of the car, and that Driffield's finger had only been grazed.

"You didn't see Huskens fire any shot, did you?" I asked.

"Not out in the alley but — "

"Did you see Huskens fire a shot in the alley?"

"Not in the alley, no."

Over and over, this had to be emphasized.

* * *

It was one long, busy day and night after another. Judge Sbarbaro was forever impatient to move the trial along and since each day was not over until midnight, there was hardly any time left for anything but sleep.

In short order, the state presented its supporting witnesses. Edward H. Law, chief of police in the Village of Stickney, told of finding Litral's body, which had been removed to the Cook County Morgue. As the policemen testified, I kept hammering at the facts in Huskens' favor. One cop agreed that no weapon had been found on Huskens at his arrest. I also emphasized how Huskens had cooperated perfectly with the police from then on. This was an essential part of the record. The truth is not merely a few selected facts; it is all the facts. I was trying to present the facts favoring Huskens, just as the state was presenting those against him.

Police Sergeant Robert E. Gibbons had been in the lobby of the Jackson View Hotel where Huskens rented a room, waiting for Huskens to return.

I asked him, "Did Alvin Huskens come in alone?"

"He did," replied Sergeant Gibbons.

"And when he came in, he walked up to you, is that right?"

"He walked up, yes."

"He did not try to get away? He never struggled with you, did he, Officer?"

"No."

"And you asked him about three bodies out in the country and he immediately told you about them?"

"Well, he said there were four."

"Four. And he immediately told you about Jack Ryan?"

"He did."

"And he immediately told you that Jack Ryan was out in front?"

"He did."

"That is all," I said.

Police Sergeant Frankie Pape, who had killed Ryan, took the stand to describe how Huskens had told officers Ryan might be at a tavern on Madison Street. They hadn't found him or Gardona there, so they went to another location. When he located Ryan, testified Pape, the ex-convict leaped at him. Pape fired five times. Ryan fell dead.

On cross-examination, I brought Pape back to the scene of that night.

"Was Alvin Huskens directing the officers there, or aiding the officers in locating Jack Ryan and Gardona?"

"Apparently he was," said Pape.

"Did he point out any house where Gardona or Ryan might be?"

"He did."

"Did he point out the building that you later entered and killed Ryan in?"

"He did."

Again the fact of Huskens' cooperation had been established.

* * *

The state had a host of technical testimony. Dr. Jerry Kearns, the Cook County pathologist, had performed the post-mortem on Litral's body. There were two bullet wounds in the forearm and the second had entered the chest and left through the lower back. It had probably taken him three or four hours to die. Skorios had had a bullet in the back of the head and a fracture of the skull; Dr. Kearns said the bullet had caused death. Steuben had been shot five times, two times in the head.

There also were expert witnesses to testify on ballistics and the scientific aspects of the case. Pellets had been taken from the 1937 automobile that Huskens had driven that night. These were compared to the guns that had been dredged up from the canal after Huskens had advised police where to look. Two guns were introduced into evidence: a nine-millimeter Polish-made Radum automatic pistol and a Japanese military-type pistol, called a Bulldog revolver. The pellets were matched with the weapons and we spent some time in cross-examining the men. Both Bellows and I attacked the testifying policemen's background. They were parading as experts; we thought they should prove they were experts. Otherwise their testimony should be judged as less than authoritative. But in the nineteen-forties, their testimony was limited, compared to the scientific proof that is generally offered today.

The background of the police ballistic expert was discovered to be very lacking. He had been on the force three years. His training was a one-day tour of the Colt gun factory. He had studied several pamphlets about the manufacturing of gun barrels and how scrolls and striations would appear on pellets fired from that barrel. Prior to being on the police force he had been a cheese-maker for six years.

Sandwiched in between the technical testimony was that of a woman who had witnessed the shooting of George Skorios. She had gotten off the street car and had been walking toward the garage in the dark when she saw "a heavy-set man bend over and fire a shot." At the morgue she had identified Ryan as the man who shot him. Another woman had heard a shot but hadn't seen it happen.

* * *

By the time the defense was ready to present its case, Healy and Bellows had worked up fine tempers toward each other and had engaged in a number of verbal fights in the courtroom. Healy was especially provoked by two defense witnesses. I put on Alvin Huskens' wife, the mother of a seven-months-old baby, who testified that the police had put her husband "in the line of fire" during the gun battle with Ryan at Gardona's home. But when Alex Napoli cross-examined her she admitted that detectives were on either side of Huskens, putting them in the line of fire, too. Huskens had to be restrained by bailiffs as his wife was questioned. Then Huskens' sister, the mother of five children, also took the stand, testifying only that she was related to him. Healy, upset, accused us of putting them on merely to arouse the sympathy of the jury. This led to another tiff with Bellows.

Healy and Bellows on one occasion were so bitter in their exchange that Judge Sbarbaro interrupted the trial and threatened contempt proceedings. After Bellows had moved for an adjournment following one stormy session, the judge warned, "If this court adjourns, somebody will go to jail."

As my major move for the defense, I put the defendant himself on the stand. Alvin Huskens, a slender, curly-haired youth, was only twenty; at the time of the crimes he had been a teen-ager. He and Gardona were both scarcely more than kids.

I went into his early life. His three-year-old brother had been kidnapped from a picture show; I let the jury ponder what effect this might have had on him. I brought out that he hadn't known anything about the previous fight between Ryan and Skorios. Then we got to the scene at the garage on that cold December evening.

"And what did you do after you got into the garage?"

Huskens said, "Jack Ryan ordered the boys who were in the garage to sit on the running board of the car."

"Who did he order to sit on the running board?"

"There was Pete Murzikias, John Driffield, Max Steuben, and Andrew Litral."

"And what did you do?"

"I sat in front of them."

"Why did you sit in front of them?"

"Because I was afraid of Jack Ryan."

"Did he tell you to do that?"

"Yes, sir, he ordered me to do it."

"Did he give you a gun?"

"Yes, sir."

"Did you point the gun at anyone?"

"No, sir. I had two guns at the time, but I didn't point them at no one."

Outside later with the prisoners in the car, he said he had handed a gun to Gardona and then had gotten right back into the car.

"Did you kick George Skorios in the head?" I asked.

"No, sir, I did not."

Then he was ordered by Ryan to drive. He told of Ryan's shooting Skorios.

"Did you take the body of George Skorios out of the car?" I asked.

"Yes, sir, I did," he replied.

"Why did you do that?"

"Because Jack Ryan ordered me to."

He described taking the body out.

"Was he alive?" I asked.

"Yes, sir."

"You knew that?"

"Yes, sir, I did."

"Did you shoot John Driffield?"

"No, sir, I did not."

"Who shot him?"

"Jack Ryan shot John Driffield."

"Did you take his body out of the car?"

"Yes, sir."

"Where did you put his body?"

"Next to Pete Murzikias."

"Was he alive when you put him there?"

"Yes, sir, he was."

"Did you fire a shot at Driffield?"

"No, sir, I did not fire a shot at him. I fired a shot about two feet over his head."

"Why did you do that?"

"Because I was afraid I would get shot myself if I didn't."

"Did Ryan point a gun at you?"

"Yes, sir. After I laid John Driffield down I walked back towards the car. He was sitting in the front seat with a gun pointed at me and said: 'Hit that guy, he is still kicking.' "

"What did you do?"

"I went back in the direction of John Driffield and fired a shot about two feet over his head."

"How far away were you from him?"

"From four to six feet."

"You could have hit him?"

"Yes, sir, I could have."

"Did you shoot Andrew Litral?"

"No, sir, I did not."

"Who did?"

"Jack Ryan."

I tried to put the gun in either Ryan's or Gardona's hands. The bullets found were all from one gun, and either Ryan or Gardona had had it. These were all significant facts, but facts do not rise, like helium-packed balloons, of their own accord. And the prosecution is not going to bring them out for you.

In my direct examination of Huskens I established that Ryan was drinking at the time and that Ryan had not told him about the previous fight, the big one that had set up the killings. Huskens was under the impression it was only to be a fight; nobody would really get hurt, no one would be killed. Possibly he was a "bad guy" by association, but not like Ryan, and he had not been aware of the bad blood between Ryan and Skorios. I pictured Huskens as being under the control and direction of Ryan and Gardona. Huskens drove, but either Ryan or Gardona told him where to go, where to stop. Even when he had fired that shot over Driffield, Huskens had been in fear himself.

Huskens had cooperated with the police, helping them locate the bodies of the slain men, cooperating in every way he could. And there was the vital point that he could have killed Driffield, which Ryan ordered him to do, but he had not. These were hardly the actions of a "mad dog killer."

Another aspect of the defense's case was to show not only the characters of the defendants but the records of the victims. The slain George Skorios had been in the reformatory for auto theft and burglary, on a three-to-ten-year sentence in 1932. Steuben had a long record of misdemeanors and had served time in the Cook County House of Corrections. He had been arrested a number of times. I was not trying to mar their reputations, now that they were dead, but it was all part of the truth.

Charlie Bellows called Bobby Gardona to the stand in his own defense. Gardona was a slender, rather good-looking young man with dark, wavy hair. He was twenty-one at the time of the trial. Both he and Huskens scowled a lot at the trial; it was pretty hard to find anything for them to smile about.

Gardona had been married about six months when the killings happened. At the time he was on probation, having been found guilty of robbery. He had met Huskens three weeks before the shootings, and had met Ryan in a poolroom. He admitted going on the ride, but he, like Huskens, denied doing any of the shooting. He said all of the shots were fired by Ryan.

From the previous testimony, Gardona's case was a tough one and Bellows had his hands full trying to overcome some of the damaging things that had already been said about Gardona.

We managed one minor surprise for the defense when we called one Dr. Grout, a general surgeon and chief of staff of MacNeal Memorial Hospital. He testified that there had been no wound on Driffield's finger. He said he had "never placed a bandage on any finger." This helped substantiate Huskens' claim that he had shot to miss Driffield.

* * *

Then, suddenly, after a long and weary back-breaking trial, both sides rested and it was up to the lawyers to make their final arguments to the jury.

Healy asked for death for both Huskens and Gardona. He went all out. In my own closing, I hammered at points that had been building slowly and carefully during the work-packed trial. The indictment for the murder of Andrew Litral stated that Alvin Huskens had shot him. But where in the evidence had the state proved this? Had the state proved guilt beyond a reasonable doubt? Ryan had been crazy drunk that night. Huskens, a youth, a teen-ager, had been afraid. He never shot anyone. He had no motive. Circumstances had placed him there. Huskens' wife had said she had never seen him with guns. Then Bellows closed in the defense of Gardona. He too emphasized the fear that Ryan exerted on Gardona. He went into Gardona's background and the environment that contributed to his plight. He argued there was reasonable doubt of his client's guilt.

On a Friday afternoon Judge Sbarbaro gave the jurors their instructions and at about three-thirty they began deliberating. It was to be a long wait. Darkness fell as they deliberated long into that cold January night. After eight hours they were still deadlocked, and at 12:30 A.M. Saturday, Judge Sbarbaro ordered them to retire to their quarters in the county jail for the rest of the night.

After breakfast, at 9 A.M. Saturday, they continued to argue. But inside the jury room another minor drama had begun. One of the male jurors had a lung ailment that now required special treatment. Under Illinois law a jury cannot be separated before reaching a verdict. This meant there was the possibility of a mistrial. Judge Sbarbaro never entertained that possibility, though. If a verdict were not reached quickly, he announced, a chartered bus would transport the entire jury to the doctor's office while their peer was provided with medical attention.

The jury room in each courtroom in the Cook County Criminal Court Building is about fifteen feet wide by thirty-five feet long and has a long conference table with twelve chairs around it, one for each juror. The jury room is behind the courtroom; on one side there are glass windows, on the other three sides nothing but solid walls. There is a lavatory for men, another for women. The door to the jury room closes as you walk out, then leads to a little hallway about four feet long and then to a second door opening into the anteroom of the judge's chambers.

In the anteroom the judge's bailiff usually has a desk. In this case there were two bailiffs, one male and one female; each was sworn not to talk to the jurors except to answer specific questions and it was their responsibility to keep the jurors from other persons. The jurors could have no food and drink unless it was ordered by the court.

In the hall there is a bell button about five feet high. The jurors had been instructed to press the button when they had a question for the judge or when they had reached an agreement.

At 10:50 Saturday morning, two hours after they had resumed deliberations, the buzzer rang. The verdicts!

The courtroom was crowded. In addition to the lawyers and other attachés of the court, the relatives of defendants Gardona and Huskens filled most of the seats. There were also the relatives of the victims.

The court clerk, in a resonant voice, read the verdict to the court and the assembled crowd:

"We, the jury, find the defendant Robert Gardona guilty of murder, in manner and form as charged in the indictment, and we fix his punishment as death."

The electric chair! The reading of that verdict touched off one of the wildest scenes ever experienced in a Chicago courtroom. Huskens' wife screamed and collapsed into a faint, sprawling between the benches onto the floor. She had to be carried out. Gardona's wife and mother both screamed hysterically and fell over. When bailiffs charged over to revive them, they were punched by some of the relatives and friends of the defendants. Policemen and deputy sheriffs hurried in and pulled Gardona's mother and his wife out of the courtroom.

Photographers were allowed in the courtrooms in those days,

and these newspapermen immediately rushed up to take pictures of the distraught wives in their emotional condition. I didn't like it. Neither did others: Gardona's brother fought the photographers; some of the men grabbed for the cameras to prevent the photographers from taking pictures of that moment of naked grief and tragedy. It was a terrible scene.

Amidst it all, Judge Sbarbaro stood up behind the bench, shouting for order, rapping his gavel sharply.

It was to no avail. Although bailiffs and policemen were seizing people and trying to move them outside, it was about thirty minutes before the courtroom quieted down. While Judge Sbarbaro kept pounding his gavel and shouting, ten deputy sheriffs formed a ring around Gardona and Huskens.

Outside the courtroom, Gardona's wife was revived in the corridor and she began shrieking and fighting all over again. "I don't want to go home," she cried. "I've got no home, nobody. Why don't they let me die, too? I want to die." She was seventeen years old.

The bailiffs dragged the distraught women down the hall to the elevators and then to the ground floor. Huskens' wife was dragged on her knees with one shoe off, lost in the confusion. Then she collapsed again.

I knew how Mrs. Huskens felt. Her hysteria was very logical, for at the moment Gardona's fate had been announced, I, too, knew what it meant. The less severe penalty is traditionally announced first, so this meant they both would get death. But in one corner of the courtroom Huskens' mother and sister sat, suppressing their feelings, waiting, as if they were the only ones there who realized Huskens' fate had not yet been formally announced.

At long last, when decorum had been restored to the courtroom, the clerk read the verdict on Huskens.

"*We, the jury, find the defendant Alvin Huskens guilty of murder, in manner and form as charged in the indictment —*"

No surprise to anyone in that courtroom, by then.

"*— and we fix his punishment at imprisonment in the*

penitentiary for a term of 199 years. And we further find from the evidence that the said defendant Alvin Huskens is now about the age of twenty years."

Huskens received the news silently and without any expression. Gardona bowed his head. They were still not over the shock of the first verdict. From Huskens' point of view, the clerk had done an unfortunate thing by reading Gardona's verdict first. Anything after that had to be an anticlimax. As far as my client was concerned, I felt relieved. He had only received what he already had. But downstairs his wife was still in a state of hysteria. She thought he had been condemned to the chair.

Bellows kept fighting for Gardona's life, seeking a new trial, then stays of execution. He was thorough, and exhausted every avenue of appeal for his client. But finally, time ran out, and Gardona died in the electric chair. Huskens was never tried in the Steuben murder. The case was closed.

CHAPTER 7

Making a Deal

IF THE CLIENT IS GUILTY, and *wants* to plead guilty, it is the duty of his public defender to work out the best deal possible for him. That means a negotiated sentence. We used to call it "making a deal."

How do you do it? There's no set way. It all depends on the prosecutor and the judge your're dealing with, the case and the defendant and his previous record. Most of all, it takes experience. You have to develop a feel for personalities and cases.

They say that no two cases are alike, but the truth is, most of them are pretty close to each other. Certainly there's no excuse for two cases with identical sets of facts, whether it's robbery or larceny or burglary, in which one defendant gets one-to-twenty and the other defendant gets one-to-five. There is nothing fair about that. A negotiated sentence should be one that is fair to the state and fair to the defendant.

As guidelines, there are the sentences that others have received in the past from other judges, and you dredge those cases up from your own experience. Of course, you can't negotiate with a prosecutor who is inexperienced. He might think everyone charged with a crime should go to the penitentiary, without even considering a probation period. Nor is it easy to work out a deal with a new judge.

Some judges, as well as prosecutors and defense attorneys, want to work everything out so that there will be no trial. Many judges in Cook County have gone about their business in this fashion and habitually left the courtroom by one o'clock. Many of them have a knack for working out negotiated pleas, and in those instances it's sometimes foolish for the defendant to contest the matter when he's going to get immediate probation rather than a trial with all its risks.

Whatever happens, the client has to be told of the offer, even if he is innocent, because the decision of taking the risk of a trial is his, and at the felony level, the risk can be great. In Illinois, a felony is any crime for which one can be sentenced to the penitentiary upon conviction, as opposed to a misdemeanor, usually a lesser crime, for which one can be sentenced up to a year in jail or a house of correction. Usually, the guilty defendant wants you to negotiate the best deal possible, and in our office 70 percent of the felony defendants pleaded guilty, a percentage comparable to those with private counsel.

Some judges and some state's attorneys hold one trial after another. You can't work out anything with them. In those cases, you take a trial or a change of venue to another court where, hopefully, you can. This is what happened in the Wola case. That case has been discussed. We were willing to make a deal for life imprisonment in the kidnap-murder. But the state wanted his neck. Which is why we had to fight, literally, for Wola's life. In the end, the victory was only what we had offered as a deal in the first place.

Lamentably, what happens to the defendant in court is not always what he and the public defender had expected to happen, as I learned as an apprentice trial lawyer in the case of one of my early clients. Thomas B. Stratter, handsome, dapper, twenty-three-year-old ex-con.

The newspapers labeled Stratter a "one-man crime wave." If Stratter was as prolific in his criminal activities as was alleged, he was a real workhorse. He was accused of twenty stickups that winter over a four-day period. His "crime wave" ended at a North Side cocktail lounge on what was said to be his seventh robbery of the night when he took a shot at the bartender, but the gun misfired. A customer lunged at Stratter. Other patrons pitched in and he was disarmed. The police came.

According to the police, Stratter bolted away while they had him on the sidewalk, waiting for the paddy wagon to arrive. They shot at him. He was hit three times. So he went to Bridewell Hospital instead of the police station. In those days this was a common occurrence. Many policemen in Chicago felt, apparently, that it was just as well to avoid the bother of trials. They held the trial on the streets, right there at the scene of the crime. Stratter was lucky he wasn't killed.

Stratter had a lot of strikes against him; especially his record. He already had three burglary convictions to his credit, one as a boy, one year in county jail, and he had served a two-to-five at Joliet Penitentiary.

Despite the loot he was supposed to have taken at gunpoint, Stratter was found to be indigent and I was appointed to represent him. A tough case. He had been caught in the act of holding somebody up with a gun. He possibly had been involved in quite a few holdups, for he was accused of twenty. Out of these, three robberies and a car theft were selected for trial.

He pleaded not guilty.

I asked for a bench trial without jury, and before we had gone too far I managed to work out an agreement with the assistant state's attorney, who agreed on a sentence of twenty-to-forty years to cover all of the charges. With the evidence such as it was, Stratter was willing to take it.

The judge knew of the agreement, but he said, "Yes, but you didn't get *me* to agree!" He then sentenced Stratter instead to a term of *forty-to-eighty* years in the pen — doubling the recommended sentence by simply having two of the robbery convictions run consecutively instead of concurrently, as the deal stipulated.

Why did he do that? Because a well-known newspaper reporter wanted to write a dramatic story that particular day and influenced the judge into giving Stratter a heavy sentence. The reporter was a very enterprising man. Some judges seemed to be in awe of him. They listened carefully to him and their decisions sometimes reflected what he had told them. At times one judge would even let him sit up on the bench with him!

* * *

It took a court battle to get one of my clients, Donald Cruzera, the deal we thought he already had.

Cruzera was charged with four counts of armed robbery. He was told that if he cooperated with the police and pleaded guilty, he would get a light sentence. I personally discussed it with Lieutenant Frank Pape of the Chicago Police Department's robbery detail and with Sam Papanek, the assistant state's attorney in charge of the case. It was my understanding that both of them agreed the state would recommend a sentence of five-to-ten if Cruzera pleaded guilty.

Cruzera pleaded guilty to all four counts.

The trial judge, Charles Doherty, however, didn't ask anyone for a recommendation. Very quickly, before anything could be done, he sentenced Cruzera to prison for a term of twenty years to life. This was unusual; he always did ask for and invariably followed the recommendation of the state. Thus, lawyers pleading their clients had confidence in him.

This came as a brutal surprise to me as well as my client. Inwardly I was boiling and I can only speculate as to whether Cruzera's outrage matched mine. But on that day there was nothing to be done about it.

Later, we sought a new trial for Cruzera in a hearing before Judge Richard Austin, the presiding judge of the Cook County Criminal Court at that time. John Branion, a black lawyer in our office, and one of the finest defenders anywhere, and I handled the case from that point on. Our petition for Cruzera charged that his plea of guilty was induced by promises of a lenient sentence if he cooperated with the prosecutors, and since the promises hadn't been kept, he should get a new trial.

Cruzera testified that after his arrest he had talked with Lieutenant Pape and that Pape told him that if he cooperated he,

Pape, would see that Cruzera received a light sentence, possibly four-to-eight. Cruzera further testified that on the trial date he had conferred with both Pape and me in the courtroom and that Pape informed us that the prosecutor, Sam Papanek, wanted eight-to-fifteen but would take five-to-ten on a plea. Expecting five-to-ten, Cruzera had pleaded guilty.

Branion then called me to the stand, for in the process I had become a material witness in the case. I testified that on the trial day I had talked with both Pape and Papanek and that both of them had told me the state would recommend five-to-ten in exchange for a plea. I had told Cruzera this. But the judge had sentenced Cruzera without asking their opinions. It was the custom for judges to ask the state for their recommendations. It didn't occur in this case.

Sam Papanek took the stand. He confirmed that he had told me he would recommend five-to-ten if the court asked me.

"Had I had an opportunity to make a recommendation, it would have been five-to-ten, as I advised Mr. Getty," he said. He said he had talked to the first assistant in the state's attorney's office about it and with Pape.

Lieutenant Pape testified that he had told Cruzera he would see that his cooperation was noted to the state's attorney and he would make a recommendation if he could but that it wouldn't be binding on the court. He couldn't remember specifically what he had said to me on the trial date.

"It's possible I made a statement to Mr. Getty concerning a recommendation that I would make," Pape said. He said he had told Papanek of Cruzera's cooperation. "There was talk of a recommendation of eight-to-fifteen or five-to-ten."

Thus, both Papanek and Pape backed up our contentions. They had done what they had promised, and now, in effect, were helping in the appeal by testifying. The trouble was, Judge Doherty hadn't given them a chance to make a recommendation — a real oversight.

Judge Austin agreed with us that Cruzera had pleaded guilty, expecting that some consideration would be given to the recommendation, even though it would not have been binding, and the recommendation had not been made. He ordered a new trial.

The state's attorney appealed Judge Austin's ruling. It went on to the Illinois Supreme Court. There, John Branion and I defended Judge Austin's ruling. The high court affirmed Austin's decision, the case went back and Cruzera finally received what amounted to his five-to-ten on a plea. He entered another plea to the indictments and was given a sentence of two-to-seven years. He was given credit for the two-and-one-half years he had spent in prison pending the appeal.

From that day on, I never entered a plea of guilty unless I had talked to the judge first.

CHAPTER 8

Promotion, Politics and the Babbling Burglar

IN THE EARLY FIFTIES John Gutknecht, who had been a Municipal Court judge, was elected state's attorney and he asked me to be his second assistant in charge of the criminal division. It wasn't an offer to be taken lightly; traditionally, the state's attorney's office had probably spawned more judges than any other single incubation site in Cook County.

I turned Gutknecht down. I felt I wasn't ready for prosecution work and, furthermore, I thought something more interesting lay ahead. I had an inkling that I might in time become head of the public defender's office. The chances looked excellent. In 1954 Francis McCurrie was slated for a Municipal Court judgeship. He won. That left his old job open.

I had had about ten years of criminal trial experience. I was familiar with the courts, the judges, procedures, and the wide variety of criminal cases that we experienced day after day in Chicago. I felt I was ready to fill McCurrie's shoes.

In Chicago, however, other matters were also important. Politics.

Though my family had always voted Democratic, I had become an assistant public defender without the sponsorship of any Democratic organization. Another lawyer had introduced me to Judge Philip J. Finnegan, who was then chief justice of the Criminal Court, and he had recommended me to Public Defender Bachrach. Later, I did Democratic precinct work and ultimately became an aide to our ward committeeman, James J. Sullivan, who asked me to speak at various ward functions on behalf of Democratic candidates and projects.

My contribution to the Democratic party, however, was relatively minor. This was through no fault of my own but was because of demography. To become a really big cog in the Democratic machine in Chicago, you have to come from a ward with a heavy Democratic vote. But I lived at Eighty-Fourth and Dante Avenue. This was the Eighth Ward, and in the nineteen-fifties it was Slovac, Polish, Irish, and Swedish. The Swedish vote was the balance of power, and the Republicans usually carried the ward, which didn't please the Democratic party when favors were handed out.

Politics, of course, has a special meaning in Cook County. In 1954, and for the next twenty years, the key to all political motion was held by one person: Richard J. Daley, who then was county chairman of the Democratic party and in 1955 was to become mayor of the city of Chicago.

By statute, a majority of the judges of the Circuit Court appoint the public defender. My elevation to the head of the office in 1954 wasn't that complicated. Richard J. Daley merely picked up the telephone and passed the word to the right men that I was to be the new public defender and that was it. The required number of judges signed the order, but the decision had been made by Daley.

In late November, after McCurrie's election, I had been called to Daley's office. I never had a real relationship with Daley. I probably spent as much time with him that day as I have at any time since. Up close, he was short in stature, perhaps five-seven, broad in both chest and shoulders. He was an immaculate dresser and then, as on every other occasion, he wore a well-tailored suit with the best of choices in shirt and tie. And, certainly on that occasion, he was a very congenial person.

He said to me, "You are going to be appointed public defender. What I want you to do is go out there and do a good job and represent those poor people."

I thanked him, and told him I would do exactly that.

Then Daley added:

"If you're out there a while and you do a good job, we'll make you a judge."

But there came a time, some years later, when doing a good job, from my viewpoint, did not make Daley happy.

* * *

Officially, it all began on October 8, 1959, in the court of Judge Alfred J. Cilella, as part of a case styled *State of Illinois* versus *Richard Morrison*. Before it was over, Chicago had been rocked by one of the biggest police scandals in its history and I, as public defender, was in the middle of it.

Because he "spilled the beans" on some of his associates, Richard Morrison became known as the "babbling burglar." But there was nothing incoherent or rambling in anything he said. His mind was very sharp, and he had a nearly photographic memory. In the process of talking freely he became a minor historical figure in the annals of our city.

Although he was still in his early twenties, it was estimated that $250,000 had passed through dapper, good-looking Morrison's hands during his youthful venture into crime. If so, none of that quarter-million was visible on the October day he appeared in Criminal Court, charged with several burglaries. Five of the indictments each carried a $10,000 bond and nobody came forward with the $50,000 that would get him out of jail or with the money it would take to hire him an attorney. He was broke, and a client of the public defender's office.

That day Morrison was being represented by Assistant Public Defender Jim Doherty. Judge Cilella was presiding. This judge wanted everyone in his court to plead guilty, even though he often gave excessive sentences, and he asked if there was "any likelihood of adjusting this matter."

"There might be, Judge," said Doherty. "There might very well be."

The judge turned to Frank C. Stanley, one of the assistant state's attorneys in the court, and asked him the same question.

Stanley replied, "We have offered — we have had a conference on it, Judge — but so far, we can't. We have reached an impasse."

They were talking about a deal. The charges were serious enough so that Morrison risked twenty years to life. He was willing to take a sentence of three-to-seven, but the best the state's attorney's office appeared willing to offer him was five-to-twenty, or maybe three-to-fifteen. Morrison wouldn't go for that. He — and Doherty — considered it excessive. Morrison preferred to take his chances with a jury.

But Judge Cilella wanted the case resolved that morning. He kept prodding Doherty, keeping the pressure on. Finally when Morrison was called before the bar, Doherty asked to be excused so he could answer ready for trial in another felony case before the chief justice.

The judge would have none of that. "The case is called now and I want to dispose of it," he said.

"Yes," said Doherty. "Well, I am asking the court to set it over then."

"Yes, that's what I want to do first. Now, is this going to be a bench or jury trial?"

"In the event it cannot be worked out, it will be a jury trial. I suggest the nineteenth."

"I have to set it down for one or the other because — "

"Yes, all right," said Doherty impatiently, "set it for a jury."

Defendant Morrison broke in. "On all of them."

"Yes," said Doherty.

"And," said Morrison to Judge Cilella, "I want to see your head man upstairs, Mr. Adamowski, before this case is even started."

He meant Benjamin Adamowski, the state's attorney of Cook County at that time.

"What is he saying?" said Judge Cilella, flustered.

"I would like to see the State's Attorney Adamowski before these cases even start, your honor, because there's a few things that aren't squared off here on these cases. And from the way it started out, nothing was supposed to be like this. Quite a few police officers are involved here, and I would like to speak to Mr. Adamowski before this case starts."

"Well," said Judge Cilella, "I am sure the assistant state's attorneys will convey that request to the state's attorney."

* * *

So there it was, in open court: an accused burglar had blurted out that "quite a few police officers" were involved. The implication behind his words was evident to an experienced courtroom observer. If he was to get a long sentence by pleading guilty, then he would take some policemen with him. Unless he was speaking empty words, this was no insignificant outburst. But there was only one way to find out what he meant.

Jim Doherty, a genial, redheaded Irishman, hurried to my office.

"Boss, you'd better talk to this fellow," he said after he had reported what Morrison had said in court. "I think there's something to it."

I went to the court to see for myself. Morrison still wanted to see the state's attorney and involve some policemen, as he had stated in court. Since he had made that statement in front of the assistant state's attorneys, I called them — Frank Stanley and Frank Wesolowski, now public defender of DuPage County — to join the conference. We took Morrison into an empty jury room and began the first of many conversations I was to have with him.

Morrison was a wee little fellow. As I was to learn, this was one reason he was so talented at his trade. He could take off a ventilator and crawl through ducts, if necessary, to get into a place. He also was a lock expert and probably could have passed an examination to be a locksmith.

"Well, Dick," I said, "since I am your lawyer and you have just accused police officers in open court, tell us what you wish to relate about any unlawfulness on the part of police officers."

"Well," said Morrison, "many police officers have aided me in burglaries, they have looted places of business, sold proceeds of the burglaries, and have some of the stolen property in their homes."

I stopped him short. "Before you continue, let me remind you that previously you have not told me you were involved in any other crimes. If you now divulge other crimes you participated in, you can be indicted for those crimes. It is your constitutional right not to give evidence that will incriminate or involve you in further crimes. Understanding that, you may or may not continue."

Morrison had a fast, crisp way of speaking, and came right to the point.

"Mr. Getty, I wish to talk my head off!" he said.

"All right."

"I am going to involve every policeman that was in on a burglary with me, the burglaries they forced me to commit, and tell of payoffs to other policemen who were tipped off by the policemen in on the burglaries. They were playing a two-way street, placing me in a trap that slowly closed. Why should I take the rap for them? Even today they are messing around. I was to plead guilty to the seven indictments and receive three-to-seven years; now if I plead guilty today the sentence will be three-to-fifteen years. If I am going to get that kind of time, they are going with me. From now on, Dick Morrison looks out for himself. Let them sweat."

It was incredible, but I felt he could be telling the truth. I was aware of the skepticism with which many people would view his story. He had a record of arrests and had served time. He wanted a lighter sentence for himself. So I explained to him that he would have to tell us about every place broken into with police assistance, including the names of the policemen, a description of every article taken, and the disposition of the loot.

Could any of the items be found in their possession now? I promised him his information would be carefully checked and his allegations investigated.

* * *

He began talking and I listened. I didn't want to believe him, but I was deeply impressed by the great detail in his story. Either he had a good memory or a super imagination.

He told us he had had an evening delivery job at a pizza place in the Fortieth Police District on the North Side. Several policemen from the Fortieth, or Summerdale, District, ate there from time to time.

"I knew most of them because I lived in that district all my life and there were a few I went to school with. At the time of June, 1958, I was on the bad side of them. I guess they thought every time something happened I was the one who did it.

"Anyways, that's what I thought. I was no angel, by all means: I'd been in trouble for quite a few things. But that was up until September 14, 1957, when I got done doing a four-month sentence for petty larceny. On that day I decided to go straight and try the other way for a change.

"Everything was going along fine until one day when I was walking down Berwyn Avenue from Broadway and this police officer named Joe Coltera came out of the liquor store there and said to me, 'Well, if it isn't the little burglar, Richie.' I knew Joe from the pizza place and I seen he was a little loaded, so I just said, 'Hi, Joe, how are things with you?' and he said, 'Well, they would be a little better if you would cut us guys in on some of your jobs.' He said, 'You know Ted Durros and some of the other fellows and we'll go along with the show. After all,' he said, 'we like nice things also.'

"Just then another cop came out of the liquor store and Joe introduced me to him. His name was Jack Dicky and he was riding a three-wheeler at the time.

"I forgot to say they were both on duty and this was their favorite hangout to pass the time away.

"Well, anyways, I said 'Hi' to Jack and he started talking about golf clubs and Joe said to him, 'Anything you need, just see Richie here. If anyone can get them for you, he can.' So, I said to him, 'I'll see what I can do.'

"To tell the truth, I don't know what made me say that to him, because I hadn't been doing anything wrong since I got out of the House of Correction in September of '57. I guess the reason I did say it to him was because it was the first time in my life a copper ever asked me to get him something cheap and I got the big idea all of a sudden that I was in with them now and to stay on good terms it would be a good idea to get the clubs for Jack.

"Anyways, I left them and said, 'I'll let you know later on.' I didn't know at the time what I was really letting myself in for, but after I told them I'd see what I could do, it seemed like everyone in Forty was asking me to get them one thing or another.

"Well, a few weeks passed and I completely forgot about the clubs and the cops until one afternoon I was eating in Nick's Restaurant under the el station on Berwyn Avenue and the whole gang came in to eat and it was then I found out that that was their main headquarters for coffee breaks and eating. When they all walked in, well, they saw me and asked me to join them in the booth and I did. We started talking and Jack Dicky asked me, did I have the golf clubs yet? Well, I said to him that they were ordered and that he would get them any day. To tell the truth I was lying to him. I guess I just wanted to stay on the good side of things. Anyways, I told him he would get them in a few days."

A month passed, Morrison said, and then one night he went to a West Montrose night club.

"At about ten-thirty that night I saw Ted Durros in there and he said to me that Jack Dicky had been asking for the golf clubs and I told him to tell Dicky I should get them within a few days.

"Well, at about eleven-thirty I was pretty loaded and got the idea to go out and get Jack Dicky his golf clubs because I was getting sick of him asking me for them. I remembered that when I used to take things out of cars in 1957 that twenty-five percent of the cars had golf clubs in them. So, I left and started up to Rogers Park to find some new convertibles, as they were the only kind I could see into the trunk to see if there were any golf clubs there or not.

"Well, I drove around Rogers Park for about an hour and went through about ten cars, but no clubs. So I decided to head up into Evanston to see if I could find some there. Well, I drove around for about a half an hour and finally spotted a station wagon that had a set of clubs in the back end of it. I started to open the vent window to get them when I spotted two police officers running toward me in the park next to the car, so I jumped back into my car, which was a 1955 Cadillac convertible, and took off. They opened fire on me and chased me through Evanston, but I finally lost them and abandoned the car and got back to Chicago to a friend's house on Grace Street.

"I was later arrested by Chicago police and turned over to Evanston and made bond. I denied everything and that morning at 1:15 A.M. August 1, 1958, it began all over again. I figured as long as the clubs were for a cop and I didn't get them anyways, I would accept their offer and start doing burglaries with them so I could get the money to beat the case.

"So, from day to day I met the cops in Nick's Restaurant at 1 A.M. and we set up jobs every night and from time to time I kept meeting more coppers that were burglars and from time to time I kept getting more cases in the Criminal Court Building and needed an awful lot of money for lawyers, bondsmen, and cops . . . ."

Needing more and more money, Morrison said, he took up an offer to pass counterfeit one hundred dollar bills — for which Secret Service agents arrested him in March, 1959. It was at this point that Morrison began "studying safes" and learned to open one "within a few minutes." His confederates on the police force, he said, "really went for that, as now they got more than just the merchandise, they got cash also." With protection from his friends in blue, he added safecracking to the nocturnal activities he shared with them.

Morrison glibly rattled off names of policemen, the burglarized businesses they had collaborated on, and came up with fairly precise dates for when the crimes had been committed. As he talked, I was impressed by the details he kept providing. I would interrupt him from time to time, as if he were on the witness stand and I were cross-examining him, and I would intentionally try to confuse him, try to trip him up. But he always came through without contradicting himself. I couldn't shake him. He would even cite the color of articles, the color of a TV set, whether it was black-and-white or a color set, and the type of wood it was.

The policemen that Morrison implicated in the burglaries were mostly from the Summerdale Police Station on Chicago's North Side. It is a district of contrasts, including honky-tonks, tenement housing, and the lavish homes and apartments along the fashionable lakefront.

* * *

We had a long session with Morrison that day in the jury room. At that point we couldn't be positive he was telling the truth, but he seemed to have too firm a grasp of details to be creating this out of his head. At the very least, such charges should be investigated. What more basic requirement of law and order can there be than that a society's policemen conduct themselves honestly and in accordance with the law? I felt personally compelled to see that the truth came out, whatever it turned out to be. As a citizen, it was my duty and this came first, but as the public defender there was more to it: I also had to try to get my client Morrison the lightest sentence possible.

The first move should come from the state's attorney. When we had finished listening to Morrison, Stanley and Wesolowski, the assistant state's attorneys, went downstairs and presumably told what they had heard to their superiors.

Nothing happened. Morrison was treated like any other suspect trying to get a lesser sentence by claiming to squeal on the cops and involve others.

It was the second time this had happened. Back in the previous summer he had told at least part of his story to a sergeant of the central detective bureau, who had relayed it to the chief of detectives. They had also completely discounted Morrison's words as unreliable and, in fact, incredible. Morrison had never been pressed for names or other details; it was dismissed as the wild, plea-copping statement of an anxious burglar.

But if the state's attorney's office didn't buy this incredible story, what could be done? Now I had to take an unusual step, merely in order to fulfill my constitutional responsibilities to my client. Because the state would not check out his story, I, as the public defender and his attorney, had to do it. If Morrison was right in his allegations, and if he became a state's witness, then he would probably never go to the pen.

But more was at stake than Richard Morrison's liberty. The integrity of a city, a police force, the whole county, was involved. If. There were a lot of if's, but the only sensible thing to do was to test them. This I set out to do.

* * *

Morrison's arrest record stretched far back into childhood. By one report there were twenty arrests, many of them in the Summerdale district of Chicago but others in Los Angeles and Las Vegas. Some were merely for "investigation" or "general principles" and the most time he had served was nine months in the Cook County Jail. The charges were usually larceny or burglary and he had been given probation on one serious case. He had not yet been to prison, but in 1959 with several charges stacked up against him, the possibilities looked good that he would. California police wanted him for parole violation. He was broke and, it seemed, his friends had left him.

The key arrest had occurred back in May. Detectives were

checking a burglary at a furniture store on North Milwaukee Avenue when a woman a few doors down called to report a man trying to break into her apartment. Detectives ran over, their guns drawn. Out of the darkness a man's voice greeted them, "Don't shoot. I'll give up." It was Morrison. He was in his stocking feet. The circumstances were, to say the least, suspicious. The furniture store had been entered through a hole chopped in the roof and the safe's tumblers had been knocked off. Burglary tools lay on the floor. They found Morrison's car parked in the vicinity, and when the inventory was completed, they found among the burglary tools — presumed to be his — two sledgehammers, a fourteen-foot scaling ladder, and a 100-foot long rope. These charges of burglary and possession of burglary tools, on top of his other troubles, indicated his chances of getting a long prison term were excellent. He was ripe for a deal, but the deal han't come through. His willingness to implicate the policemen seemed perfectly understandable.

With Jim Doherty as my right-hand assistant, we began digging at the truth, testing with facts every detail that Morrison had told us. We conducted our investigation independently of the Chicago police and of the Cook County state's attorney's office. I had four investigators on my staff at the time and I put two of them on the job. We worked ten to twelve hours a day and then sat up nights writing reports. Everyone was under secret orders. In something as sensitive as criminal charges involving a substantial number of policemen, there was no other way to do it.

Our men went to contact the owners of the stores that Morrison mentioned to us. *Was your store burglarized?* we would ask. *Yes,* the reply invariably came. *What was taken? What were the serial numbers? Where were the articles manufactured?* It took a while to get a list of the serial numbers we needed. In order to obtain some of them, we had to write to the manufacturers of the guns, motors, and tires that had been taken. There was a long list of stolen items and anything that could be checked was checked. TV sets. Evinrude boat motors. Household furnishings. Guns. There was a mountain of details, all of which had to be kept secret.

We compiled detailed rosters of the loot that had been taken in each burglary. Each list also provided the information found on police records, such as the time of the burglary and when it had been reported and who had investigated it. To organize Morrison's information we made up index cards that contained the burglaries and pertinent information on each one, such as which policemen were alleged to have been involved. We ended up with ten major burglaries that had been committed on nine different nights. Morrison mentioned others and he told of jobs he had heard some of the policemen talking about but which he had not gone on. We felt that on these ten burglaries the state could obtain enough evidence to convict. They had taken place from October 1, 1958, to July 8, 1959, slightly over a nine-month period, and a wide range of stores was included: two different tire companies, a gasoline station, a furniture store, a music shop, a radio and appliance store, a cocktail lounge, a marine supply, an automotive store, and a drugstore.

The total losses reported by the burglarized stores reached thousands of dollars. A furniture store counted its losses at $2,660; a tire company listed a partial loss of $4,822.52; the automotive supply reported $355.03 taken from its safe, plus about $1,000 in goods. Several of the losses were under $1,000.

We also made up inventories of stolen merchandise that Morrison said could be found in policemen's homes. The inventories included the exact descriptions of stolen items and the serial numbers of such articles as guns, outboard motors, and certain household appliances. Along with this, we made a list of the names and addresses of eight policemen whom Morrison said were involved with him in the burglaries. Quietly, we checked the dates of the burglaries against the duty records of the accused Summerdale policemen. Again, Morrison's story held up.

Our investigators also located a reel of a tape recording that could be used as evidence to support Morrison's claim that he had paid a $2,000 bribe to a suburban police officer.

Nor was that all. Morrison also charged that two policemen had switched evidence in the police custodian's office in order to help Morrison win an acquittal in court. The evidence was a stolen camera, and this disclosure turned out to be one of the more complicated maneuvers that Morrison had pulled off during his collaboration with his buddies on the police force. We located a man to whom Morrison had sold the disputed camera and obtained a statement from him that helped to confirm Morrison's charge.

* * *

After Morrison had told us his version of the camera switch, I took a look at the transcript from that case. Morrison had been picked up "under suspicion." and in his car the police had found some items, including a Polaroid Land camera that had been stolen in the burglary on West Lawrence Avenue. At that trial, before Morrison went broke, he was represented by private counsel.

The owner of the burglarized store took the stand to describe the break-in, and identified the loot — $139.51 in cash, a Polaroid camera, a radio, some flash bulbs for the camera, some four-cent stamps, a roll of film for the camera, and some liquor — nine bottles of Haig and Haig, gift-wrapped for Christmas. He had identified these items in the Summerdale Police Station and now, in court, he verified that the exhibit was his property.

The storekeeper testified that, although the camera belonged to him, he didn't have the serial number.

Was there any way he could distinguish that camera from any other one?

"Yes," he said, "you'll find a negative in there with a picture of my office on the last exposure."

But Morrison was a very proof-conscious person and he produced a receipt for the camera, which his lawyer now presented to the court. Then, in order to break the stalemate, the assistant state's attorney asked the storekeeper who was in the picture in the camera. One of his mechanics, said the man; he had taken the photo in his office and there was a TV set in the office that would show up in the picture, once it was developed.

"That's my picture!" said Morrison.

The court ignored Morrison's claim.

Morrison's lawyer then asked the storekeeper for the location of the serial number on the camera.

"I couldn't even tell you," said the complainant.

Morrison, however, eagerly volunteered the information. He found the letter P and 1-20-59. He said, "That's when I bought the camera, eight months ago."

"Eight months ago?" asked Judge Morrissey.

"Yes, sir," said Morrison.

"Just a minute — " said his attorney.

The judge continued. "Where did you buy the whiskey?"

"The whiskey was given out as Christmas presents around Christmas time. I can account for everything in the car," Morrison insisted. He had been arrested in April, closer to Easter than to Christmas.

"This radio, too?" asked the storeowner.

"Yes sir; it belongs to my grandmother," replied Morrison.

As unlikely as might seem Morrison's explanation of the Christmas gift-wrapped Haig and Haig and the other items, the case now revolved around the camera. If the picture inside it, indeed, revealed the storekeeper's mechanic, then Morrison was tied to the crime. If, however, the picture proved to be of Morrison, as he claimed, then his other explanations would appear just as credible. The issue was clearly drawn. One was right and the other was wrong, and now the truth could be ascertained. The state was directed to submit the camera to the crime lab to make a reproduction of the picture. This would decide the matter once and for all.

The picture was of Morrison. There was a TV set in the background.

Morrison was off the hook.

The storeowner theorized in court that the camera may have been switched, but Judge Morrissey found that too hard to believe.

Now, that cleared up the mystery for us. Knowing that the storeowner had accurately described the contents of the camera, Morrison had set about to rearrange the evidence more to his own advantage. He had gone to one of his policemen friends and said, in effect, "Here's a camera just like that one. Take this camera right over there to the evidence department and then put the one there in my car." Morrison claimed this was done. The identification card was changed and the incriminating camera was brought back to Morrison, who immediately got rid of it.

It was a very serious charge of police collusion with a criminal to thwart justice, and a very complicated manipulation. It had to be nailed down, at least partially, before it could be accepted. How could we be sure Morrison wasn't lying? Well, he told us who had the key camera now. The camera had the film in it with the picture of the storekeeper's mechanic. How was that for proof?

The story came out officially, later, after I had turned over the results of my investigation to the state's attorney. Assistant State's Attorney Wesolowski questioned Morrison for the record, weeks later. Morrison was testifying about Officer Carlson, the policeman who "set up the fix" when he was caught.

"Did Carlson participate in the burglaries with you?" asked Wesolowski.

"No," said Morrison. "He was the man in case we got caught in the place. He was the man that set up the fix to get me out of it."

"At that time you switched the Polaroid Land camera in that case?"

"No. It wasn't that time."

"Subsequently, the Polaroid Land camera was switched?"

"Later on."

"You obtained a Polaroid Land camera from some friend of yours. It was a used Polaroid Land camera. You took a picture of yourself or had someone take a picture of you with a television set behind you with a plain background, is that correct?"

"I did."

"What officer replaced that camera?"

"The switch was to be made with Officer Carlson. I gave the camera and my picture in it to Officer Carlson. He gave it to Officer Appleton."

"You don't know that of your own knowledge?"

"I don't know that, but I found that out. Appleton switched it the day before it came to court on the process. He went down and picked it up. The day before, at night, I met Officer Carlson at the Granville el station. It's on the North Side. He gave me the man's camera and he told me the other one was in the police department."

"You did what with the camera you got back?"

"I sold it to a fellow named George on Catalpa Avenue. I sold him the camera. That is what I did with the Land camera. I didn't want no part of it."

"The camera used as evidence?"

"The first time in front of Judge Morrissey, the man's camera was there with his picture in there. We switched it during the time it was supposed to be sent to the Polaroid people to get the picture developed. We switched it the day before it came back. I gave him the picture of me and they took that the next day, and sent it to the crime lab and it came back of me because it was all set up. I have the names of the people that took the picture."

"What are their names?"

Morrison supplied them.

* * *

Little by little, we had completed our investigation. Two months after Morrison's accusations in court, I presented the state's attorney's office with a bundle of documentary evidence lending indisputable credence to Morrison's charges. He had a good memory. We hadn't been able to shake him. I suggested that secret search warrants be obtained and that the policemen's homes be raided simultaneously.

Soon, other things were also rolling. Morrison voluntarily took a polygraph test, and the results of it firmly convinced the men in the prosecutor's office that the "babbling burglar" was telling the truth.

In January, the official interrogation of Morrison by the state's attorney's office began. He told the story of police involvement in his burglaries from start to finish, beginning with that day he had met policeman Joe Coltera coming out of the liquor store and had been greeted with: "Well, if it isn't the little burglar, Richie." He told of his first job, trying to get the golf clubs and how it had escalated from that point.

He began by listing his police confederates, at least eight of them soon to become publicized as the "the burglars in blue." They were, besides Coltera and Dicky, Ted Durros, Chris Massos, Chuck Forini, Walter Skarla, Bill Sullivan, and Jake Chandler. He gave names, addresses, and sometimes telephone numbers. Then he went into the mechanics of the operation and how the burglary ring first started working.

The first job he did with the policemen was a tire and auto store, which he set up with Dicky, Ted Durros, and Coltera. Morrison had another friend, a non-policeman, open up the store and then the two of them loaded up expensive tires, TV sets, radios, electric shavers, shotgun shells, and guns into their cars while policemen (he mentioned Coltera and Dicky) patrolled the area to make certain "everything was okay." Then after Morrison had loaded down his car with merchandise, at about five-thirty in the morning, he notified Dicky he was through with the job and left. Morrison took the loot to his garage, where the officers were to pick it up the next day when they were off duty. The split was for the policemen to get the merchandise, Morrison the money, if there was any.

The following day Morrison met several of the policemen at

Chris Massos' apartment. Although not in the Fortieth District, Chris Massos had promised cover in case a call came in, Morrison said, for which he had asked for a set of tools, a set of tires, and a good shotgun. Morrison named Dicky, Coltera, Durros, Massos, and Sullivan as being present at this division of the spoils. The men started squabbling over "who was going to get what."

Morrison said, "They were sort of peeved at Chris because he got the Browning automatic shotgun and the set of tools and he wasn't even around the area at the time. But I had promised all these items to him and I had to give them to him. So, they started splitting up these items and Bill Sullivan took a whole box of radios."

"What is a whole box?" asked the interrogator.

"He took about fifteen to twenty radios."

"Small transistor radios?"

"Small Zenith radios."

"And table models?"

"And table model radios. He took all of these because they were the only things he could get."

"Did Chris Massos get a radio?"

"Chris Massos got a set of tools, Browning automatic shotgun, and he got a little Admiral pink table model radio, and a clock radio — I can't remember the brand name of the clock radio. He got a bunch of shotgun shells, he got a couple of electric shavers, and I believe he got a transistor radio out of the situation, too. Bill Sullivan got — we mentioned what he got."

"That's all marked down here."

"Getting back to Chris Massos, he also got a set of tires. Joe Coltera got a set of tires for his car, and Jack Dicky got a set of tires for his car. Jack Dicky also got a television set. I think it's a twenty-one-inch portable. Joe Coltera got a seventeen-inch portable. Jack Dicky also got a pump shotgun. Ted Durros also got a pump shotgun with a case of shotgun shells. And they got various miscellaneous items like shavers, transistor radios, and table model radios. That's all I can remember that was split up at the time. When I gave the set of tools to Chris Massos we opened it and there was $460 there. I got that. That was my cut of the situation, seeing that was the only cash around.''

''Have you seen any of the items in their homes?''

''I seen all these items in these police officers' houses. I seen the shotgun in Ted Durros' house. I seen the TV set at Joe Coltera's house. Joe Coltera also got an AM-FM Zenith radio and Ted Durros got an AM-FM Zenith radio, and I seen all these items in their homes up to six months ago.'' Later he pinned it down. ''The only homes I was in were Chris Massos, Ted Durros, and Joe Coltera. Those were the only three homes I was in. However, through conversation with these police officers I've learned that all these other items were in the homes of the other police officers.''

* * *

From that joint venture, the cooperative burglaries grew. Morrison would meet the policemen late at night during their duty hours at the usual restaurant and they would talk about future jobs. ''Sometimes we drove through the district and cased places up and down alleys for the next day or that night.''

The next target was another tire store. The policemen themselves had cased this job. Durros, Coltera, and Dicky told Morrison that there was nothing but a padlock on the back door. Morrison checked into it, verifying their observations. Then one day the officers went ''shopping'' in the store, deciding on the items they would want Morrison to get for them later. Again, they decided on TV sets, radios, batteries, and tires. At night Morrison broke the lock, entered the store, and brought out the ''shopping list'' items the policemen had ordered.

In that job, Morrison himself took about thirty cases of spark plugs, along with television sets and record players. He later sold some of the spark plugs to a gasoline station on South Ashland Avenue. But a few days after the burglary, Chicago detectives, learning of his sale, nabbed him on the street. They took him in for possession of stolen spark plugs.

Morrison wasn't worried about the spark plug charge. How could they ever prove the plugs were stolen? The articles had no serial numbers or other identifying features. But, for other reasons, it was a touchy moment in his life. Back at his apartment was merchandise he had stolen for the policemen. If the detectives searched his home, they would have a strong case against him.

Just as he was sweating over it, his policemen friends visited him in the back of the lockup. He told them of his problem. "If they got rid of the stuff they would have a hard case to beat," he knew. The friendly cops got his keys, went to his apartment, and moved the TV sets and a record player. Morrison breathed easier.

Morrison's story continued. "Well, as time went on things started getting out of hand. A few days after that tire store they started wanting to do almost anything. They even wanted to knock off food stores in the district. The next thing was the gas station. That occurred on Catalpa and Clark, a Sinclair gas station. They wanted anti-freeze for their cars for the wintertime and they didn't want to pay the two dollars and something for the anti-freeze. They noticed the open window and they wanted me to go in and open the doors. I went in and opened it up and there was two sets of tires they got."

The interrogator from the state's attorney's office repeatedly pinned Morrison down for specific details and names of those involved in a particular job. And Morrison always had a ready reply.

"You didn't see any officer take anything out of this gas station?" he was now asked.

"Oh, yes."

"Which officers did you see?"

"Joe Coltera, Bill Sullivan and Ted Durros, those three officers. They backed the squad by the station."

"Can you mention what they took?"

"They took the batteries and tires and all kinds of polish."

"What number was the squad car?"

"207. Now, 120 came later on."

Sometimes, Morrison suggested the job himself.

"There was a music store on Balmoral and Clark. I told Joe Coltera that I needed some money for one of the cases, so I picked this out myself to do this job. I went in through the back door and the call came in. Joe Coltera heard the call. He said he heard the burglary-in-progress call given out from the squad operator. They gave a burglary-in-progress call and Joe heard the call in the Fortieth District station. He just happened to go in there to check the book to see if there was anything up for them. They usually went in to check the book. He happened to hear this call and he happened to know it was me in the place. He shot down there in 207 and blocked the street and he hit the window in the place with his spotlight. It was a music store. I can't remember the name. The guy had an intercom in the place. That's how the owner knew someone was in there. He ran down from his apartment into the street. He heard me making all this noise in the place.

"As soon as I entered the place I picked up a cigar box. I was lucky to find it. I had the money in my pocket when Joe came on the scene and hit the window with the spotlight. Ted Durros and Chris Massos knew I was there. I talked it all over with them at the el station on Berwyn. I told them to cover for me. It was supposed to be one of my nights.

"Joe Coltera blocked the street from the Bureau car and the other car came around the alley. I got over the fence and my car was parked down the street. So, I took off.

"I met Joe an hour and a half later. He said, 'Jesus Christ, was that a close one!' He told me he drove eighty miles an hour to get to the scene. So, I gave him all the money that was in the place. It was a couple of hundred dollars. I never got a chance to get to the safe. I gave him the money. I said, 'I don't know how to thank you.' I said, 'Here's all the money I got from the place.' He said, 'All right.' I told him he deserved the money for getting there that fast and he took it. I didn't get nothing out of that; I just got away. I was glad to get away."

* * *

In the middle of December, 1958, Morrison said, he "cut them off" of burglaries because he was busy handling counterfeit money, which necessitated his traveling over the country, and he no longer needed them. But the counterfeit passing ended in his arrest.

"So, I came back after the Secret Service busted me on the counterfeit money on March the fifth. I had to start with them to get money for my cases. They were getting pretty hot because I ignored them for a couple of months. In fact, they asked me a couple of times, 'When are you going to come back and give us a job?'

"Anyways, I started with them in the middle of March. They wanted liquor and they wanted meat for their freezers and they wanted various frozen food and everything."

They had found a food mart on West Thorndale right by an alley. The policemen — he named Durros, Dicky, Coltera, and Sullivan — had crowbars, with which Morrison opened the front door. They and Morrison drove to the station so all could get their cars.

They returned and parked their cars on the market's parking lot. Then they loaded the squad car with food, drove to the parking lots, and transferred it to their own cars.

They had a close call on that job, recalled Morrison.

"We were all running around in the store until I happened to think, 'Who's listening to the calls in the squad?' Joe said, 'Jesus Christ, somebody's got to listen to them.' I said, 'This is all your stuff. I'll go listen to the calls in the squad.'

"So, I went to the squad car and I was sitting there. They were coming out with bacon and hams and everything you could think of in the store, real expensive foods. They kept filling the back seat of the squad. This was around two-thirty to three o'clock in the morning.

"All of a sudden, a '57 Cadillac pulled up in back of the squad 207 in the alley. I started to get out of the car to tell these guys they got a call over the air. I don't remember, I think it was a burglary-in-progress call.

"Anyways, I was about to tell them when I seen this Cadillac pull up. It was the sergeant of the North Shore Patrol. I figured if he sees me and all this stuff in the squad, everybody is dead. I figured the best thing was to jump into the squad and drive around. The best I could do was drive away and ditch the stuff in the squad car under some porch or in the alley and come back with the squad car with nothing in it.

"So, I had to think fast. I seen this North Shore Patrol sergeant walk to the door where the coppers were running around with the food baskets filled with stuff. I didn't know what to think. I didn't know if this North Shore sergeant was to go there and check that door or not.

"Anyways, I took off and when I came back they were still there. They said, 'Where the hell you been?' I told them, I said, 'Jesus Christ, the damn sergeant came up behind me, I didn't know what to do. I'm dirty and maybe he knows who I am. I didn't know if he could recognize me or not. I didn't know if he was coming to this store or not.' They said, 'We almost had a heart attack ourselves.' They said, 'We had our guns drawn on him. We all laid low in the store.' They said, 'He went to the store next to us and checked the store; he didn't even see us in the store.' I said, 'Jesus Christ, is that a break!' "

Morrison said the food was split up by the policemen the next morning after they got off duty. "They all got about $500 worth of merchandise from what they told me." They were all in uniform and on duty at the time of the burglary, he said.

The revelations went on, as Morrison searched his memory for the record. He told of Jake Chandler's proposing the burglary of a tavern he had once owned but had sold. "He said, 'I know how to get in. He [the new owner] keeps it in the same place I kept mine, all the liquor and everything.' So, I said, 'Wonderful, let's go!' He said, 'I don't want to do it while I'm on duty, we'll do it on the day I'm off,' adding, 'I don't want to cut these other guys in, just between you and me.' So, I said, 'Well, all right.' " They opened up the cocktail lounge and took out fifteen cases of liquor, a camera, and a large set of tools. Then they did an encore that night, crossing the street to a TV repair shop. "We broke in through the back window, and we took out all kinds of stuff. There wasn't much in the store to take out; when we got into the place it was a bum deal. There was just a recorder and various items.''

Later Chandler, he said, introduced him to another police officer in the Thirty-Ninth District who talked up a bakery job. ''They said they had three or four thousand in the oven and it was very easy to go in. They wanted half of this money, Chandler and this other copper.'' Morrison went in. He found $38 in the oven. Dismayed, he hunted all over, even the basement, inside barrels.

''I gave the place a complete search and found nothing. I said 'Jeez, how am I going to tell these guys there is only $38 worth of pennies in the whole place. So, anyways, I told them. I said, 'Well, look, fellows, I never screwed anybody in my life.' I said, 'You can have all the money, but don't ever tell me again about a job you guys got lined up for three or four thousand. Go find yourself another sucker. We're through!' That's when I cut these guys off.''

As spring came on, he told how Sullivan, Massos, and Dicky had been anxious to get outboard motors, water skis, and other items for Lake Michigan outings. He stalled them, but one night at a night club ''they grabbed me right out of the place. They said, 'You are opening this place whether you like it or not; we've waited two weeks and your're going to open it up for us.' ''

He promised to knock the window out of a marine supply business about two-thirty in the morning, but the cops would have to carry out the motors. By this time, Morrison had so many cases against him that he didn't want to risk another charge. With a burglar friend, he knocked in the whole front window in a matter of seconds, first taping the window to prevent noise from the breaking and falling glass. Then the policemen came by and chased them away. Fifteen minutes later, he said, the policemen walked in the front window, as if they were investigating the break-in, and selected their outboard motors.

But Morrison was curious.

''I wanted to see how they did it, whether they took the stuff out Broadway or the back way. So, we hid in the bushes and we seen them coming out with the big outboard motors. I told my buddy, 'We'll scare the shit out of them. We'll walk like pedestrians down the alley.' So, we did that. All of a sudden we seen them both stop. They both stopped with outboard motors in their arms. They said, 'Don't move, somebody's looking at us.' That's the exact words they said.

"So, I busted out laughing and I said, 'You crazy jerks, it's only us.' So, they bawled the hell out of us for staying around there. They told us we scared the hell out of them. They put the motors in the car and they said, 'Go in there and try to get the gas tanks and try to get the automatic starters, they've got them mounted on the boards.' They said, 'Try and get the automatic starters.'

"So we went in and I tried to get the starters off and the gas tanks. I got the gas tanks stashed in the bushes but I couldn't get the starters off. In fact, I wasn't too interested in getting them off."

That summer, Morrison said, the policemen went water skiing on Lake Michigan with the motors.

* * *

By this time Morrison needed about $50,000. He had several cases pending against him, including the big federal charge on the counterfeit money. But he had a moment of inspiration one day when he spotted a safe in a Walgreen's drugstore window. "I said, 'Jesus Christ, that's it! I got to start studying safes.' "

Morrison was a brainy fellow. In order to learn about safes, he went to the logical source of information: a safe manufacturer. Claiming he represented a large juke box corporation and would be buying twenty or thirty safes, Morrison impressed the safe firm's representative. "He showed me every kind of safe he had, books, diagrams, and it was wonderful. Right overnight I learned almost everything there was about a safe from this fellow. I saw one I wanted for myself and I gave him a $2,000 order. But I never did order it. I told him I would send him a check Friday, but I never did."

While he boned up on safes, he pulled more burglaries with police officers. They opened up a meat market. There was a safe in it. Morrison ripped into it and pocketed $1,300 in cash. Then he called the policemen in to loot the store. Morrison kept the money; the policemen, the meat. He said he ate steaks at some of their houses after that and "they were eating steak every night."

Later, he said, Durros and Massos became interested in better furnishings for their apartments. One rainy night they got together with him at the restaurant and went to a furniture store on North Broadway. Morrison opened the back door and took drapes and a big armchair. Then he notified Coltera, "It's open." Morrison later recalled which officers appeared and, to some extent, who took what. A $75 early colonial chair went to Skarla. Another got a "big marble table" and took it home. "He told me where he chipped it rolling it through the store." They took out drapes by the bales. "They didn't tell me how many bales they took out of there, but from what I heard they took quite a bit. They were real expensive. They've got them hanging in their apartments now." Morrison said he didn't get a dime out of the haul but just opened the store to help them out with their apartments.

Later, when Morrison lined up jobs, Massos drove him and the tools he would need to open the safes.

"On one job I told him how I would enter the place, and every half hour I would come through the hole up there and signal him down on the street. I said, 'If anything goes wrong, if a call comes in, you come and hit the front window with the spotlight and hit the roof. I'll know something is up.' He said, 'Okay.' I entered the store two hours later after he dropped me off. He kept circling the block. I saw him in the streets and there was this Flash cab parked right out in front. He kept sitting there and sitting there. Finally Chris came up to him and chased him out of there. This was the night of this burglary. He chased the guy out of there. He told him this was no place to hang around.

"He chased him out of there and then the watchman came to check the doors. All of a sudden Chris came and hit the window with the spotlight and he hit the roof. I was up on the roof at the time. I still hadn't entered the store. I was still trying to get into the hole, trying to get the hole the right size. I looked over and seen him talking to this guy. I jumped off the roof on the other end of the building and I hid in the bushes until he met me. He told me the watchman came and he chased him away and I said, 'Okay.'

"I went back on the roof and when I got into the store the sergeant-lieutenant came around. He came right up to the front window and this safe was in the front window. I put my body beside the safe and he didn't see me. He just kept on driving along. Later on I said, 'Jesus Christ, who was that?' He said, 'It was the sergeant.' He said he couldn't do anything about it. He said the best thing to do was to let him go through the shopping center and inspect it. He said so many things were happening in the district that the sergeant-lieutenant was checking it out.

"Well, when I went to the door of the safe, the safe was open. They forgot to close the door of the safe that night. That was a square door; the round door was locked. That's where the most money was, twenty or thirty thousand dollars all the time before the pickup. However, the change kept behind the square door was all I was interested in at the time. At the time I couldn't open the round doors. It would take around three hours. So I just messed around with the change compartments which had about two or three thousand dollars in each one of them.

"So I just walked in and the door was open and I took all the money out and left the place through the side door. They even forgot to put the main padlock on it. It was a big padlock, really strong. Nothing could cut through it. Evidently the store manager forgot to put it on.

"So I left the door open because Massos wanted to get the camera and some liquor. I couldn't take anything else because I had a hard enough time carrying the change. It weighed about a hundred pounds."

There was $1,600 in cash, as it turned out, and Morrison gave Massos $400 of it. Later, when the burglarly was reported, it was Massos who officially investigated it.

Morrison told of the conversation he and Massos had the next day. "He told me, he says, 'Jesus, when I got in there with the store manager he couldn't figure how they had got into the place, so I took him over and showed him the roof. I said to him, 'Is that the way your ceiling usually is?' The store manager said, 'Holy smokes, that's the way he came in!' So they went up and checked the roof.

"The safe wasn't even touched except for the inner compartments. Massos said he told the manager, 'Say, if they took the hinges off the door, I'll reimburse you for everything that was taken out of the safe.' He told the manager that. The manager said, 'What do you mean?' He showed the door to the manager and how the bolts were still on the door. The manager said, 'You're right, I didn't see that.' He was telling me what a dumb jerk this assistant manager was. He said he kept saying to the store manager, 'Looks like an inside job.' He told him they must have had the combination to the safe; that was the only way to open the door without damaging it. The store manager was certain the door was locked, but nobody knew it wasn't except me and Massos. Anyways, that was this conversation that took place between Massos and this store manager."

That was Morrison's swan song as a burglar working with the policemen. Shortly afterward, he was arrested by the downtown detectives.

But like an afterthought Morrison brought forth one more burglary job from his memory. A shoe store on Devon Avenue had a fire sale of about 20,000 shoes. Policemen from the Fortieth District were guarding it. One night, according to Morrison, he and four policemen got into several cars, including one squad, and loaded up "tons of these shoes." They filled thirty or forty large cartons with shoes, estimated in value at $13,000 to $14,000: a neat night's haul. "We took every one left in the place. The insurance company couldn't figure out where the shoes went. No one knew." One of the officers, Bill Sullivan, was drunk that night; he went into a show lounge and sold shoes for two dollars a pair. Later he almost piled up his car going through a stop light, running onto the sidewalk, almost crashing into a drugstore.

"He was real drunk. They all chewed his ass out for doing that stunt."

* * *

Transcribed, Morrison's long interrogation came to seventy-seven pages of revelations. It was an amazing, incredible document. Yet, as true as I believed it was and as now the state's attorney believed it to be, it did not mean the policemen Morrison mentioned were criminally guilty. Like any other defendant, each one first had to be *proved* guilty in a fair trial.

The stage was now set for the next, dramatic development. In order to gather concrete evidence, the stolen articles had to be found in possession of the accused men. Morrison said some of the goods were there. The homes had to be searched.

The secret simultaneous raids on the homes of eight policemen got under way on January 14, 1960, on a wet, cold Thursday night when the temperature was in the low 30's. The rain was turning to snow. That night was selected because it was a good one on which to find a man at home. Frank Ferlic, first assistant, and Paul Newey, chief investigator from the state's attorney's office, obtained search warrants that afternoon. They then lined up the chief of uniformed police, his deputies, and the chief of detectives and his deputy. Later they met in the designated room of a downtown hotel with the captains and lieutenants. Ferlic and Newey gave the police officials sealed envelopes containing the names and addresses of the policemen to be taken into custody. There were eight arrest teams — one for each suspected policeman — with a captain and a lieutenant of city police and a state's attorney policeman on each team.

The envelopes were opened after the teams had got into their cars. Each order directed them to enter the particular home at exactly 10:30 P.M.

At the appointed time, the teams entered the homes of Ted Durros, twenty-six; Chris Massos, twenty-six; Jack Dicky, thirty; Walter Skarla, fifty; Joe Coltera, forty-three; Jake Chandler, twenty-nine; Charles Forini, forty-five; and William Sullivan, twenty-eight. Needless to say, the policemen were completely surprised by the midwinter's night raid. They were taken to a room in their "staging area" downtown and Ferlic questioned them in the presence of five court stenographers while police officials restively waited outside. All eight were suspended by Police Commissioner Timothy J. O'Connor. After Ferlic was through questioning them, he turned them over to their superiors who took their badges and relieved them of duty. Each was booked on burglary charges and released on $3,000 bond and served a subpoena for his appearance before the grand jury the following Monday.

While the policemen were being questioned downtown, the owner of one of the large stores that had been burglarized was taken from home to home, identifying articles that had been taken from his business. Goods identified as stolen were found in seven of the homes, all but that of Sullivan, where no loot was found. The recovered merchandise included TV sets, radios, draperies, tires, guns, an outboard motor, gasoline tanks, cigarette lighters, furniture, batteries, and anti-freeze. Their total estimated value was somewhere between five and ten thousand dollars. It took four patrol wagons to haul it all to the state's attorney's office at Twenty-Sixth and California, where it filled two rooms.

By dawn it was snowing in Chicago, and nearly freezing. That day Chicago's *American* hit the streets with an equally chilling 96-point, all-capitals, six-column headline:

8 CITY COPS SEIZED, ACCUSED OF THEFTS

It was suddenly big news, not only in Chicago, but all over the nation. Reporters interviewed everyone in any official position, including myself, and even dug up victims of the burglaries. Police Commissioner O'Connor was quoted as saying, "This is a crime that calls to heaven for vengeance." Morrison was quoted as to how the burglaries had started. A major police scandal had exploded in Chicago!

* * *

Mayor Richard J. Daley was in Florida enjoying his first vacation in years when he first heard of the Summerdale Police scandal. It came as a great shock to him. He had taken great pride in the Chicago Police Department, seeming to personally identify with it, almost as if it were an extension of his personality. Recognizing the arrests as a crisis of major proportions, he immediately ended his vacation and flew home to Chicago. He arrived on Sunday and issued a terse, urgent two-paragraph statement.

"I have directed Commissioner O'Connor to bring me a full report today of everything that is known and that has transpired since the apprehension of the members of the burglary ring.

"The public may be assured that every possible step will be taken to bring to justice every officer and person directly or indirectly responsible for these crimes, and betrayal of the public trust."

He was soon to call it "the worst police scandal in Chicago's history."

Three days later, five more policemen were arrested, three for allegedly extorting $1,200 from Morrison, and two for conspiracy to obstruct justice — Edgar Carlson and James Appleton on the camera switch.

The prosecution of the Summerdale case was to be no simple matter, complicated by the political picture in Chicago at the time. The state's attorney, Benjamin Adamowski, was a Republican; Mayor Daley, of course, was a Democrat. Considering their past postures toward each other, conflict seemed inevitable.

Adamowski, a dark, robust man of about 180 pounds on a five-nine or five-ten frame, had once been a Democrat. Under Mayor Kennelly he had been corporation counsel. His ambition was to run for mayor and become Chicago's first Polish-American mayor. But Richard J. Daley, entertaining ambitions of his own, had defeated both Mayor Kennelly and Adamowski in the Democratic primary. Later, Adamowski had broken with Daley and the Democratic organization. He ran for state's attorney as a Republican, secured backing — and won. It was a major accomplishment.

When the Summerdale scandal burst open, Adamowski seemed to view it as another round in his battle with his archfoe Daley. At one point he even hinted that the Mayor might be called before the grand jury. "There is no question about Daley's responsibility in this police mess," he was quoted. He indicated that Daley might even be subpoenaed. Eventually, Adamowski demanded mass polygraph tests for all 11,000 Chicago policemen, insisting that the tests be administered by someone outside of Chicago.

With headline following headline and with almost everyone making a statement or allegation, the political complexities of the case often overshadowed the questions of law. And the fact that I, a Democrat, had dumped the scandal in the lap of Adamowski, a Republican and Daley foe, tended to confuse my own role in the public mind.

By the time the amended estimates of loot taken by Morrison and his confederates from stores in the Summerdale and Rogers Park police districts over the two-year period had reached $100,000, I felt compelled to clarify my position. So I issued a statement of my own. I began with the hope "that this will not be a political issue" and that all would cooperate in the cleanup, just as, during war, partisan politics are forgotten.

"The police knew of these accusations in July. They would not listen. We investigated. Then the state agreed that Morrison possibly was telling the truth. We did not wish publicity, but the truth came out.

"This was given to the state's attorney to prosecute and not for political reasons. He is the elected official. He controls the grand jury. The evidence in this case was not turned over to the state's attorney because he was a Republican, but because he was the people's elected prosecutor. The people of this county have a right to vigorous prosecution. To now resort to further arrests without evidence, to demand lie detector tests, when one is not considered as evidence in any court, and to indicate guilt by association are methods foreign to our administration of justice.

"The state's attorney should prosecute the policemen he has evidence against and not conduct a political campaign. He must prosecute in several thousand other cases in the criminal court where police detection has apprehended and gathered evidence against criminals awaiting trial. Discrediting police in general will only weaken his prosecution in these cases. The police force is not all bad because of a few."

* * *

Summerdale was a hot political issue during that Presidential election year of 1960. Mayor Daley didn't have to think twice to realize that a mishandling of the Summerdale case could mean serious political trouble if it simmered on into the primaries and then into the general election in November.

Developments in the Summerdale case vied regularly with the top national news. And symbolic of the walloped public image that Chicago policemen now had was the song reported in the Chicago *Daily News*. Said to have been heard in a saloon close by the Fortieth Police Station, its tune was that of an oldtime, popular song:

In the good old Summerdale,
In the good old Summerdale,
Stealing down a shady lane

With your pal from jail.
You loot my house, I'll loot yours;
We'll have a time making bail.
You'll be my lootsy-wootsy,
In the good old Summerdale.

Discounting demotions and resignations of certain minor officials, the first victim was Police Commissioner O'Connor. He resigned on January 23, slightly more than a week after the arrests. His temporary successor, Captain K. V. Phelan, shook up the department. By early February, a special grand jury was investigating the scandal.

Who would replace O'Connor? This was important politically, for his successor would inevitably serve as a symbol — cleanup or coverup. The Mayor hastily assembled a committee to select the new police director. Candidates from all over the country were to be interviewed. At the head of the mayor's committee was Orlando W. Wilson, the fifty-nine-year-old dean of the School of Criminology at the University of California at Berkeley. On February 22, a week after Chicago had been named the winner of the National Cleanest Town Contest for the one million-and-over category, pushing ahead of Philadelphia and New York, Orlando Wilson was chosen as the new police commissioner. Presto! A cleanup image had been established.

Indictment of the accused policemen soon followed, and then the legal skirmishing began.

In all, thirteen policemen were indicted as a result of Morrison's statements: the eight arrested that first night; James Appleton and Edgar Carlson, charged with conspiracy to obstruct justice on the camera-switching case; Lewis Holdmen, Carl Holland, and Ray Bailey, all charged with extorting money from Morrison for overlooking a burglary.

The cases of the eight Summerdale defendants were assigned, through seeking changes of venue, to the only woman on the Criminal Court bench, Judge B. Fain Tucker. In July she dismissed four counts in the eighteen-count conspiracy indictment — the heart of the state's case — by sustaining the defense's motion to quash. The same month Judge William V. Daly dismissed the extortion charge against Bailey under the Fourth-Term Act. Bailey had not been brought to trial within 120 days, which was the fault of the state's attorney. In September, Judge Frank R. Leonard refused to hear the case against Appleton and Carlson; and in October, a month before election, Judge Daly quashed three counts that were the heart of the case against Holland and Holdmen. It was beginning to appear that Morrison's accusations would not go beyond the headlines that they had wrought.

The state appealed Judge Tucker's quashing of the eight indictments, however, and in the November, 1960, term of the Illinois Supreme Court, Judge Tucker's quashing decision was reversed. She had agreed with a defense motion that the wording of the indictments was not specific enough, but the high court overruled her on all points.

Politics continued unabated throughout all this. In the November, 1960, general election, Adamowski sought reelection as state's attorney — planning later, some thought, to use the office as a springboard to unseat Daley as Mayor. He was opposed by Democrat Daniel P. Ward. Dan Ward, selected to run against Adamowski, had been dean of the DePaul University law school for several years. A tall, friendly fellow, he had been aloof from precinct politics; a legal scholar, his was a scholarly approach. He was a friend of Art McGloon's and I had met him on several occasions. Although I took no active part in the campaign, I did help Ward indirectly by supplying him with information on his opponent's record of lost cases, particularly the number — which was large — that had been dismissed under the Four-Term Act. One of the accused policemen had gone free under the fourth term, and before that I had liberated a number of my own clients under that provision of the law. Who was closer to his performance in the Criminal Court and had a better overall view of his record than the public defender?

Ward won in November. In December he became the new

state's attorney and inherited the prosecution of the Summerdale cases.

Meanwhile, the trial of Appleton and Carlson on the camera-switch case had gone to Judge Daniel Covelli's court. In early December, following testimony in which Morrison took the Fifth Amendment forty-six times, a jury found them guilty. Carlson was handed nine months in the county jail, Appleton a $500 fine. The convictions were appealed to the Illinois Supreme Court, but they stuck: Morrison was ruled a credible witness.

* * *

Since the time his story was accepted by the state's attorney's office, Morrison had been, for all practical purposes, a temporary ward of the state. As the state's star witness, he was housed in the witness quarters on the fifth floor of the county jail. He was to spend approximately two years there. Keeping him happy there was to be a problem. Because he was my client, it became my problem. The case dragged on and on. Defendants asked for continuances. Meanwhile, Morrison periodically got restive. There were times when he said he wouldn't testify. He complained that sometimes the food was not up to par. He was used to the best, and he found fault with anything less than that. He had his share of steaks. He had radio and TV. He was permitted to make telephone calls and they took him out for rides from time to time, but the incarceration eventually began to wear on him. He let it be known that he remained in the jail by choice. He told me he could get out anytime he wanted to. He knew the structural defects; he once told the warden he could have got out of "that flea trap" at his convenience. Throughout the long wait I listened to his complaints and when I could, I tried to do something about them. I found him to be a very congenial fellow. He was friendly to me. He sent me greeting cards on holidays and on my birthday.

Finally, in June, 1961, following a series of pre-trial hearings, a jury of twelve women was selected to hear the case of the eight policemen in the sweltering seventh-floor court of Judge James B. Parsons, a black judge who was later to become a distinguished federal judge. It was the first time that a black judge had presided over an important criminal trial with an all-woman jury. Sullivan, in whose home no evidence had been found, asked for a bench trial, so that Judge Parsons would decide his fate while the jury would determine the verdict on the other seven policemen.

Although Adolf Eichmann was on trial in Jerusalem around this time for mass murders of Jews during World War II, in Chicago the Jerusalem trial was eclipsed by the Summerdale case. My own role in the trial as Morrison's counsel was not in the arena of legal gladiators but quietly out of the spotlight. When Morrison testified, I was in the courtroom to advise him, if necessary. I was his lawyer, even though he was not on trial.

Morrison was the star of the trial. The whole case hinged on him. He became the target of the defense attorney's fire from the opening moments of the trial. This was a new role for me, to be on the side of the state. It was a new role for Morrison, too. The defense lawyers protested immediately to Morrison's testifying, and then to almost everything he said.

The array of opposing attorneys was impressive, or perhaps formidable, depending on which view you had of it. Prominent attorneys Barnabas Sears and Charles M. Rush had been brought in to prosecute, assisted by Daniel McCarthy and Louis Garippo from the Cook County state's attorney's office. Sears was a former president of the Illinois Bar Association. Rush was a senior trial lawyer in another firm. Charles A. Bellows was chief defense counsel, flanked by attorneys Marshall Schwarzbach, Julius Lucius Echeles, George Cotsirilos, Stephen Levy, and Morris Meyers. These were the batteries from both sides that Morrison faced in the witness chair.

Morrison, a tiny figure as he faced the various imposing figures of the prosecution and the defense, took five days to tell his story. Following the direct testimony, his cross-examination began. After two days, he was showing the strain; his eyes blinked and his shoulders sagged. He had to ask Bellows to repeat questions and took long pauses. Bellows, always a shrewd and persistent cross-examiner, kept pushing him, getting him to admit that, at times, he was guessing, and that he was testifying in order to help himself out of deeper trouble.

The first major attack on Morrison's testimony came when the defense moved for a directed verdict of not guilty, basing the motion on the contention that Morrison was a known thief and perjurer. Judge Parsons considered the motion. After almost prayerful deliberation, he ruled that Morrison was a credible witness. The "babbling burglar" could be believed. Now it was up to the jury to decide to what extent he should be believed.

The defense then produced its own full-scale presentation.

The case went to the jury and deliberations began at 5:02 P.M. on Wednesday, August 23, 1961. At 9:17 P.M. a verdict was reached. Meanwhile, the bench trial of Sullivan continued before Judge Parsons. Parsons ordered the bailiff to ask the jurors to stand by until the lawyers, defendants, and their families could be rounded up.

All seven defendants in the jury trial were found guilty, but since there were varying degrees of involvement in the series of burglaries, there was a wide range in punishments. Skarla and Forini escaped with $500 fines. Judge Parsons then set the specific terms for the other five. The judge sentenced Coltera, Chandler, and Durros to two-to-five years; Massos, two-to-three; and Dicky, one-to-three. The judge then found Sullivan guilty, sentenced him to six months in the county jail, and fined him $1,000.

Sullivan was a fine-looking young man. I just hated to see him involved in the scandal. I had known his father, who had attended DePaul University law school while he worked as a policeman at night. The father later became a captain. Young Sullivan was the youngest of the lot to be indicted and it seemed he had been drawn into the crimes as a result of the bad influence of some of the others.

Only the five sentenced to the pen appealed. In January,

1965, the Illinois Supreme Court unanimously affirmed the convictions. In October of that year the U.S. Supreme Court refused to hear the case. The ex-policemen had exhausted their legal remedies. The next month, after a six-year fight, they surrendered to the sheriff's office at Twenty-Sixth and California where it all began, to go to the penitentiary.

What happened to Morrison? All of the cases against him in Criminal Court were dropped. That was the purpose of his cooperation in the first place. But after the trial of the eight policemen, he still faced a federal charge of passing counterfeit money. He pleaded guilty and asked for leniency. His testimony in the burglary conspiracy trial became a factor there too. U.S. District Court Judge Julius H. Miner gave him three years probation. Morrison was free. He vowed it would be his last court appearance.

What the Chicago *Tribune* called "one of the greatest scandals ever to rock Chicago" was officially closed.

Then, like a nagging epilogue, in January, 1966, the residents of the Fortieth District petitioned the city for a new name for their police district. "Summerdale" still evoked unpleasant memories. So it became the "Foster Street Station."

For me there was to be a personal epilogue, as I experienced some unexpected repercussions from the Mayor's office.

* * *

Back in the early fifties when I was Francis McCurrie's first assistant, an inmate of the county jail — who was a client of mine — insisted that he had been sold an apple by the jail commissary for the outrageous price of twenty-five cents. It was my obligation to my client to see that his complaint was voiced. So I brought it out in open court.

Frank Sain at that time was warden of the county jail and ran the commissary. He was very unhappy about the story of the two-bit apple. He called my boss, McCurrie, and told him I shouldn't be making statements like that in court. I got called down for it. Sain got the nod to run for sheriff of Cook County.

It soon appeared, after the Summerdale scandal, that I had inadvertently stepped on bigger toes than Frank Sain's when I had listened to the babbling burglar and had followed through. Mayor Daley was miffed. He seemed to blame me for the whole notoriety of the scandal. Soon after the eight policemen were arrested in 1960, Daley called my ward committeeman, James J. Sullivan, into his office. Why had the Summerdale case hit the newspapers before he knew of it? Why hadn't it been called to his attention? He had perhaps been as proud of the Chicago Police Department as of any other single segment of city government.

It came as a great surprise to me that Daley held me personally responsible for what had happened. Since I was not thinking of currying his favor, I had seen no reason to go to the mayor's ear with the routine administration of my job. But if he had expected someone to warn him about the case, there were many others who could have done so. The trouble had been that they had not believed Morrison's story, so they had not passed it on to the mayor. But they had the basic facts and could have enlightened him. Why hadn't *they* been held responsible for not properly investigating Morrison's charges? Considering the number of people involved, I assumed that somebody *had* tipped the Mayor off.

On the surface, the Summerdale case never affected my relations with Mayor Daley. But the word went out to his protege-secretary and the man closest to him, Matthew Danaher, that my name was mud. Danaher didn't tell me himself, but the word was passed on to me that the Mayor had said, "Wait till he's looking for a judgeship — and he's just not going to get it!"

Outwardly, the Mayor remained friendly toward me. From time to time I would pass him in City Hall or we would meet at Democratic functions. I always spoke to him with a "Hello, Mr. Mayor," and he responded with a cheery "How are you, Jerry?" He never refused to talk or to return my salutation.

As the years slipped by, I was considered for slating on the Democratic ticket for judgeships, sheriff, and state's attorney.

Considered. Every time a vacancy developed, my name would be mentioned; my prospects usually would be rated excellent — until the matter reached the inner circle.

In 1962 I appeared before the eighty-man county committee of Democratic slatemakers as a potential candidate for sheriff of Cook County. Newspapers labeled me a frontrunner. Nothing happened. In 1966, when Dan Ward was appointed to the Illinois Supreme Court, that left his powerful state's attorney job open. Again, I was a leading contender, but John Stamos was appointed by the Cook County Board to fill the unexpired term. (Under the law, the County Board fills vacancies.) Later, Stamos was given an appellate judgeship, and Edward V. Hanrahan was slated and was elected as state's attorney.

Twice I was sponsored for the bench by my ward committeeman, Sullivan, once each for the Municipal Court and the Circuit Court. Later when I moved to Dolton, a South Side suburb, I was sponsored twice more for a judgeship by my committeeman there, Patrick O'Block. Although I didn't have the driving desire to be a judge that others may have, I think any lawyer would like to sit on the bench for a while, unless he is making so much money in private practice that he can't afford it. The public defender's salary was not much below a judge's salary, but I had devoted many years to representing the indigent in a manner that had gained recognition throughout the country, which in turn was a credit to Cook County and Chicago. Most people in the legal profession thought I deserved this recognition.

At least twice I went in to see Mayor Daley, to personally ask for a promotion to a Circuit Court judgeship. He had, after all, promised as much if I did a good job as public defender. But most of all I wanted to discover from a personal interview if the message that had been passed down to me from Matt Danaher was true.

The Mayor never said no. Each time he said he'd consider my request seriously. But after a while it became evident that the original, indirect message was absolutely accurate. Mayor

Daley considered judgeships as his to dispense as he saw fit, and he clearly did not intend to award one to me. Although the bar associations had given me high marks, loyalty was the prime requisite to Daley, and he had decided in his own mind that my representing Morrison was an unforgivable act of disloyalty.

Loyalty, in Daley's criteria for selecting judges, ranked well above legal ability. Candidates were selected to satisfy ward committeemen or to reward a lawyer who had done the party a very good favor or who had done as much for Mayor Daley personally. Some judicial candidates wouldn't know how to get to the courthouse. One evening I received a call at home from a judge who was a friend of mine to be on the lookout for a newly elected judge on a coalition ticket. When he got to the Criminal Court Building I was to show him around. I waited and waited. He never appeared. Finally I went looking for him. He was two blocks away, trying to get into the Marshall High School on a day the school was closed.

My personal epilogue to the Summerdale case didn't end so neatly. Instead, it became a forcible reminder of a lesson I had learned years before as a public defender. In this office, you travel a lonely road. Your clients are poor and they have no power and the next day they are gone. You are by yourself. You cannot grant favors. You do not control anything. The only thing you can do is give the poor and unfortunate a fair and impartial trial to the best of your ability.

It was all right with me. This was a great vocation, and I never regretted it.

CHAPTER 9

Protecting a State's Witness

SOMETIMES THE PUBLIC DEFENDER finds himself on the other side protecting the constitutional rights of a defendant who has turned state's evidence. That's what I did for Richard Morrison. The state's attorney can't be expected to do that at the same time that he is prosecuting the case. The witness's own involvement may result in a light sentence or a discharge. However, without this defendant's testimony the state would not have been able to convict the real culprits and bring their crimes to a halt.

* * *

In these cases I was cast in an unaccustomed role; to a certain extent, I was using my talents on the side of the state, helping to gain a conviction. Yet basically I was doing the same for these clients as I had for thousands before them — protecting their constitutional rights and getting them the best deals possible under the circumstances.

Gloria Rusella and Albert Warpek were charged with being part of Tony Rusella's gang that robbed wealthy North Side and suburban homes. Gloria was Tony Rusella's trim, brunette, twenty-six-year-old wife. She and Warpek had become state's witnesses.

Officially, my appointment came in Chief Justice Joseph J. Drucker's court on that July day of her arraignment, when the clerk called out her case: "Gloria Rusella."

Judge Drucker said, "Gloria Rusella, do you have an attorney?"

"No, I don't," she said.

"The court will appoint the public defender to represent you."

Bernard Winsberg, the assistant state's attorney in that court, stepped forward to notify the defendant he was providing copies of the lists of witnesses and the three typewritten confessions she had given to the police.

I said, "I will acknowledge receipt of the confessions of Gloria Rusella and on behalf of Gloria Rusella in all indictments we will waive the reading of the indictments, and since I have just been appointed, enter pleas of not guilty."

Judge Drucker assigned the indictments to Judge Abraham W. Brussell and I was formally her attorney. At a later hearing I would change the pleas of Mrs. Rusella and Warpek to guilty, a normal thing to expect in cases dealing with state's witnesses, and obtain a severance of their cases from their co-defendants.

At that time, Warpek was under guard in the witness quarters of the county jail where Morrison spent so much time, and Gloria Rusella was being guarded by state's attorney's police at a suburban motel. She said she had informed because she was afraid of her husband, whom she said had threatened her and her three children. She and Warpek — and especially she — were "hot" witnesses. Already one gang member had been murdered and another had suddenly vanished and was believed to have been killed.

The leader of "Chicago's gang of terror bandits," as the newspapers called them, was Tony Rusella, a forty-one-year-old ex-convict. Being sought along with Rusella was Walter Dosser, an ex-hairdresser accused of having taken a prominent role in several robberies and singled out as a torture expert.

Statements from Mrs. Rusella implicated her husband and several of his associates in fives crimes in which they:

1. Looted a suburban Lincolnwood home of more than $5,000 in furs and jewelry during a robbery in which the owner, his wife, and their children were threatened with torture.

2. Took $21,150 in another Lincolnwood home robbery.

3. Prowled a Lake Shore Drive apartment and took furs and jewelry valued at more than $7,000.

4. Seized more than $8,000 in furs and jewelry the same night in another home burglary.

5. Took jewelry valued at more than $8,000 in their most savage crime, a home raid in New Trier Township, in which they stripped three women and tortured them with lighted cigarettes, molested a child, and viciously beat the man of the house.

Mrs. Rusella was arrested a month before I was appointed to represent her when police found her digging up a canister of stolen jewelry in her backyard near Joliet, Illinois, near Chicago. She had had enough of being forced by Rusella to participate in crimes and had arranged with the Joliet police to be caught. Once arrested, she talked freely. Within a short time, the police had rounded up all suspected members of the gang except two — Tony Rusella and Walter Dosser.

Excerpts from her statements portrayed the gang's modus operandi and the details of the cases. For instance, in the $21,150 Lincolnwood home robbery, Tony Rusella had got his lead — according to Gloria Rusella — from a woman who played cards with one of the victims. The victim-to-be, it was reported, had a five-carat, square-cut diamond ring, a black onyx watch with diamonds, and other expensive jewelry.

"A few days later," said Gloria Rusella, "Tony sent me to the women's apparel store owned by [the victims] at Devon and Western Avenue. I saw Mrs. Franklin and she was wearing a large diamond ring. Tony then made plans for the robbery.

"A few nights later I drove our T-bird with Tony and Walter [Dosser] with me. Tony got out of the car and told me to drive Jimmy [Barceloni] and Walter to the Franklin home.

"Tony told Walter, before we left, that Tony or I would call the home and that one of them should answer the phone. Tony also told them to try and disguise themselves with Mr. Franklin's clothes and to take scarves or something to hide their faces. That was it. So I drove Walter and Jimmy and dropped them off. I saw them go through the woods toward the house. I left and picked up Tony again.

"I stopped at a drug store and called the Franklin house about 9:45 P.M. Walter answered the phone and I told him it was me, and he said, 'Hi, honey, call back in ten minutes because I have company.' So I waited ten more minutes and called again. Jimmy answered the phone and said that he and Walter would be leaving in five minutes. I told this to Tony and we drove over to pick them up.

"When Tony and I got to where Jimmy had his car parked, Jimmy was gone and Walter was standing there holding a pillow case with the furs and the costume jewelry. Tony told Walter to put everything except the good jewelry and the money in the alley behind the houses. Tony sent me home with the good jewelry to my home in Joliet. Tony counted out $1,100 in cash in front of me."

The most savage scene took place at the Clevy home where Mr. Clevy was badly beaten and his wife and child tortured.

About two months before the crime, Mrs. Rusella said, George Holcomb, a twenty-three-year-old doorman at a beauty salon, gave Dosser a duplicate set of keys and an auto license number. Holcomb frequently lined up potential robbery victims in this way.

"Walter Dosser," said Gloria Rusella in her statement, "brought the keys to our apartment and told Tony and I that these keys belonged to a Mrs. Clevy from Winnetka and that they were good keys for a job because he knew the woman from the beauty shop, that she was a millionaire, that he had seen her wear three different diamond rings, one of which was supposed to be at least a ten-carat stone. This information was related to Dosser by Holcomb."

Rusella, she said, paid Holcomb for the information and keys. Tony then checked the automobile license number with the Illinois secretary of state's Chicago office and learned the

Clevy address in New Trier Township. Then Tony and Gloria drove around the area of the estate, studying the streets and terrain.

"Tony was very impressed with the home, although he said the area would be very hard to get into.

"Then a couple of days after that, Tony, Walter Dosser, and I drove out to the area of the home. Tony and Walter then began making plans for the best route in and out from the home."

About 1 A.M. on another occasion, they drove to the Clevy place and dropped Dosser off. An hour later, after he had tested the key and had gone into the mansion, they picked him up. He had made a thorough examination of the house and was impressed by its extravagant furnishings.

The next day Rusella brought Jimmy Barceloni in on the plans, and the three men and Gloria Rusella mapped out the job in a tavern on Montrose Avenue. Rusella told Barceloni to bring his own galoshes and a long coat to cover all of his clothing. Since he had been nabbed once by police because of a footprint, Rusella insisted on galoshes on every job. The long coat was to protect the other clothing in case there was blood or other identifying substances. The galoshes and coat could be disposed of easily.

While Rusella gathered in a supply of strong adhesive tape and rope, his wife shopped for large woman's stockings to be used as masks. On the morning of the Sunday night crime the two of them drove to the North Shore where Tony rented a set of master keys from a man who handled keys and guns for the gang. The keys were guaranteed to fit any make of General Motors car. They then stopped at the Lake Forest Oasis where Tony jotted down the number of a pay telephone that would later be important in the night's operation. The rest of the day they spent sunning themselves on Lake Petite and talking over the night's business.

At 9:30 that Sunday night, she said, she and Rusella met Dosser and Barceloni. Rusella had three revolvers, masks, rope, and the master keys.

"Tony then gave Walter and Jimmy the master keys and told them to go and steal a car. Walter and Jimmy were walking around trying cars with the keys and Tony was getting mad watching them fumble. Tony got out of the car and tried the keys also on several cars, but he didn't have any luck either. So Tony told them to walk over to a parking lot and he got in the car with me and we followed.

"Walter and Jimmy stole a blue Pontiac and then we drove over to where Jimmy had his Cadillac parked. I got into Jimmy's Cadillac and drove to the 3400 block on North Spaulding. Jimmy followed me with the stolen blue Pontiac, and Tony and Walter followed in the T-Bird. We parked and I gave Jimmy's keys back to him. Jimmy parked the blue Pontiac in the same block and Tony told Jimmy and Walter to walk to the nearest tavern. Tony and I had to pick up Al."

"Who is Al and how does he figure in this robbery?" asked her interrogator.

"Albert Warpek," she said, "During the previous week, Tony called Al and told him that he would like to see him, and Al told him that Tony could pick him up the next day at 1800 South Ashland at about 5 P.M. The next day, Tony took a cab and picked Al up and brought him to our apartment. In front of me, Tony and Walter Dosser laid out the plans to Al regarding the Clevy robbery. Tony told Al the reason he called him in on this job is because he knew that Al needed money and that they expected to get a good haul from this robbery."

They started out in two cars, with Rusella and Gloria leading the way. Barceloni and Warpek had been told by Rusella that Dosser was to be in charge.

"Jimmy then pulled away, following our car, which I was driving. I drove to Edens Expressway where I got on at the Kimball entrance and I drove to the Willow Street Exit where I put on my directional signals for them to get off, which Jimmy did. I kept driving straight. Tony and I drove to the Lake Forest Oasis and waited. This was about 2:30 A.M., Monday morning.

"At about 3 A.M. Tony told me to go and stand in the phone

booth with the number that Tony gave Walter. I went into the booth and stayed in there till about 3:15 or 3:20 A.M. and then the phone rang.

"I answered and it was Walter Dosser. He said, 'Hi, honey, how are you? Let me speak to my other friend.' I then gave the phone to Tony. Tony talked to him for a while, then hung up. After he came out of the phone booth. Tony told me they were in the house, that they had it under control, that they were getting ready to have the safe opened, and that they would be leaving the house within the next fifteen minutes.

"Tony and I waited around the Oasis for another five minutes. We then went to the car and I drove very slowly to our meeting spot in the 3400 block on North Spaulding. We parked kitty-corner from Jimmy's brown Cadillac to wait for Dosser, Barceloni, and Warpek. We waited till about 4:30 A.M. and it began getting light out and Tony began getting worried because they weren't back. He then told me to start the car up and drive him down Belmont to some busy corner where he could get a cab, that he would take a cab and go home and I was to drive to Tower Road to pick them up, which were the plans in case they had trouble.

"We drove about six blocks and Tony told me to turn around for one more look. When we arrived back in the 3400 block on North Spaulding, we found Jimmy's brown Cadillac gone; so we knew that they had come back. We circled the block a few times looking for Dosser and we couldn't find him, so we drove to our apartment. When we arrived there, we found Dosser waiting for us there.

"Dosser was very upset and told Tony that they didn't get anything except $130 in cash; he showed us two or three strands of pearls, one of which was blue, and he started telling Tony the details of what happened in the house, as to the treatment he gave the people, such as 'that I left them for almost dead,' and that if Mr. Clevy lived it would be without an eye because he kept poking the eye with his thumb. Tony kept telling him to shut up, he didn't want him talking in front of me.

I heard Dosser tell Tony that he had hit Mrs. Clevy in the head with the gun several times. This is about all I heard that morning. Tony made Dosser take off the suit he was wearing, I think it was gray, because the suit had blood on it. Tony put the suit in the bag, along with two masks, and told me to take and throw them into the first alley I saw, which I did."

The delay in the gang's timetable that night had been necessitated by the time used to torture the residents of the Clevy home. There were five: Mr. and Mrs. Clevy, their eleven-year-old son, and two women servants. The women were ordered to remove their clothing and they were burned with lighted cigarettes. Both Mr. and Mrs. Clevy were beaten, the husband so badly that he almost lost the sight of one eye. The boy sustained a badly wrenched arm.

After the robbery, Gloria Rusella drove to Joliet and back. In Chicago she met Rusella and Barceloni in a North Side tavern.

"Tony and Barceloni began discussing the Clevy robbery. Barceloni said to Tony that he thought Dosser was crazy; that he did things that no normal person would do; that probably all of the victims are in the hospital from the treatment they received from Dosser. Tony asked Barceloni what he did with his mask and rubbers and Jimmy told him that the other two guys were running so fast that he could not keep up with them, so he took his mask, coat, and rubbers and threw them in the forest preserve in the vicinity of the Clevy home. Tony got furious and told Jimmy how simple-minded he was and that it was no wonder that he was in so much trouble. Tony said he better not hear that Jimmy had told his father or anyone about this robbery.

"Tony then told Jimmy that he had information that they missed a lot of money and jewelry in the Clevy home. Tony then took a newspaper showing Mrs. Clevy wearing a ring and Tony said 'Why didn't you guys get this?' Jimmy answered, 'Those people did not have anything. If she is wearing a ten-carat ring in the picture, she rented it.'

"Tony said the reason that Dosser acted the way he did with the Clevys was because Mr. Clevy had hit him in the eye and that the contact lens that Dosser wore had cut his eye and that Dosser was too ashamed to let Jimmy and Al know about him being hit in the eye.

"Tony continued that if Barceloni and Al would have helped Walter instead of just following him and standing around, they would have made a good haul. Tony then said that on the next big job he was going himself to make sure that all orders were followed out.

"When we met Dosser in our apartment after the robbery, Dosser gave Tony $25 and said the other dough was split up in the car between Al, Barceloni, and himself."

About a week later, she said, Rusella put the Clevy pearls and other stolen jewels in a canister which he buried in their backyard in Joliet. This was the canister Gloria was digging up when she arranged to be arrested.

Another Lincolnwood home robbery had been set up after George Holcomb, the car parker, had had duplicates made of the wife's car and house keys while she sat unawares in the North Side beauty salon for which he worked. In that robbery, she and her children were threatened with torture and her husband was slugged; more than $5,000 in furs and jewelry was taken.

Holcomb was later found shot to death in a West Side alley. Another car hiker at a hotel restaurant, believed to have been involved in supplying keys similarly to the Rusella gang, vanished at this time; police believed he may have been killed. Police theorized that fear of Holcomb's being a narcotics addict may have led to his death — that once arrested and deprived of drugs he would talk readily of his and others' complicity in various crimes.

The beginning of the end for the gang had come earlier that year, before Gloria Rusella's arrest, when a wealthy suburban victim identified one of the gang members from his picture, even though he had been masked at the time. She recognized him as being an employee in a jewelry shop that she had patronized. He was arrested. Then a few weeks later, acting on a tip, the police staked out at the home of an intended victim. Three men attempted to raid the home. Two — Harry Baziol and Jacky Lake, were shot to death by the police and another — Roland Tiblier — was wounded and captured. They were the newest members of the gang. Rusella had a pattern of recruiting young members for a particular job and then dealing them small portions. But Tiblier, the survivor of the police ambush, felt he and his two dead buddies had been set up as decoys, to confuse the police into believing the gang had been liquidated. He became a witness. Then Albert Warpek was nabbed and he too resented Rusella's treatment of him. He talked and became a state's witness — and my client.

By the time Gloria Rusella had given her story and was under the protective custody of Roswell T. Spencer, chief investigator for the Cook County state's attorney, Tony Rusella and Walter Dosser were fugitives. Sometime later they were arrested near Ypsilanti, Michigan, where state troopers spotted them driving on the wrong side of the road. Held in the Washtenaw County Jail in Ann Arbor under $100,000 bond each, they at first agreed to extradition. But once before a judge, they balked. Then another surprise — Dosser waived extradition, and was returned to Chicago in manacles and leg irons. Rusella fought extradition to the end.

In the Cook County state's attorney's office, Dosser was picked out of a nine-man lineup by Mr. and Mrs. Clevy and by Mrs. Franklin, three of the gang's victims.

At his arraignment several days later, Dosser stood mute in court, refusing to answer Acting Chief Justice Brussell's questions. Ruling that Dosser was standing mute before the court, Judge Brussell ordered me to talk with Dosser. I did for several minutes. Dosser said he planned to plead not guilty. I agreed to represent him temporarily, through the arraignment for four robbery charges, but I pointed out to the judge I couldn't defend Dosser at his trial. "I already represent two other defendants and there would be a conflict of interest," I explained, indicating my clients Warpek and Gloria Rusella. If he was indigent, the court would have to appoint some other attorney to represent him.

Following his extradition from Michigan, the arraignment of Tony Rusella brought forth a stormy court scene in keeping with his rambunctious personality.

"Tony Rusella," the clerk intoned, calling the case.

"Are you Tony Rusella?" asked Chief Justice John S. Boyle.

Rusella said, "I want to know why my wife is living like a queen in some of the biggest hotels in the City of Chicago. Who's paying the bills for her?"

"Now, quiet," said Judge Boyle. "You are here for arraignment for three charges of robbery. That's all you're here for."

Rusella went on.

"I want a change of venue to Moscow, to Africa — "

"I'm asking, have you got a lawyer?" asked the judge.

" — or to Fidel Castro's regime, where I can have an impartial trial."

"You're here to be arraigned on three charges of robbery," said the judge. "I'm not interested in any charges you may make or anything you may say. You're here to be arraigned. You know what an arraignment is."

"Yes," said Rusella. "I want to know where my wife is at today, and what they did to her, who poisoned her."

"Have you a lawyer?"

"I don't need no lawyer."

"Have you a lawyer?"

"No. God Almighty is my lawyer. I'm speaking the truth. My wife is guilty. She said she's guilty. And I'm innocent until I'm proven guilty. Give me a break."

"Have you the means to hire a lawyer?"

"Never mind about means. The man upstairs is my lawyer."

Ignoring Rusella's claim of celestial counsel, Judge Boyle said, "I'll appoint the public defender to represent you. He's right there."

I was standing nearby. Judge Boyle had indicated me.

"He's Roswell T. Spencer's man," said Rusella.

"Your honor, in this case — " I began.

"Let me out of here," interrupted Rusella.

" — I represent Mrs. Rusella," I continued.

"Now, that's all right," said the judge.

"I ain't doing nothing," said Rusella.

A policeman had moved forward, and the judge said, "Take your hands off him. He's here to be arraigned. Let counsel make a statement. You remain quiet."

"I want to go home," said Rusella.

"I'm sure you do," said the judge.

"Your honor — " I began again.

"Wait a second," said Rusella to me, "you're not my counsel. I don't know anything about you, mister. You're working for the state. I can't be tried fairly in this here court. No, sir, you're not my attorney."

"You're not going to be tried," said Judge Boyle.

I said, "I don't want to be your lawyer. I'm telling the judge here that there will be a conflict of interest."

"You're not my lawyer," said Rusella.

"I'm asking the court not to be appointed," I said.

"My wife is in open adultery," Rusella said. "It's her testimony that brought the indictments down."

"I couldn't defend you," I said.

"Quiet," said Judge Boyle.

"Let me go home," said Rusella.

"Continue with your statement, Mr. Getty," said the judge.

"Your honor," I said finally, "there would be a conflict of interest here. I've been appointed to represent Mrs. Rusella."

Finally Judge Boyle had Rusella taken out of the courtroom until he quieted down. Rusella accused the deputy sheriff of kicking him. He refused to accept two Chicago Bar Association lawyers appointed for him by the judge. Then he refused to plead to the indictments that had been returned by the grand jury. The judge entered pleas of not guilty. At last Rusella was arraigned.

That was the beginning of a long case. Sanity hearings were held for both Walter Dosser and Tony Rusella. Juries found both to be sane and therefore able to stand trial. Both men were then tried for the Clevy robbery, found guilty by a jury, and each was sentenced to sixty-to-one hundred years in prison. Dosser then entered pleas of guilty on two other indictments and received ten-to-twenty-five on both, to be served concurrently. Tony Rusella didn't enter a plea to the other indictments, so the state dropped them. Jimmy Barceloni was never tried; he received a heavy sentence of twenty-five to fifty years after he was found guilty in a narcotics case. That would keep him off the street for a long time.

Gloria Rusella and Al Warpek went free. The armed robbery charges against both clients were dropped as a reward for their cooperation and testimony. I had represented them throughout the long case and had advised them of their legal rights. Gloria was in protective custody the whole time, and had been moved from one motel to another as a security measure.

She said she had participated in the crimes only because she was afraid of Tony and his terrible temper. The last time I saw her, she intended to divorce him, and move to another state.

* * *

The other notorious case in which I represented a state's witness involved a hired killing.

A hired killer is possibly the lowest of human beings. Defending a person accused of being a hired killer brings its own peculiar pressures to the lawyer. He must do his best for the client, and make certain his constitutional guarantees are invoked. He also must never forget that no one, his client included, is guilty until proved guilty. It is not a popular, or an easy, position.

In this particular case, my own pressures were relieved to some extent because my client, Leonard Edwin Durlan, turned state's evidence against his uncle, Byron Emory Carter.

And before the case was over, I had been called — reluctantly — as a defense witness for Carter although I was representing Durlan, whose interests were in conflict with Carter's.

The case began when a man kidnapped Edward R. McGannity, the fifty-five-year-old international president of his union. The union official was driven to the southwest side of Chicago, where he was shot in the head and left dead in an alley.

Subsequently two men from Detroit — Carter, forty-one, and Durlan, thirty-seven — were arrested and accused of being the hired killers of McGannity. Carter was in the Michigan penitentiary at the time, on a forgery conviction. Eventually both were extradited to Chicago to stand trial for the murder.

Durlan was indigent and I was appointed by the court to represent him. He was a tall, lean, muscular man whose reflexes reminded me of a caged panther. He was nervous and always chain-smoked when he was allowed to smoke. He gave you the impression that he might spring in any direction at any moment, a tough guy, indeed, not one you'd want to meet on a dark street when he was bent upon mischief.

In my first conversation with him, he indicated that he would turn state's evidence and testify against Carter, his uncle. He placed all the blame for McGannity's death upon Carter. As we talked about his defense, Durlan poured forth, in staccato fashion, how Carter had induced him into it by claiming McGannity was only to be roughed up. He insisted he had never had an inkling it was to be a murder and he pleaded with me, "I know I'm in bad, and I'm hooked. Please get me out of this the best way you can."

I proceeded to do just that.

But I almost lost my client when, housed in the state's attorney's witness quarters at Twenty-Sixth and California, he apparently changed his mind and slipped out of the witness quarters and fled the city. When the FBI recaptured him in New York, he also faced federal charges of interstate transportation of a stolen vehicle and kidnapping of an Illinois salesman during his flight. When he returned to the Criminal Court Building he was in handcuffs, guarded by two deputy U.S. marshals.

It was our first meeting since the escape.

"How was your vacation?" I asked him.

"Rather hectic," he said. He was chain-smoking nervously and was rubbing his wrists where the handcuffs had been.

Until the trial, Durlan remained in federal custody in the witness quarters on the third floor of the county jail. The whole section was under constant guard by the state's attorney's police and had its own entrance by elevator. Durlan feared for his life, but there was no danger because he was apart from the rest of the jail population. The state didn't want anything to happen to its informers.

Durlan's decision to turn state's evidence against his uncle left Carter fighting alone. The state had already announced the intention of seeking the death penalty. The prosecution's case was based primarily on evidence that had been gathered by the FBI, nailed down by Durlan's forty-one-page statement in which he told the FBI of going from Detroit to Chicago with his uncle. Durlan stated that they were hired by McGannity's rivals in the labor movement and that he thought that McGannity was only to be beaten up. He told of seeing Carter shoot McGannity and that this had come as a surprise to him.

The day before Carter's trial began, I formally withdrew Durlan's plea of not guilty and entered a plea of guilty for him. I told Judge Napoli that I had discussed and explained the possible circumstances to the defendant. Then, to verify it for the record, I said to my client, "Is that correct, Mr. Durlan?"

"Yes, Mr. Getty," said Durlan.

"You want to enter a plea of guilty?"

"Yes, I do."

"Durlan, you have heard what your counsel has stated here today?" said the judge.

"Yes, your honor."

"That you are desirous of withdrawing your plea of not guilty to this charge of murder?"

"Yes, your honor."

"And you wish to enter a plea of guilty to the charge of murder?"

"Yes, your honor."

Judge Napoli further made certain that Durlan understood the consequences of his act, that he had waived his right of trial by jury and that the court could give him any sentence from fourteen years in the penitentiary to death in the electric chair. This done, a plea of guilty was entered, which meant an automatic severance of Durlan's case from Carter's.

The next day Carter's trial began with the selection of a jury. Then the state marshalled its witnesses and evidence while I, as Durlan's counsel, remained in the background. Durlan testified to Carter's having made a long distance telephone call in a supermarket. After the call, he said, Carter told him he had been talking with a Chicago labor terrorist, whom he named, "a guy I used to be in business with." Then Durlan said Carter told him, "You can make yourself a couple of hundred dollars by helping me beat up a guy." Durlan was told the job had been muffed before. Two days later, he said, they drove to Chicago and for a day they trailed after McGannity. Durlan admitted kidnapping McGannity near the labor union's office and taking him to Carter. But he said he thought they would only beat McGannity up and that he was completely surprised when Carter shot McGannity. Durlan testified that, at Carter's instructions, he took the .32 caliber pistol to a South Archer Street tavern, where he placed it in the toilet tank.

A Chicago Police Department ballistics expert, John C. Stauffer, testified that the pellet taken from McGannity's head matched the pistol found in the tavern toilet tank. Another witness testified that Carter and Durlan stayed in her home at the time of the murder, thus placing them in Chicago at the time. Other testimony included that of a telephone operator who testified to handling a collect call from a Detroit supermarket wall telephone to a telephone booth in a Chicago North Side tavern on the date Durlan said Carter had made the call.

Carter's attorneys, Warren Carey and James R. Chapman, had been appointed for him by Judge Napoli from the volunteers available from the Defense of Prisoners Committee of the Chicago Bar Association. This was necessary, for if the public defender had been appointed, there would have been a conflict of interest, since I was already representing Durlan.

As the defense presented its case, I — to my surprise — was called as one of its last few witnesses. Realizing it was part of the defense's move to discredit Durlan's testimony, I protested to Judge Napoli that I was entitled to maintain confidential my conversations with my client. The defense argued that Durlan had already modified this privilege by testifying on cross-examination that he had made no agreement to swap his testimony for a light sentence.

Judge Napoli ordered me to testify as a defense witness. I could not invoke the lawyer-client privilege. I took the stand. In essence, I testified that I had discussed a sentence recommendation for Durlan but that my client did not know of the offer. Assistant State's Attorney Mackoff was then called by the defense. He confirmed my testimony. But he also admitted that his office had not sought indictments against Durlan for a number of acts connected with the escape from the witness quarters in May, although the federal authorities had indicted Durlan for kidnapping and auto theft.

The state asked death for Carter. The jury found him guilty of murdering McGannity but did not recommend death. This left any term short of death up to the judge.

The next day Judge Napoli sentenced Durlan on his plea of guilty to murder. Mackoff, for the state, recommended the minimum sentence, despite Durlan's long criminal record, "for his cooperation in testifying against Byron Emory Carter, the real killer." Durlan was given fourteen years in the Illinois State Penitentiary. But that didn't mean he would be free after serving eight and a half years of the sentence; he had another sentence in Michigan, six-and-a-half-to-fifteen years for armed robbery and a parole violation there, plus his federal trouble, to which he had pleaded guilty.

As for his uncle Carter, his motion for a new trial was denied and Judge Napoli sentenced him to the penitentiary for a term of from ninety-nine to one hundred fifty years.

Newspapers said it was the first time in twenty years that there had been a conviction in a Chicago gang-style killing. Well, it was the *first* time I could remember that a hired killer had been convicted in Cook County, and it was doubly ironic to me personally that the public defender, a criminal defense attorney, had played a small part in securing that conviction.

CHAPTER 10
3,100 New Clients!

ONE TIME I WAS SWAMPED — practically overnight — by 3,100 new clients.

All of them were black. They had been arrested in the Chicago riots that followed the assassination in Memphis of Dr. Martin Luther King, Jr., on April 4, 1968. In every case, the public defender was appointed. For five grueling days and nights, the hours blended together into one body of time as my staff of fifty-four lawyers and I manned the courtrooms, twenty-four hours a day, for the emergency round-the-clock bond hearings.

The rioting had begun in Chicago on April 5, the day after the Nobel Peace Prize winner's death. The first news of trouble that we in the public defender's office had was from the state's attorney's office, on the floor below us in the Criminal Court Building. They had police communication. By that time I could look out my third-floor office window and see, on the West Side, towering black smoke angrily boiling skyward. I could see the flames of a building burning at Madison and California. Eastward along Madison and Jackson and on those streets that lead toward the Loop downtown and the central city of Chicago, I could see the same sights. The stores along Madison Street were being firebombed. We learned later that they were also being looted; pictures were taken of people carrying TV sets and clothing and other items from the stores. All this was in the black ghetto area. We turned on the radio in the office for up-to-the-minute news reports, for we knew it was only a matter of time until we would be involved, once the police began rounding up the rioters. They would become *our* defendants. You could bet on it.

The rumors varied. Some reported a high arrest number; others not so many. But I was not long in getting a reliable hint: Chief Judge John S. Boyle's office alerted me that there would be bond hearings all night. The courts would open up at 5:30 P.M. for the night sessions. It was up to us to get ready. I passed on the word to the assistant public defenders, the investigators, and the secretarial staff. We still had a few hours.

Thomas P. Cawley, now an associate judge, was my first assistant in the criminal courts trial division and now I assigned him to take charge of our personnel at Eleventh and State, which is the central police station, and the location of the bond court. A likeable Irish six-footer, Tom was in his late thirties and had the necessary experience to handle the deluge of clients. He did a superb job. I was in constant touch with him and with some of the other assistants.

The turmoil began on a Friday afternoon, which was a bad time for Tom to have to round up everybody. Some of the assistants were out of the office. It took hours for Tom to locate them all and give them their assignments. But he found them, and we had our lawyers in the courtrooms on time. For the next five days, until April 10, we kept our lawyers rotating in four-hour shifts around the clock as black citizens were herded in to the police station. Naturally, they arrived without counsel, and Judge Boyle had issued orders that only the public defender and his assistants could be appointed to bond hearings in those cases. Although we had the manpower and the experience, we were strapped to handle these in addition to our normal caseload.

Soon additional courts were opened, until there were four bond courts going simultaneously. As each lawyer's four-hour stint ended, he was relieved by another assistant public defender and so it went, a fresh wave taking over, one shift after another, for five days and nights. By Sunday, hearings were being held in what was then the House of Correction, and I personally represented many in hearings that day.

The purpose of bond is to ensure that the defendant, if released, will return to court for his trial. A bond hearing should bring forth the pertinent facts on this issue. Is he reliable? Are his roots in the community? Does he have a prior criminal record? On the basis of guidelines I had worked out following the winter of 1967 Chicago riots, these questions were to help determine bond on the cases that normally would come out of such incidents. With these facts in hand, the judge then would set bond accordingly.

But now, with the city torn apart by rioting, many judges were processing the cases very slowly, apparently reasoning: "They're still rioting. Why set low bonds on these people so they can return to do the same thing? They might commit more serious crimes if we let them go."

It was all up to the judges. We interviewed each client and made recommendations. We made our motions. The judges did not always agree with the public defender's motions.

By Saturday, the second day of the riots, the police stations were jammed with arrested black people. The district stations couldn't handle them all and started taking them directly to the Central Police Headquarters at Eleventh and State for fingerprinting, photographing, and marshaling into court. Additional policemen had to be assigned there. Judge Boyle ordered that all judges be assigned to the riot courts, so that state, defense, and judiciary were on a ceaseless round-the-clock schedule.

As the number of arrests grew, the police failed to keep pace — they could not compile the defendants' records in time. Consequently, the judges had no prior criminal history sheets to guide them in the bond hearings. In many cases, the problem was even more aggravated. Many arrests were recorded improperly. It became difficult to locate records. Some persons gave aliases. As more people accumulated in the jails, confusion proliferated. Those who gave false names were soon lost. When friends or relatives came to get them out, there was no record of them by their true names. We had to comb the jails to find them.

The charges leveled against our clients ranged from violation of Mayor Daley's emergency youth curfew to burglary. Bonds of $20,000 and $25,000 on burglary charges were common. So we began taking steps to have bond reduced in the cases where it seemed excessive, where bond apparently was being used to incarcerate the individual. As we obtained copies of the jail records, we began making the information available to the volunteer organizations and relatives of the defendants who were interested. We began interviewing the defendants in the county jail and House of Correction — in the first week interviewing 900 persons as we prepared motions for bond reduction and trial.

At this critical time we also had help offered us from the American Civil Liberties Union, the Chicago Bar Association, the Cook County Bar Association, and the newly formed Chicago Council of Lawyers. There were several hundred such volunteers. But initially we were forced to turn them down. On the whole, they sent young lawyers. My assistants, accepting some volunteers at first, soon bogged down as they gave these volunteers hasty seminars in the technicalities of a bond hearing. Some of the volunteers had been bringing in matters of evidence, which is not involved at all in a bond hearing. We couldn't afford to conduct *ad hoc* seminars at a time of such great pressure. Later, when the pressure was off, we were able to work with the volunteers.

As the riot cases inundated the courts, the normal operations of the Cook County judicial processes came to a virtual standstill. Traffic court, for the most part, was suspended. Continuances in other regular matters were given *en masse*.

The big issue by now was that of lowering bond for the thousands of arrested persons. Under pressure from the Chicago Bar Association, ACLU, and other groups, Judge Boyle gave in, to some extent, and bond reduction hearings began. Few defendants were affected at first, but on Easter Sunday, April 14, more than a week after the riots began, the tempo stepped up. In most instances, the defendants were brought into the courtrooms in groups of from five to fifteen. Some judges held individual hearings. Others did not.

On the Monday following Easter, trials began and continued until June 28 on all regular court days at two in the afternoon at the Criminal Court Building. At first, other organizations, most notably the Chicago Bar Association, were assisting my office, but by mid-May we were doing practically all of the legal work, in all handling about 70 percent of about 6,000 court appearances, in which there were 2,700 dispositions. By that time the vast majority of the defendants were out on bond and able to hire lawyers of their own. Out of the original arrest number, only 718 were finally indicted in the criminal court and we were appointed for only 117 of these.

For those who were indicted and eventually tried, what kinds of defenses were offered? Well, the one word that most accurately characterized the riots was *confusion*. Many of the defendants were picked up for just happening to be on the scene; they were looking on and breaking no laws whatsoever. Others were actually seen carrying large amounts of foodstuffs and clothing from stores. But because of the sheer volume of arrests, the prosecution had a special headache. What actually did the policemen see when it came down to a specific case? Invariably, in all the turmoil, they had not written down the witnesses' names. Very often the state couldn't locate the right witness or the policeman couldn't remember essential details or he couldn't identify the defendant. On the other hand, the defendant would deny he had done what he was charged with. Only a small portion were convicted. Those who had been picked up for curfew violations were eventually discharged.

About the only positive result that came out of the "Martin Luther King" riot was that the judicial establishment adopted a demarcation point for handling future riots: until 300 had been arrested, the defendants would be taken to police headquarters at Eleventh and State for bond hearings; after that, they would be taken to the Criminal Court Building at Twenty-Sixth and California.

The April, 1968, riots were the worst ones we had in the sixties, but not the only civil disturbances, by any means. There had been two other major riots during the previous two years. In July, 1966, at the time of the Chicago nurse murders, the police were so busy struggling with rioters that it interfered with the investigation of the eight slayings. Another group of riots erupted in the winter of 1967, with snow on the ground.

The winter, 1967, riots served as a kind of preview of what we were to have when Dr. King was murdered. The black defendants were herded into the police station and had high bonds slapped on them. In one case, a bond of $25,000 was set for a defendant arrested for burglary in connection with the rioting. The public defender asked the judge:

"May we have a short hearing just to get some background information on this youth?"

"How old is he?" asked the prosecutor.

"Nineteen," said the young black defendant.

"Denied," said the judge. He looked at the prosecutor. "What's your date?"

"February 20th, your honor."

"I respectfully ask for a shorter date," said the defender.

"Denied," said the judge; "you're going to have to understand the gravity of these offenses."

"Judge, the gravity of the offense is burglary."

"Oh, no, no, no. As I said, the environment of the offense is important. Robbery is a grave —"

"But, Judge, at this point, Judge, there is no disturbance. Why incarcerate these people before there is a hearing?"

"Call the next case."

This scene, in variations, was repeated in case after case. The Illinois division of ACLU termed such use of bail to detain arrested suspects as "shockingly unfair." By the time bail was reset at a more realistic level, many had spent as much as three weeks in jail.

Cases such as these led me to formulate the guidelines for seeking personal recognizance bonds for worthy individuals arrested during disturbances. Though these guidelines proved workable, they were virtually nullified by the courts' actions during the riots triggered by Dr. King's death.

A few months later, in August, 1968, our city became the battleground for the nationally-televised riots that erupted during the Democratic National Convention.

I learned of the trouble just as the rest of the country did, as I watched the convention on television at home. Immediately, in case another major riot was in the making, I called Tom Cawley and placed him in charge of the public defender's bond hearing operations at Eleventh and State. But compared to the riots back in the spring, the August episode was minor. The arrest number never surpassed 300; therefore, the Criminal Court Building was never opened up for bond hearings. Furthermore, most of these arrestees had friends who soon came up with the 10 percent cash bonds that could liberate them. I allowed them to use a phone and set aside space for this purpose in our offices in the Criminal Court Building.

Unlike the earlier riots, the Chicago incidents of August were instantly televised by the networks, so that Americans all over the country were suddenly "there," listening to eyewitnesses, seeing the police in action. The police's handling of demonstrators at Grant Park was harshly criticized. For instance, sociologist Anthony Platt, a director of the Task Force on Demonstration and Protest and Group Violence, called the episode a "police riot," reiterating what Chicago *Daily News* columnist Mike Royko had said, that the biggest threat to law and order was the Chicago Police Department.

But behind the scenes, out of the lens of the inquisitive TV cameras, an important legal point was proved that went unnoticed: When you have an organized public defender system, you have an organization that is always ready — immediately — to protect the rights of the individuals arrested in a crisis.

In Chicago, we learned to be ready for the worst. Much of the time, it came.

CHAPTER 11

A Casualty of War

THE CASE OF JOSEPH LESNA is a study in investigation and a defense that never was.

It began with a series of mysterious homemade bomb explosions on the South Side stretching back to August, 1967. This is what occurred:

1. A bomb made out of a piece of pipe was picked up by an unwary worker in a cement company. The bomb exploded and blew off the man's hand and injured a fellow worker. Two injured.

2. On April 13, 1968, a railroad electrician was killed when he picked up a length of pipe along the tracks near the Calumet Skyway and 103rd Street. One dead.

3. On the Fourth of July, 1968, a boy innocently kicked what seemed to be a water canteen on Calumet Beach near 102nd Street. It was a bomb. Four injured.

4. On Easter Sunday, 1969, a bomb exploded in front of a South Commercial Avenue apartment building. None injured.

5. The next day, a bomb in the toy department of Goldblatt Brothers' store at Ninety-First and Commercial Avenue exploded when a woman picked it up from the counter. This was a "tip" bomb, which if tilted sideways over three degrees would

set off the firing mechanism; it consisted of a paper bag in which a juice jar was wired to an eight-inch, powder-filled pipe. One killed, nine injured.

Thus, over a period from August, 1967, to April, 1969, less than two years, South Side bombings in a relatively small radius had produced a casualty toll of two dead and fifteen injured. But thousands of others, as a result, were terrorized by the bombings. Who knew where the next bomb would be or whom it would kill?

Police and members of the bomb and arson squad began scouring that section of the South Side where the bombings were concentrated. They began a door-to-door interrogation, searching for suspicious persons, hunting down clues. Soon several policemen discovered, from talking to neighbors, that a guy named Joseph in a nearby building acted kind of strange. So they went looking for him on South Exchange, in a working class neighborhood where most of the residents were of Polish and Croatian ancestry.

In mid-afternoon on Monday, April 14, a detective from the bomb and arson squad knocked on the door of the apartment where Joseph Lesna lived.

Then all hell broke loose.

According to police, the man answered the visit with gunfire from the other side of the door. A detective, William McInerney, was hit in the chest. He became the first of several casualties that day, but lived. Several minutes later, though, Detective Jerome A. Stubig and Sergeant James R. Schaffer were mortally wounded by automatic rifle fire and a hand grenade. They died before they could be taken from the scene.

By now the man inside, Lesna apparently, had barricaded himself with rifles at the seven windows in the apartment. Police rushed reinforcements. An hours-long siege began. Finally there were as many as one hundred and fifty policemen in the area, and perhaps a thousand spectators crowding the police lines, trying to catch a glimpse of the dangerous action. It looked as if war had come to the South Side as the police encircled the bullet-splattered old building where Lesna was holed up. There was a police helicopter, a sniper team, fire engines, and a truck carrying high-powered searchlights that flooded the three-story building with light.

Inside, Lesna was a very busy man. The police estimated that he fired a thousand rounds of ammunition and heaved out at least ten bombs and grenades during the six-hour battle. The building was soon pockmarked by police bullets that also had blasted out all of the window panes.

The siege ended that evening when Deputy Police Superintendant James M. Rochford, joined at one point by Lesna's brother, convinced the sniper, after more than an hour's discussion, to put down his weapons and surrender.

Two policemen were dead. Seven, including two civilians, were injured.

Although Lesna didn't become a public defender client until his arraignment, we were, in a sense, in on the case soon after his capture.

Investigator Leo Ranachowski, a husky former scuba diver for the Evanston Fire Department who later became chief investigator for the Illinois Defender Project, was home with his family that night, watching television, when he first heard of the siege. As Ranachowski recalls it, "While we were watching the Miss America contest, Joel Daly, one of those super-duper newscasters, who had just come to Chicago, came on with a bulletin that there was a shootout in progress. I knew there was a good chance that in a shootout like that, if the guy survived it, he would probably be one of our cases. I called George Brobst [another investigator for the public defender] and asked if he had a tape recorder at his house. He did. He taped the ten o'clock news. By that time Lesna had surrendered."

The tape recording of the ten o'clock news became the first item in our voluminous file on Joseph Lesna. Such tapes and newspaper clippings sometimes are essential to the defense, especially if the case becomes so notorious that a change of venue is sought because of the excessive publicity.

Ranachowski later was assigned to investigate the case. He went to the scene of the shootout and photographed it from as many angles as possible. Since it meant including a three-story building, this was very difficult. But the greater challenge was photographing the apartment without seeming to be nervous. Bomb experts from the police department had gone through the apartment. Police found fifty-four unexploded bombs in the house and in the yard. The search took twenty-three hours. "If they missed one," Ranachowski told Tom McCurrie and Ed Downs, who were with him, "we're all gonna go bye-bye!" But the bombs apparently were all found and defused safely.

The police said Lesna had told them he set his bombs to demonstrate to people "what the Vietnam war was like" and he had placed the bomb in Goldblatt's department store to destroy war toys. They found a small arsenal in his apartment when he surrendered: seven rifles, two shotguns, grenades, thirty homemade bombs, a grenade launcher, and 2,000 rounds of ammunition. Where had he got it all? He wouldn't say.

The day after the siege was Lesna's forty-second birthday. He was arraigned in Felony Court on two counts of murder (the two policemen) and held without bond in the county jail. He had no lawyer and the public defender was appointed to represent him.

I talked to Lesna, a husky, crew-cut six-footer, a brooding Marine veteran of both World War II and the Korean War, for the first time on the day he was arraigned. We went into a room adjoining the judge's chambers. He impressed me as having some sort of mental disease. Aside from what he had done, he just didn't sound or act like a normal person. I decided then that the first step would be to have him examined by psychiatrists.

For the record and for the benefit of the public, I made a statement. "In view of the bizarre circumstances, a mental test is indicated. We will represent him throughout the coroner's inquest and trial proceedings."

My preliminary impression was confirmed by Ranachowski's official investigation for our office. It probably could be said that, in essence, Lesna was one of the most tragic casualties of our wars, eventually bringing great personal tragedy to others here at home whom he had never seen before.

Lesna had joined the Marine Corps at age sixteen to fight in World War II. He saw action on Okinawa but escaped injury. After his discharge he had worked for a chemical company. His supervisor there, who had had an opportunity to observe Lesna over a period of years, had found him to be a hard worker — "the harder the job, the better he liked it" — but believed he probably was mentally disturbed.

Lesna, who took his war service very seriously, volunteered for Marine service in the Korean War and went on active duty in May, 1951. He became a corporal. In 1952 two highly significant things happened to him. In Korea, he flipped a coin with a close buddy to see which of them would go on patrol. The buddy went out instead of Lesna and never came back. His buddy's death affected Lesna deeply. Some time after that, Lesna himself was wounded in the war, as enemy mortar shrapnel hit him in the hands, face, and buttocks. He was hospitalized for six months for these wounds and for malaria and was finally discharged with disability. One of his fingers and part of another had had to be amputated.

Rehired by the chemical company after the Korean War, Lesna was more of a loner than before. He seemed to have been completely changed by his experience, emotionally all torn up. Although his hand was not a factor in his work, and to that extent did not disable him, he seemed almost to blame his fellow workers for his injury. One day during lunch a fellow worker reported that Lesna raised the hand with the amputations and announced, "You pussies are going to pay for this!" He was still a hard, tough Marine, and the others were afraid of him. At one time he got into a fight on the swing shift. Eventually he became too difficult for the others to work with and the company let him go. On his last day at work he threatened some of the other workers and threatened to kill one. He cried and whimpered. He had reached his limit.

After that his deterioration continued. He never married. He lived with his mother and sister on the Veterans Administration disability payments he received. When she died in 1962 another stage in his decline began. He never got over losing her and kept a 1962 calendar in his room with marks on it indicating events in her poor health and her death. He lived in one room of an apartment shared with his sister and brother-in-law. He became increasingly withdrawn, sitting in his room, refusing to answer the door or phone, and taking flowers to his mother's grave on Sundays. He became the neighborhood character, flying into rages at kids, carrying his brown zipper bag everywhere he went, and vowing to one day wipe out all the "snipers" around him. No doubt, his being holed up in that apartment for more than ten years had itself contributed to the final deterioration.

By systematically going back in Lesna's life for more than twenty years, a pattern of gradual, progressive deterioration became evident. It was clear that if he were ever to stand trial, the defense would be insanity at the time of the crime. But first impressions of Lesna seemed confirmed by my subsequent conferences with him. On these occasions, he just wouldn't cooperate with me as we discussed his possible defense. As time went on, I knew he couldn't stand trial. He didn't know the extent of the crime and he couldn't cooperate with counsel. In order to stand trial both were required.

If, of course, he should recover his sanity, and was adjudged sane, I would defend him on the basis of his having been insane at the time of the crimes, but now recovered.

For several months the case was complicated by the impressions of Dr. William H. Haines of the Behavior Clinic, who considered Lesna legally sane and able to stand trial. In August, 1969, Dr. Haines visited Lesna and diagnosed a "paranoid schizophrenic reaction," but stated that Lesna knew the nature of the charges and could cooperate verbally with his counsel.

Then in January, 1970, Dr. Haines examined Lesna again in his cell and concluded the defendant knew the nature of the charge but was unable to cooperate with his attorney. Lesna had lost sixty pounds by then, reported the psychiatrist, and felt I was working against him. "He indicated he wanted the electric chair at that time and he objected to his attorney wanting to get him two life sentences."

I withdrew from the case, assigning it to an assistant, Edward J. Downs, who presented the psychiatric evidence at the sanity hearing for Lesna. Dr. Haines testified to Lesna's war-connected mental disturbances and as to how he had deteriorated through the years. He told of Lesna's very strong feelings about his military service: "I got the impression he would not hesitate to kill anyone who had not been in the service." He had an obsession with weapons and with death, Dr. Haines reported. "He kept weapons in his house in order to protect his sister in case of a riot as the Chicago police would be incapable of rendering protection until the arrival of the National Guard." The psychiatrist concluded that Lesna showed signs of paranoid and schizophrenic reaction and was not able to cooperate with counsel.

Judge Louis B. Garippo ordered the jury to render a verdict of mental incompetency, based on Dr. Haines' findings, and Lesna was committed to the Illinois Mental Health Maximum Security Institution at Chester.

Joseph Lesna was not the first — nor the last — American war casualty whose mind broke with reality upon returning to civilian life. In his own mind, apparently, he was fighting the Korean War all over again. But what made his deterioration so dangerous to society was that his technical know-how had not atrophied at all. He could make any kind of bomb there was, short of an atomic one. That made him a holy terror, and provided a tragic personal postscript to the Korean War, seventeen years later.

* * *

He was a young black man, twenty years of age and just up from Mississippi, charged with armed robbery and attempted murder, all shot up, another client of the public defender's office.

The police claimed he had used a sawed-off shotgun in the holdup, but that wasn't the worst of his problems at the moment. The arresting cops had shot him three times — in the forearm, in one leg, and in a testicle. Although he lived, the remainder of his injured sexual organ had to be removed surgically. And now compounding his plight was the fact that one of the policemen had had his scalp cut open during the arrest. The other policeman said the suspect had clouted him with a board or piece of pipe.

It looked like a bad case and the state didn't make it seem any cheerier with the sixty-to-eighty-year deal they were willing to make. A deal that the defense rejected as excessive.

I have always believed that the public defender should try to know as much about the state's case as the prosecutors themselves. This means making a thorough investigation, a facet of the defense that many lawyers don't properly appreciate or understand. The investigator does the spade work. He digs up witnesses and facts. The defense lawyer also directs the investigator to specific things he is looking for. The client's life or liberty may well depend on what he finds.

Public Defender Investigator Leo F. Ranachowski drove out to the scene of the arrest and started looking. As he entered the basement room where the suspect had supposedly injured the police officer and where the arrest and shooting had taken place, Leo was almost brained by a low, jutting pipe. He suddenly realized that if a man ran in there fast in a tense situation in which he expected resistance, he could easily cut his head open on the pipe and think he had been attacked by someone. That low pipe, then, could have caused the cop's scalp injury.

He also found a fourth bullet hole in the room in which the arrest and shooting had occurred. The policemen had sworn that they had shot three times and no more. They were absolutely positive of it. But now Leo dug out a fourth bullet from the wall plaster. It was from a .45 caliber pistol and he was able to match it with the policeman's gun. The dug-out bullet had missed the client. This rebutted the official account that only three shots had been fired.

Obviously, the official version, that the suspect had viciously resisted arrest, could only serve to aggravate his legal condition. Any jury could be expected to take that into consideration. But now these two factors — the jutting pipe and the fourth bullet — changed things radically. Both indicated the policemen had probably not been attacked as contended, and that the suspect may not have resisted arrest after all, and that the cops might have been overzealous. It had been proved beyond any doubt that they were mistaken about the number of times they had shot, although they had sworn they were positive. Could they be sure that the suspect had hit one of them; might not it have been the low pipe?

The prosecution was now on the defensive, for the jury was very much aware of the significance of these two matters. Sixty to eighty years in the pen? Suddenly, the case started looking better.

The jury found the suspect not guilty of armed robbery and attempted murder of the injured police officer, but he was found guilty of aggravated battery and armed violence. It looked as if they wanted him to have probation. The judge sentenced him to two concurrent terms of two to five years in the penitentiary. On appeal, the sentence for aggravated battery was reversed.* A far cry from sixty-to-eighty.

A proper investigation made the difference.

* * *

Although it often is overlooked, it should go without saying that a thorough investigation is essential to a good defense — whether the client is innocent or not.

Many times, pre-trial investigation discloses that what the defendant told us is not true. When we acquaint him with the

**People* v. *Brown* (275 N.E. 2d 163).

facts of a detailed investigation, he usually will enter a plea of guilty. He can take for granted that the state also has the evidence to disprove his claims. Now, knowing the truth of the case, we are in a better position to get the client a more realistic sentence — maybe even probation, depending on the circumstances.

No defense counsel can intelligently advise his client until he has made an independent investigation of his own. Many "confessions" are made by innocent defendants. Some of them have emotional and mental quirks. A few give false statements under pressure. Quite a few defendants may confess to the maximum degree of a crime when, in fact, they are guilty only to a lesser degree, such as when a man confesses to murder when actually he is guilty of manslaughter. A poor, ignorant defendant often has no inkling of the legal meaning of intent.

An investigation by the defense is essential for these reasons. But because of its importance, there is left a gray area in our system of criminal justice. The defendant who is not indigent, for example, can afford to hire counsel, but he frequently does not have enough money to hire an investigator. That man may be more handicapped than he would be if he were indigent, for then he could have his case investigated by a man from the public defender's office.

It is axiomatic that a defense lawyer — or any other! — should never ask an adverse witness a question unless he knows the answer in advance. The only way to prepare for this is to have the investigator talk to every witness before the trial. In our office, the investigator writes down everything he is told by a witness and then has the witness sign it. This is to insure that the witness does not change his statement later. If he does change what he has said, then the investigator can be called to the stand to testify to the earlier statement. This is but another brick in the legal checks-and-balances system to make the truth surface, to keep the truth flowing.

The investigator searches for lost witnesses or potential witnesses. Frequently the defendant may tell you that certain people were present with him at a particular time. Maybe he knows them only by nicknames or first names or perhaps he was introduced to them only that evening. But they may provide him an alibi, proving he was at a specific place at a certain time, instead of committing a crime miles away. The investigator has the chore, usually a very difficult one, of finding out who they were, the type of persons they are, and he takes statements from them.

* * *

During the forties and early fifties, and even after I became public defender, I used to go out and investigate cases for myself. I would go out to the scene and get the flavor of the environment. Invariably I would come upon important information or witnesses that I otherwise would have missed. This was especially necessary in those earlier days, for we had a small investigative staff. In 1964, the office expanded to allow us five investigators for all of Cook County.

Although they were armed only with Polaroid cameras, with which they took pictures that later might be used as evidence, our investigators were never attacked or in real danger. Probably it has been to their advantage that they weren't armed, despite the places an investigator has to go and the people he has to find and talk to. Investigators from the public defender's office go everywhere. They are working for the underdog and the most dangerous places are those inhabited by people who consider themselves underdogs. These are the haunts of the poor. Our investigators are always sent in pairs when there is a hint of danger, and they identify themselves right off. ''We're here to help this man. Do you know So-and-So?'' Their job is also their protective armament.

The unexpected pops up routinely for the investigator. One investigator, off to interview a witness, found his way barred by a growling lioness! The lioness, it turned out, held a key to the case. The defendant was charged with burglarizing a business. The owner of the business used the lioness for a watchdog. The defendant allegedly had worked a day at the business and had made friends with the lioness. This was the police's theory. The investigator took a picture of the lioness. In the process he discovered the lioness was not really as ferocious as had been believed. She liked people. A stranger probably could have got by her.

Not only does the investigator wear out a lot of shoe leather, he also subjects himself to eyestrain as he examines records: Police, arrest, jail and penal, hospital, medical, and employment records, and transcripts. He may obtain official records of weather conditions at the time of the crime. In addition, he is called upon to serve subpoenas.

The better acquainted the investigator is with scientific methods, the better he can perform. The defendant has the right to review all scientific evidence that the state may introduce. Either the investigator or the trial lawyer or both should review it. For this reason, the investigator, as well as the trial lawyer, should have a working knowledge of fingerprints, a working knowledge of firearms, ballistics, blood types, autopsies and polygraph tests. He may have to provide information on hair and semen specimens or handwriting comparisons. He should know about arson and the various forms of arson, in order to recognize what is effective as state's evidence. He often has to obtain experts for the defense in scientific fields. Finally, because of all the interviews he will have to conduct — ranging from policemen to Skid Row characters to scientific experts — he must know how to talk to people in a personable way and get people to talk to him.

The training of these key staff members in the public defender's office is a problem in itself. There are no special training schools for defense investigators, although there are certain courses at various schools that are helpful. A decade ago, even these were unheard of. There are police schools that the man can attend, but the County Board, which funds the public defender's office in Cook County, has never allocated funds for such training in the public defender's annual budget.

This has meant that, largely, an investigator has had to single out his own direction and learn through the accumulation of experience.

The fact that the County Board has not allocated funds in this area is only one aspect of its failure to keep pace with the growth of population and of crime — indigent crime — in Cook County. The public defender's office has been there all these years, working overtime, but the inadequacy of funds has made it difficult — sometimes impossible — to handle each case as it should be handled. The holders of the purse-strings are proud of the public defender's office. They relish the compliments it gets from time to time for defending the poor. But they are reluctant to spend the money necessary to do the job completely. The poor who get in trouble don't possess a political organization that can exert the pressure. It's as simple as that.

Theoretically, we all believe that every man, rich or poor, guilty or innocent, should have his day in court. But in a county that has a population of six million people, as does Cook County, it takes a tremendous amount of money to get the job done. The County Board had responded only with window-dressing. We had defended the poor, but we had not had sufficient personnel and funds to do the job thoroughly. All the activity was in the front window where the world could see it, while the essentials that the public was less aware of, such as the defense investigation, were forced to remain unseen, carried out under unusual burdens in the best way we could.

CHAPTER 12
The Assistants

WHEN HAROLD SULLIVAN WAS an assistant public defender and an apprentice trial lawyer, the two of us were examining the veniremen in one of his first jury trials. I had completed the process for the defense on the first panel of four jurors, and Harold took over for the second panel. He soon demonstrated that he was learning fast.

"You know what?" I said when he returned to the counsel table. "You're doing a good job — I'm going to let you finish by yourself!"

I walked out of the courtroom, leaving Harold responsible for the last two panels and the trial itself. He had assisted me in several jury trials previously. I thought he was ready.

Harold was a bit trembly inside, he told me later, but he soon recovered, completed the jury, and rendered a competent defense. He had taken a huge step toward becoming a fine trial lawyer.

Today Harold is a judge. At last count, there were seventeen judges in Cook County who had been in the public defender's office while I was head of it.

But whatever their ultimate goals, young lawyers come to the public defender's office for one common reason: to acquire solid trial experience. And they do. If you can try a criminal case in Cook County, you can try any kind of case anywhere. This is the magnet — experience that is as valuable as gold — that draws them to a job that in 1968 offered an $8,400 starting salary — about that of a rookie policeman, who didn't have to go through law school. (By 1972 it was $10,800.)

To nobody's surprise, many assistants later enter the private practice of civil law, a much more lucrative endeavor. It was a major problem for me to keep good assistants. Some, like big boisterous, hearty Jim Doherty, who was my first assistant for years, were committed to defending the poor; it was more than a job with them — the money was secondary. Others like him came to the public defender's office primarily for trial experience — and stayed. But many others left for greener pastures. I couldn't offer them salaries that were commensurate with the jobs they were doing. The problem evolved into an annual pitched budget battle with the County Board, which I never won, except partially.

Although they were few, I also had the other kind of assistants: political parasites, or payroll sluggards, who looked upon the job as a sinecure. Most of them I removed, but a few were so protected by the political patronage system of Cook County — and had such powerful political clout — that I would have hurt the office, as far as future budget requests were concerned, had I fired them. One of them wouldn't even show up regularly in court or in the office! When transferred to the appellate division, these individuals handled one, sometimes two, appeals a year — scarcely an admirable performance. These few damaged the morale of the other lawyers in the office, but most of all they were a liability to themselves — they never became the competent lawyers that they could have been.

Without a large budget, it was especially difficult to hire and keep black lawyers. The relatively few blacks who do finish law school are able to command top salaries from corporations that hire them as their token black attorneys, thereby proving there is no discrimination in the company. But in those jobs, they have little or no contact with the cases that involve most of the black Americans who need legal help — the poor blacks haled into criminal court. In Cook County approximately 60 to 70 percent of our indigent defendants were black.

We were fortunate to have on our staff, for many years, one of the greatest black lawyers in the country — John Branion, an assistant public defender who joined Benjamin Bachrach's office in March, 1931, and stayed with it until his death in 1966. It's quite possible that John Branion represented more defendants charged with murder than any other attorney in the United States.

John was born in Mississippi around the end of the last century. He had wanted to be a lawyer from the time he was a boy. He told us, "I used to sneak into the courtroom in Tupelo and watch trials in progress. All the attorneys knew who I was, so they would let me sit in the back row and watch the proceedings."

His father was a laborer and died when John was seven; his mother died when he was thirteen. But being an orphan didn't deter him. He became a bellhop in Memphis, a stockyards worker in East St. Louis — all to earn money to attend Rusk College in Mississippi. He served in World War I and later attended the University of Chicago law school, still working his way through, now by waiting on tables by day and firing a furnace by night. After law school, he went into private practice for eight years before he joined Bachrach's staff.

I was astounded that John Branion never became a judge. For some reason, he was never placed on the Democratic ticket, even though his trial experience and his legal background made him a natural. Most of all, he had been a law partner with William Dawson, a black powerhouse lawyer and later a Congressman from the South Side. Dawson had the clout. He could have had John slated for a judgeship.

One day Dawson was in my office and I brought it up.

"I don't see why you don't put John on the ticket."

"Well," said Congressman Dawson, "John don't want it."

Perhaps. John Branion wasn't a politician and, then as now, the selection of judges was primarily a political matter in Cook County. But he would have made a fine judge.

In my early days in the public defender's office, when the staff was relatively small, at least once a month we'd all go to one of our houses for dinner and play penny-ante poker afterward. John was the only black person in the office and people would look at us funny when we were out together. As far as I could tell, it didn't bother any of us. John was fully accepted by his peers, white or black, in every sense of the word.

From his younger days, John had known many of the judges and he had their respect. He was diligent in protecting his clients' rights, and he was a good research lawyer. Sometimes he would doze at the counsel table and someone would glance at him and whisper, "I think he's asleep." But let the state's attorney make one wrong move and John would leap to his feet and shout with feeling, "Your honor, I object!"

He never retired. Toward the end of his long career he had an operation. It confirmed that he had cancer — so widespread that the doctors just sewed him back up and sent him home to die. Even so he didn't give up. He returned to the office and worked for about a month. But by the time we had organized a dinner to honor him, he couldn't attend. He was too ill. His wife and their son, a doctor who had studied in Switzerland and specialized in obstetrics and gynecology, came. Soon afterward John Branion, one of the country's finest but unsung lawyers, died.

I had learned from John Branion during my own years as an assistant, and I had learned from the judges as well. One of the first innovations I made when I became head of the office was to assign each assistant to a specific courtroom. The idea came from a judge. Previously, many clients had complained that they hadn't seen their lawyer or had had little contact with him. But now the assistant could keep in closer touch with them. The system helped client, assistant, and judge. This I had learned

from Judge Abraham L. Marovitz who, when I was a
tant, had requested that I be assigned to all of the indig
in his court.

* * *

Some of the most valuable experience that the assistant gets comes at that time before trial, virtually at the beginning, before there is any action in the courtroom. First, he must examine the case with the client. What will be the client's plea? Only the client can decide that, but he invariably can profit from legal counseling. The assistant public defender analyzes the case with him. It may be a bad case, but if the client wants to plead not guilty, then the assistant must carry through — it's his duty.

If the client says he was home in bed when the crime was committed and he insists this is true, then you ask him who else knows that he was home. (Maybe he *was* home.) You try to locate witnesses. If you can't find any and it looks like he may not be telling the truth, then you explain to him how it is going to appear to a judge and jury. You analyze it with him. If he still wants to go to trial, then you go to trial on that. After all, it's his decision whether to plead guilty or stand trial.

Explanations do not always sound as spontaneous as the client may believe. Time after time I've heard a client say, "I stepped into the alley to urinate and I found this TV there. The window was broken and there were some TV's outside and I thought, well, maybe they'd left them there, so I picked them up." These are old stories in Chicago, and the new assistant defender soon hears them. Since he must analyze the case for the client and seek witnesses if the client says there were any, the chances are that the client will soon see how his story sounds to others, and plead accordingly.

Witnesses can be a problem. Alibi witnesses are almost invariably from the same social and economic class as the defendants. In some cases, they may be Skid Row characters. Or ex-convicts. They'll be poor, certainly. So they become fair game in the state's campaign to discredit them — simply because of their social and economic background. But who else would the defendant logically be with? We all seek the company of those in our own social and economic classes. As perfect an alibi as it might be, who would expect these people to be dining with a bank president at the swank Pump Room of the Ambassador Hotel on North State Street at the time of the crime?

You can't be sure without investigating that things didn't happen the way a client claims. No matter how improbable it sounds, he may be telling the truth. Some circumstances can be incredible. I know from personal experience.

A few years ago, after my second wife, Gracia, and I had married and were living in suburban Dolton, I had to rush out one cold wintry night to see a client. Gracia's light blue Mustang was outside and she asked me to take it. I had been upstairs and now I went out with a set of her keys (we had several sets around). Outside, I saw a light blue Mustang on the street, its engine running. Well, I thought, Gracia had warmed up the car for me. How nice! It was severe, freezing weather and it felt good to be in a warm car. I drove off to meet my client, a half-mile away.

Next door, our neighbors had company. Their visitors had driven up in a light blue Mustang. But when they went outside to drive off, their car was gone. Stolen right there in quiet, peace-loving, law-abiding Dolton! They reported the theft to the police.

On the way home I noticed that something was different about the way the Mustang steered, but I didn't give it serious thought. When I arrived back home, I parked the car and went inside. As I realized later, I left Gracia's keys on the car seat.

The police had been there during my absence. Everyone was concerned about the stolen car. Shortly, the police returned. The stolen car had been located in exactly the spot where it had been stolen from.

Everything was in order. The keys were in the ignition. The car had not been damaged. But there was one small mystery: an extra set of keys on the seat. The police picked up the keys. An identification tag said they belonged to Gracia S. Getty.

Fred Moore, our chief of police, returned them to a puzzled Gracia.

"We found them in a car and we don't want any explanation," he told her, therewith closing the case.

How had Gracia's keys got into a stolen car?

No doubt I would have been believed had I explained it to the police, but at the time I didn't want to become the subject of a news story, even a humorous one, linking me to a stolen car. So I kept my mouth shut and maintained the mystery.

But what if some poor black kid had come up with a story like mine?

Who would have believed him?

CHAPTER 13
Sex Crimes

ONE OF THE CASES that I remember best came to me by default. The assistant public defender assigned to it was ill and couldn't appear in court. Francis McCurrie, public defender at the time, tried to get a postponement, but it was impossible. So I had to try it, even though I wasn't familiar with the case. Right off I had to pick a jury.

The defendant was a fellow about thirty who had spent the day of the alleged assault hanging around the saloons on South State Street. About seven-thirty that evening he had wandered over to LaSalle Street. This was the supper hour for some girls who had been working overtime at the LaSalle National Bank. All of the girls but one went back together to the bank after supper. One tarried. When she returned the door was locked. The defendant came along about that time and found the girl by herself. He seized her and took her to a nearby alley adjacent to the bank where he made her bend over and he entered her vagina from the rear.

At that time the jury set the penalty for both rape and murder in Illinois. The rape victim was a lovely looking young woman and she had the sympathy of the jury and, apparently, practically everyone else in the courtroom. And there was no doubt that the defendant had done the act.

Often while a jury was out I would listen, along with the assistant state's attorney, just outside the jury room during deliberations. This was always by agreement with the prosecutor, and, naturally, with the judge's permission. It was strictly for educational purposes, enabling us to present our cases better to the next jury. There was no invasion at all of the jury's privacy. It was too late to have any effect on that particular case. But the experience was valuable as a way to gain insights for future cases. You never knew what they would do. Often a jury would seize upon and argue a point we lawyers hadn't emphasized, which wasn't significant, and which, in fact, wasn't a part of the evidence. It helped us be clearer next time and put emphasis in the right places. It helped the next jury.

In this case the defendant was probably lucky. All of the jurors wanted to take him out of circulation so that he would never again commit rape. This meant possibly a life sentence, which would do it nicely. But one woman juror, a buyer for a department store, held out. She thought twenty years in prison was enough and she absolutely wouldn't give him one day more. Why give him more than enough?

"After about twenty years in prison, he won't be using that thing any more," she argued. "He'll be all cooled off."

She won out.

She didn't know that with a twenty-year sentence he would be out in about eight years and would only be about thirty-eight!

Rape, incest, perversion — all of the so-called sex crimes that are committed by poor people came regularly to the public defender's office. Almost invariably, this meant defending a youth or a man in a case in which the complaining witness was a girl or a woman. Since rape is always a male crime against women, and because the same is nearly always true of other sex crimes, my clients in this category were always men. The nature of these cases, to some extent, amounted to a courtroom battle of the sexes, and my role in them was never an easy one. Because I was always assigned to the side of the male defendants, I was consequently cast as an adversary against the woman who may have been victimized. It was a role I would not have voluntarily chosen, in most instances. It is a difficult situation for everyone concerned. The woman is assuredly subject to humiliation, having to testify publicly about such deeply personal acts. But the defendant's life or liberty depends on a vigorous and searching cross-examination; he is entitled to it under the law. As painful as it sometimes was for the female complainant, and for me to have to do so, I was obliged to question my client's accuser thoroughly in my efforts to help surface the truth. There is no shortcut to determining guilt or innocence. It was never a pleasant chore.

In the earlier days, if a male had sexual relations with a girl under sixteen even with consent, he could be charged with statutory rape. In many cases, the girl would be developed and sexually knowledgeable beyond her years. Judge William Lindsay, for one, used to say snidely, "Some of these girls ought to have their birthdates tattooed on their navels." In 1967 sexual relations with a consenting girl under sixteen was changed to "indecent liberties with a minor" — a lesser charge.

We also had many incest cases. One that I remember was the jury trial of Benjamin Richards who was charged with having sexual relations with his daughter. But it was not that simple. We learned that the defendant's wife had a boy friend. The boy friend was trying to get rid of the husband and so was the wife. They put the little daughter up to accusing her father of having sexual relations with her.

In the trial I brought this out about the boy friend, who always gave the little girl money to run to the store for candy or a soda. She would necessarily be gone for quite a while, giving the boy friend a lot of time. It became obvious to us all that the daughter knew much more about sex than her years would suggest. The defense was that the charge was not true and that Richards had been framed. The jury bought it. He was found not guilty.

* * *

Sex cases are always tough.

"Crime against nature" in the case of Harold Skelton

meant a homosexual act, but just because he pleaded innocent and I thought we had a strong defense didn't mean it was to be an easy fight. Originally there had also been a second charge, indecent liberties with a minor, but the state had dropped it.

Clyde Lucas, who said he was fifteen years old, had arrived in Chicago from Arkansas on the Fourth of July; the offense had allegedly occurred about a week later. He had been staying with an uncle, but that night, at about two-thirty in the morning, he had left to go to an aunt's house. His aunt wasn't home. It was three o'clock by then. He needed a place to sleep. A man nearby suggested he try the police station. On the way there he met Skelton and asked him where the police station was. Then, Lucas testified, Skelton forced him off the street into what was then a prairie, acting "like he had a gun in his pocket," and kept him there an hour. He said his trousers were taken off by Skelton, who then committed fellatio. Afterward, at 4:30 A.M., four police officers stopped them on the sidewalk and questioned them for fifteen minutes.

There were some inconsistencies in the state's case. There were only three policemen, according to the officers who took the stand. They said it was 4 A.M. or shortly before 4 when they stopped Lucas and Skelton and on cross examination they admitted the defendant had been quizzed only five minutes, not fifteen. I further elicited from the lawmen that the defendant had no weapon on him when they arrested him — an important point. They also admitted taking the boy aside and talking to him; it could be seen how this could influence his complaint.

Skelton the defendant took the stand. He had a previous police record and although it was for larceny and not a sex offense, it certainly didn't help him. But he did have some things in his favor. He told his story in a straightforward way. It was a good story. He said he had got off work at 2 A.M. His girl friend met him and he took her to a hotel. He left the hotel at three to get a drink. Returning to the hotel he met the youth Lucas, who approached him and asked where the police station was. So far, so good. It was 3:45 A.M.

Then as he talked to the youth and walked a few feet with him, the defendant testified, the policemen "threw a light" on them and stopped them. He denied ever being in the weeds or prairie. He denied taking Lucas's trousers off and having relations with him. He had always denied it.

My goal in closing was to make clear to the jurors precisely what the significant and salient facts were. I pointed out what I considered glaring discrepancies in the state's case. The state's attorney's doubt over Lucas's age: if he was really fifteen, why had they dropped the second, lesser charge of contributing to the delinquency of a minor? Did they know his age? Would a boy of fifteen be wandering the streets at 3:30 in the morning?

The defendant's version sounded more like the truth. "Why," I said in summing, "his girl friend was waiting in a hotel room a short distance away!" Why would he delay returning to his girl friend to perform fellatio on a fifteen-year-old boy? The alleged crime did not fit. "The police officers admit they took the boy aside and talked to him, and the complaining witness says they did. Here we have a boy from Arkansas, frightened by police officers in the city of Chicago, ready to say anything after they talked to him. He was thinking of his own welfare. He was rehearsed as to what he had to say, right up until he took the stand at two o'clock yesterday. There is nothing but doubt, doubt, doubt in this case from beginning to end. I ask that you return a verdict of not guilty!"

They did.

* * *

Logic is always a tool in the courtroom and can be a weapon for either the prosecution or the defense. But logic should be a means of getting at the truth, especially if the state's case has serious structural flaws. A trial that shows what I mean is that of Stephen Balchi, accused of raping a housewife a few blocks off Lake Michigan on the near South Side. He also faced an assault-with-intent-to-murder charge.

Mrs. Ida Lipton testified that her husband sometimes worked nights at the pier on the waterfront. It was on such a night that she went to a girl friend's house. She left for home around 3 A.M. As she was walking home, a man came upon her and said, "Turn around, you're going with me!" He put his arm around her waist. He cut her on the neck. He took her to his apartment. They were at his place one hour, she said, during which time he raped her twice. Then, after agreeing to meet him again, he took her home, five houses away. She got home at 4:30 A.M.

On cross-examination, I brought out that she had been married three times. She said she and her girl friends had smoked and talked and drunk only coffee. But the girl friends did not appear to substantiate what she had been drinking that night or at what time she left them.

When arrested, Balchi had a knife in his pocket, along with a watch that Mrs. Lipton had accused him of taking.

The defendant maintained he had not used force and that she had consented to having sexual relations with him. He said he met her at Forty-third and Lake Park, a business district, when she came out of a tavern. Although they passed people while walking together, she made no outcry, nor did she make a break to escape on their way to his apartment. He said they had spent three hours, not one, together in his apartment.

Several points had to be brought out for the defense: She was out alone on the one night her husband was away. She waited some time before complaining. Her neck scars were deep, but there was only a little blood on the pillow case to support her claim. Furthermore, the blood on her dress was on the wrong side. She was cut on the left side, which is where the scar was, but the blood was on the right side of the dress. She also had admitted lying down herself on the bed, weakening her claim that force was used.

Some serious questions were raised. If he had intended to rape her and rob her of her watch, would he have taken her to his own home where he had lived for the past two years? It was not the tactics of a rapist, to use his own home as a setting. Nor had she called the police or anyone else when she finally got home. She had gone to sleep. She didn't file a complaint until ten o'clock the next night — four and a half hours after her husband got home (he had worked a night-and-day shift), eighteen hours after the act. Was this the action of an outraged woman? And what about the cut? Had she already had the scar when she met Balchi that night?

The jury, which we had selected easily with only one venireman excused, saw what I was driving at. They found him not guilty.

* * *

Sometimes, like any other criminal proceeding, a rape case may become more than a mere rape case. Principles of law may be involved, carrying it further than the original trial court, possibly even to the state supreme court. In some instances it may even "make law," setting a precedent that will guide other lawyers and courts in future cases.

Which is what happened in the Waldet-Grine case.

Eric Waldet, twenty, and Fred Grine, nineteen, were charged with forcible rape. In this trial, I represented Waldet in the joint bench trial. The defendants waived a jury trial.

The complaining witness, Mary Gumbly, was eighteen. With the assistant state's attorney questioning her on direct examination, her story was this:

She left a dance around midnight with a girl friend. The girls drove to a lounge, where the girl friend danced with one of the men who worked there. While they were dancing, a man came over and sat down with Mary Gumbly, introducing himself as "Bill." She identified him as being Eric Waldet. Waldet asked her to go and eat some place and she said no, because it was late; she would rather go home. The girl friend left with the man she had danced with. Mary got in the car with "Bill" or Waldet. In the car Waldet introduced her to his friend "Gene," whom she later learned to be Fred Grine. She told them to take her home. But "Gene" said he had to pick up his girl friend first, which wouldn't take long. Grine later turned off on a dark street; he said he had to go to the washroom. He got out, then Waldet got out. When Waldet returned he threw his arms around her and tried to kiss her.

In condensed form her story from that point continued:

"I shoved him away and again he threw his arm around me and started feeling my leg. I told him not to get any ideas and he said, 'I have those ideas already, there's nothing you can do about it, and don't think you are going to get out of it.'

"I raised my hand to push him away and he grabbed it and twisted my arm behind me and shoved me back on the seat. My head got caught under the steering wheel, and I was kicking and fighting him off, and he pulled my dress up, pulled my pants and girdle down. I asked him to please stop and I started praying and he said to me, 'Shut up, remember there are two of us and only one of you.' He got on top of me and put his leg between my two legs and all of a sudden I felt something hard against my leg. I don't know what it was, and then before I knew it there was something in my private parts and it felt like a knife stabbing me. I was shoving him off and I guess he got disgusted and he got off.

"I was getting up and Gene, or Fred Grine, then came and pushed me down again and got on top of me and he did practically the same thing that Eric Waldet did. I was trying to shove him off, and told him, 'You are hurting me.' Then he put his private parts in mine and I don't know where but I got a burst of energy and turned over on my side. He got off of me and got out of the car and told me to get dressed. I got dressed. The two of them were going to get back in the car, but I told them to let me out and I would walk home. They insisted in driving me home."

When they were a half-block from where she lived, she testified, "I got out of the car and I ran home as fast as I could. When I got in the house I called the police and I woke my mother. I didn't say anything to my mother until the police arrived."

On cross-examination, I brought out that she had had one drink at the party and another one at the lounge that Waldet bought her. When she got into the car with Waldet, she sat between the two youths. She did not object when they turned off the route that would have led to her home. Although they passed a large chain store warehouse with many trucks around, she hadn't hollered or screamed. Nor had she screamed or tried to leave when they parked on the gravel road and got out of the car. When Waldet tried to get romantic with her she had struggled, but when he removed her pants she had not hollered or screamed.

"When my girdle was removed, I didn't holler or scream because I was too scared," she said.

I asked her, "Then your legs were split apart?"

"They were forced apart."

"You didn't holler or scream then, did you?"

"No, I didn't; I was too scared."

"You didn't roll over on your side or wiggle your body, did you?"

"I tried."

"Did you wiggle your body?"

"Yes, I did."

"Did you roll over on your side?"

"I tried."

"You tried?"

"That's right."

"Then you say he put his private parts into your private parts?"

"That's right."

"Did you holler or scream then?"

"No. I just told him he was hurting me and I asked him to stop."

During the interval between Waldet's leaving the car and Grine's entering it, she hadn't got up and run, she said. Nor had she cried out when Grine put his arm around her and shoved her down.

"Did you bite him?" I asked.

"No."

"Did you move your body?"

"Yes, I did."

"Which way did you move your body?"

"Almost every way possible."

"You kept squirming around?"

"Yes, I did."

"Your head was underneath the steering wheel?"

"Not at that time."

"Where was your head then?"

"It was on the seat."

"Did you bump or bruise your head against the steering wheel?"

"Not that I remember, that there were any bruises."

"There were no marks or bruises on you at all, was there?"

"No, there weren't."

"Were there any marks or bruises on your thighs?"

"No."

"You were examined by a doctor, weren't you?"

"Yes, I was."

"There were no cuts, scratches any place on your body at all, was there?"

"No, there weren't."

"And how long was Grine in the car with you?"

"I don't know how long he was in the car for sure with me, but then Grine got out and he told me to get dressed."

She put her pants and girdle back on and straightened her hair. They drove her toward her home.

"You talked to the boys while they were driving you?" I asked.

"They talked to me."

"And you answered them, didn't you?"

"Just what I had to. They asked me where I lived and I told them."

A half-block from her home she got out without saying good-bye. She told of the police coming and of her going to the hospital twice.

"You told me that you put your pants and girdle back on, is that right?" I asked.

"That's right."

"Your pants weren't torn, were they?"

"No, they weren't."

"And the girdle wasn't torn?"

"No, it wasn't."

"And the jacket, that wasn't torn, was it?"

"No."

The state presented policemen's testimony as to what they had seen upon being called and as to the girl's identification of Waldet and Grine. The doctor reported that he found numerous spermatozoa in the smear test of her vagina.

Then the state attempted to introduce statements taken from Waldet and Grine at the police station, but the defense objected. We charged they were not voluntary statements. The state offered no evidence to disprove our allegation. So, in a crucial move, the judge sustained our objection. Later the assistant state's attorney would attempt to do indirectly what he had just been told he could not present as evidence, or do directly.

The state rested.

I opened the defense's case by calling Eric Waldet to the stand. He contradicted Mary's testimony on several points. He said he had about five bottles of beer as they sat together at the lounge and that she had four mixed drinks. He denied they had ever discussed going to get Grine's girl friend.

Waldet's version after they parked, in condensed form, was this:

"I put my arm around her and I kissed her. She did not object to my arm being around her. I was in the car with her about ten minutes. I had intercourse with her. At no time did she kick at me or strike at me or scratch me, nor did she scream. I did not shove her down in the seat nor did I twist her arm. I did take her pants off, but I asked her to pick up her dress and she helped me take them off. She took off her own girdle. I did not force her legs apart. She never tried to shove me off. I never told her to shut up. I then got out of the car and Mary was still in the front seat.

"Fred Grine then got into the car and he was in there about ten minutes. He then got out of the car. They straightened themselves out and then we all got into the car and Mary was driven home. Mary told Fred where she lived and he said, 'I will drive you home,' and she said okay. While we were driving Mary home she was telling Fred how cute he was. She also gave me her phone number. When the car stopped I got out of the car and told her I would walk her to her door and she said, 'No, it is pretty late.' And that is when I asked her for her phone number and she gave it to me."

He then testified as to his arrest and how he was questioned in the state's attorney's office.

"They asked me questions and I made answers. They asked me to sign a statement and I placed my signature on the statement. I heard the statement that was previously read in this trial. There were parts of it I did not state myself."

At this point I asked him, "Was this question asked of you: 'Q. Now she still continued to resist you, did she not? A. Yes sir.' Was that question asked of you and did you make that answer?"

"I did not make that answer."

"Was that question asked of you?"

"That question was not phrased like that. No, sir."

"Was this question asked of you and didn't you make this answer: 'Q. Did she continue to keep her legs together and resist you?' "

"No, sir."

"Was this question asked of you and didn't you make this answer: 'Q. How did you get her legs apart? A. I pushed my knee there'."

"No, sir."

"Was that answer made by you?"

"No, sir."

He testified that he had relations with her in the car but that she never in any way attempted to get out from under him or out of the car.

On cross-examination, Waldet testified that Miss Gumbly took off her girdle and that he helped her take off her pants. He said he put on a ''protector'' and had intercourse with her. He later witnessed Grine on top of her.

Fred Grine then took the stand. He told of meeting Miss Gumbly at the tavern and later driving to a secluded street. After relieving himself he returned to the car and saw Waldet was having sexual relations with her. Grine went behind the car and watched the trains nearby. Waldet got out of the car and told him, ''She is waiting for you.'' Grine got into the car and had sex with her. She did not resist him; afterward, she told him to kiss her and he did.

During the cross-examination of Grine, the state prosecutors introduced a line of questions that brought me to my feet with objections.

''Did you have anything to drink at all that day?'' asked the assistant state's attorney.

''No, I don't believe I did,'' said Grine.

''Again calling your attention to a conversation with the police captain, was this question asked of you and did you make this answer: 'Q. Were you intoxicated? A. I had been drinking earlier in the day but I was not intoxicated.' ''

I bounced up.

''Objection.''

''On what grounds?'' asked the judge.

''He is reading from a statement that hasn't been introduced,'' I said. ''We haven't seen it.''

''You don't have to see it,'' said the judge.

''He is reading from a statement,'' I repeated.

''If you want to see if this statement is correct —'' the judge began.

The prosecutor broke in. ''I am not introducing anything; I am asking him if he said it. How does he know what I am reading from?''

''I know you are reading from a statement in which our objection to reading is that duress was used at the time it was taken,'' I said.

The state's attorney said, "I am asking whether or not that question was asked of him by the captain and he made that answer."

My contention was, "You have no right to read from a statement when there is an objection on the grounds of duress."

"How do you know I am reading from a statement?"

"You are reading from something."

"Objection overruled."

The prosecutor resumed. "Was that question asked of you and did you make that answer?"

"Yes, sir," said Grine.

"You did not say that to the captain?"

"Yes, sir."

"Do you sometimes use the name Gene?"

"No, sir, I never use that name."

"Was this question asked of you and did you make this answer when you were being questioned by the police captain: 'Q. On the evening of June 14th after meeting the girl, did Eric and yourself use your own names, and when Eric introduced you to the girl, what name did he use? A. We called ourselves Bill and Gene. Eric introduced me as Gene.' Was that question asked of you and did you make that answer?"

I rose. "Objection for the same reason. At the time that statement was taken from the witness, duress was used."

Grine said, "I did make that answer, but it was a forced statement. I didn't want to make that statement."

"It was a forced statement?" asked the prosecutor.

"Yes, sir."

"Was this question asked of you and did you make this answer: 'Q. Was any promise made to you to make this statement? A. No, sir. Q. Was any threat made to you or were you abused in any manner? A No, sir.' Were these questions asked of you and did you make those answers?"

"Yes, sir."

"Object." I knew this case would have to go to the Illinois Supreme Court.

"Overruled," said the judge.

Grine said, "I had to submit to that answer. I wrote the telephone number that Mary Gumbly gave to Eric Waldet when we let her out of the car, in a book, but that is not the book that I wrote it in. I lost all my papers when I was arrested. The police took two such books from me."

When Grine had finished, the state put on three rebuttal witnesses: Mary's girl friend, who said they had each had two drinks at the lounge; an assistant state's attorney assigned to the sex bureau who had read Grine and Waldet's statements to them and handed them copies at the time; and an arresting policeman who testified that he found only one book on Grine and that Grine told him he had been drinking earlier in the day.

Testimony was then over. The lawyers began arguments. The state waived opening argument. After we had summed up for the defense, the state's attorney began.

"But your honor has a duty which is far deeper and far greater than to just judge these two defendants. Your duty, in fact the duty of all of our judges, is attached to society at large, and when the two conflict, namely, the interests of society conflict with those of an individual, with all our safeguards and all our reverence for the rights of the individual, his rights must give way; and now, your honor, we have before us two young men who have shown society that they care little for our laws and our rules. They have acted against one of us, namely, Mary Gumbly. Your honor knows the conditions that exist in this country —"

"I am objecting to any inflammatory argument," I broke in, "and this is certainly starting to be such."

"The judge fixes the punishment," snapped the prosecutor.

"They are not convicted yet, or maybe you don't understand that!" I shot back.

"Go ahead," said the judge.

The state's attorney did. He asked for guilty verdicts. He got them. The judge fixed punishment for each at twenty-five years in the state penitentiary.

The battle was far from over. We appealed. I thought we had

a good case for the Supreme Court of Illinois. I wrote the brief and argument that went to the court in Springfield.

Of the nine errors I assigned to the trial, one referred to the assistant state's attorney reading from the alleged statement of Grine. I had objected to its introduction because duress had been used by the police and the statement was not voluntary. The court had sustained my objection. I also contended that the court admitted prejudicial evidence against the defendants over objections when the court permitted the state to cross-examine from an involuntary statement.

When it reviewed the case, the state's highest court took note that Grine's statement had not been introduced into evidence nor had the officer to whom it was given been called as a witness; yet the trial court had allowed the state's attorney to read from the statement on cross-examination, over defense objections. Citing a number of cases, the Supreme Court of Illinois stated that "it is established that admissions by a defendant in a criminal case are not admissible in evidence unless freely and voluntarily given by the defendant."

The opinion continued:

"Here, as in the cited cases, the alleged statement or confession is no part of the case, and all the record shows is that Grine admitted making a statement, which he testified was forced. If defendant's testimony is true, and there is no denial of it, his statement was not made freely and voluntarily but was obtained by force and the answers put down were not those that he wished to give. . . . It was, therefore, error for the court to permit the prosecution to cross-examine from the statement and thereby achieve indirectly what it could not do directly. . . . To hold otherwise would destroy the guarantees of due process of law which protect an accused from the use of confessions, statements, or admissions obtained by force, coercion, or violence."

The justices had spelled it out clearly: A statement, such as Grine's, cannot be used in a trial when it is claimed to have been obtained by force or intimidation and that claim is not disproved by the state. If the court does not conduct a hearing on this claim, then the statement cannot be used to impeach the witness on cross-examination.

And at the end, in the right-hand corner of the opinion, were those words that mean so much to defendant and defender alike:

"Reversed and remanded."

The Waldet-Grine case had made new law.

CHAPTER 14

Murder, Murder, Murder

IF THERE IS A KIND OF HOMICIDE that hasn't been committed in Cook County, I haven't heard of it.

Strangers kill strangers. Friends die at the hands of friends. Relatives take the lives of relatives. Lovers die in fatal quarrels. Kids in gangs slay other kids, or adults. Children murder their parents. Parents kill their children. Name it; it has been done.

Half or more of these cases turn out to have an indigent defendant, meaning the public defender must represent him or her. It's never pleasant work defending in a murder case. But whether he likes it or not, whether he is personally horrified or deeply saddened by the crime, it is the public defender's job. He is neither judge nor juror. The public defender is obligated to work in the best interests of his client. As I have written in a legal article, "He must be a partisan. Personal feeling is not the test when the defense of an accused person is concerned."* I had no choice but to follow the dictates of the constitution and court decisions: to see that my client received the best defense

*Cornelius J. Harrington and Gerald W. Getty, "The Public Defender: A Progressive Step Towards Justice," *American Bar Association Journal* (Vol. 42), December, 1956, pp. 1139–1142.

possible and therefore a fair trial under our adversary system of justice. You could count on the state's attorney's office to provide the best prosecution possible.

Murder cases are nerve-wearing to all concerned: friends and relatives of the victim, witnesses, the prosecutors, the judge, the jury, the defendant, and the defense lawyer. There are many pleas of guilty: often this is best for society and the individual. Many cases must be contested because of the circumstances. In others, the defendant insists on a trial. In the final analysis, the defendant has the last say as to his plea. It is, after all, his life or liberty that is at stake.

In these, as well as in the nonmurder cases, I was operating in a sort of vacuum of a living thing called The Law and the Evidence. A criminal defense attorney, whether public or private, has to condition himself to this. He can't afford to become emotionally involved with his client. He works in a narrow area: knowing and presenting the evidence and the law in the best light for his client. This is to the best interests of his client as well as himself. In some cases, especially those that I appealed, I hardly knew or rarely saw the client. For his own sake, the defender must do his job with as little wear and tear on his emotions as possible. This doesn't mean he won't work long hours or that he will fail to pursue all avenues that may benefit his client, no matter how heinous a crime the client is accused of; he is sworn to do this. But a lawyer who overidentifies with his defendants may be signaling personal trouble: if some of his clients are sentenced to long terms in the penitentiary or to the electric chair, he himself ultimately runs the risk of a nervous breakdown or high blood pressure or ulcers, perhaps even a heart attack or a stroke. In some cases, however, his problem is in the other direction, that of not letting himself be so repelled by the often revolting facts in the case, to the extent that he loses his sense of logic and objectivity. Many of my clients have been despicable. Representing them was far from easy and getting them a fair trial became a major chore.

There is always sorrow when a life has been taken, even in self-defense. But the saddest cases of all are those in which a mother is accused of killing the baby or small child she has borne.

Two such cases instantly come to mind. Early in my career I was appointed to defend a twenty-nine-year-old housewife charged with drowning her two young children, aged seven months and three years, in a bathtub. It was one of the most pitiful cases I have ever encountered. At the inquest she screamed, "Give me the chair!" and she tried to commit suicide by beating her head against the bars of the county jail. In court, her hair was disheveled and she could hardly stand by herself. I couldn't even communicate with her. The court ordered a mental examination and the psychiatrist found she didn't know the extent of the charges and she couldn't cooperate with counsel in her own defense. That made it official. She was sent to a mental institution.

* * *

Another mother, Christina Putmer, twenty-two, was charged with murdering her week-old-daughter on the day they both came home from the hospital, a steaming-hot August day in her stuffy two-room apartment close to Lake Michigan on the South Side where I had grown up.

The baby died while the husband was out briefly that evening and Mrs. Putmer rushed to a neighbor's door, crying hysterically that something was wrong. When they got back, the baby was lying on her bed with a plastic diaper tight around her neck and over her mouth. Mrs. Putmer fell to the floor, crying, and told of a Negro man's taking her watch after demanding money. They tried to revive the baby, but failed. Firemen and a doctor came, too late. Her baby was dead. The next day, during questioning, a policeman found her watch in a suitcase, whereupon Mrs. Putmer admitted tying the diaper herself and making up the story about the Negro intruder.

It was a pathetic case. Mrs. Putmer was from another state, had married over her parents' objections, and her husband had brought her to Chicago. Her parents had a large home; in this huge, strange city she lived in a little flat in a teeming neighborhood. She and her husband were broke most of the time. She couldn't take it. After the birth of the baby she had been moody and stared into space, according to her husband; then when she had called her parents, her mother had rebuffed her, refusing to talk to her. Her husband was out of work; often they didn't know where their next meal was coming from. "Sometimes I think of turning on the gas and ending it all," she had written her parents. It was as if in that one fatal moment she had taken out all her frustrations on the helpless infant. She said the baby was fussing; she went to it, leaned over the crib, and "everything went black." Afterward she realized her baby had been strangled with her own diaper.

A psychiatrist testified for the defense, explaining that in his opinion she was suffering from post-partum psychosis, a mental disorder of deep depression that sometimes accompanies the birth of a baby; he said she could have been temporarily insane when she committed the act, although he believed her sane at the time of the trial. Sanity in such an instance could be restored by a sudden shock, he testified, such as she had undergone.

The state offered no evidence that Mrs. Putmer was sane at the time of the act, and this became one point that I hammered at in my closing argument. We — Art McGloon was in the case with me — had presented evidence that she was insane at the time of the act. *"It is the duty of the state to prove that she is not insane,"* I argued, as I also sought to prove it had not been premeditated, by showing that she had actually made plans for the child's future.

The judge instructed the jury, among other things, that "in order to find the defendant not guilty on the ground of insanity, such insanity must be so clearly proven as to raise a reasonable and well-founded doubt of defendant's guilt when the whole evidence is taken together." Of course, we had contended to the contrary. We had introduced evidence she was insane when the act was committed. The state never met this issue. The jury returned a guilty verdict and gave her fourteen years in prison, the minimum sentence for murder in Illinois.

Because the state had not proved her sane beyond a reasonable doubt, after we had presented evidence of insanity, there were solid grounds for appeal. In my motion for a new trial, I wrote, "The court erred in instructing the jury." With her family backing her financially, Mrs. Putmer now appealed with private counsel, and the Illinois Supreme Court reversed the conviction expressly on the grounds I had argued. A new trial was ordered. But there was no second trial; instead, the charge was reduced to manslaughter and a negotiated plea worked out. She pleaded guilty, was given three years' probation, and was allowed to return to her hometown with her parents.

* * *

In one case, the defendant had shot and killed his wife in 1938 — before I became a public defender — and was found to be insane. He was sent to the state hospital for incarceration and treatment. In the late 1950s his daughter, who had been ten at the time of the shooting, and his sister visited him and notified our office that they believed him now to be sane. This was true; during the years there had been an improvement in the methods of treatment and he had responded.

I brought him back to Chicago on a writ of habeas corpus. At a sanity hearing, psychiatrists testified that he was sane and had been sane since 1952. He was pronounced legally sane. The state's attorney dropped the murder charges. My client, now a white-haired, stooped man with a heavily lined face, was reunited with his family, twenty-two years after his tragic nervous breakdown.

* * *

Sometimes, mothers were the victims, and their children, the defendants.

However vile the crime, a boy who slew his mother was entitled to legal counsel. If he was poor, that meant the public defender. In such cases, there usually was no doubt that the boy had caused his mother's death, although the circumstances might vary. I always asked for a bench trial, without a jury.

Frank Haddick was fifteen, the middle child of five children in a suburban township near Chicago's southern edge. He was charged with killing his forty-year-old mother with a .22 rifle. He had been absent from school earlier in the month and that day he had not gone, a matter that his mother had "discussed" with him that morning, he testified. Then he asked her permission to take his rifle outside. He claimed he bumped the gun against the door jamb and that it fired accidentally. There was that possibility — for the first shot. But it was a bolt-action singleshot, and Mrs. Haddick had been shot three times in the head. It was not a case to relish, but it was my job to do all I could for the client.

I managed to find fifteen character witnesses for the boy, not usually an easy accomplishment, and this meant the boy must have had a lot of good in him, despite the terrible thing he had done. As one witness followed another, a picture emerged of the conditions in which he and his family had lived. Their home was an old shack. When the police had gone into it, they told me, they opened drawers and rats ran out. Young Frank had worked part-time at a restaurant nearby and they had given him leftovers for the family. He had also worked as a caddy at the country club and used the money to buy school books and clothes. The head of the Cook County Behavior Clinic testified that Frank had had "some emotional disturbance deeper than neurosis" on the day of the shooting. "It could have been rage emotion — he had lost control of himself," the doctor said.

Frank, a lean-looking boy with a sorrowful face, took the stand and told of getting permission to take the gun ratshooting, for which his mother gave him four bullets. He loaded the gun, pulled back the pin, and started out through the kitchen, where his mother was washing.

"The gun fired as my arm hit the side of the door. My mother fell on the floor. I went over by her. I felt for her pulse. She was just laying there."

"Did she move? Did you hear her say anything?" I asked.

"No."

"What did you do after that?"

"I reloaded the gun."

"Did you fire it?"

"Yes."

"Did you reload the gun a second time?"

"Yes."

"Did you fire it?"

"Yes."

"Why did you do that?"

"I don't know," he said, breaking down into violent sobbing.

After a while I asked him, "You can't explain it?"

"No."

"You didn't have an argument with your mother, did you?"

"No."

"You loved your mother, didn't you?"

"Yes!" he said, his voice high, breaking, and emphatic. "I loved my mother. She was good to me."

He told of covering her body with a blanket and then going outside to play with his five-year-old sister, helping her make mud pies. Later he made jelly sandwiches for both of them.

On cross-examination, Assistant State's Attorney Irving Lang emphasized that Frank had been in the yard almost three hours after the shooting and that he had signed a self-incriminating statement to the police. He brought up the matter of Frank's truancy from school, about which Mrs. Haddick had questioned him, and of her calling the principal. Then he went into the shooting and Frank told of aiming, closing his eyes and shooting the second and third shots, "to keep her from suffering."

"If the first shot was an accident, as you say, why didn't you run for help?" Lang asked.

"I don't know," said Frank.

Lang asked for a twenty-year sentence. I asked the court to defer sentencing for six months and permit a psychiatric study.

Then the judge announced his decision. "He is guilty.

That is my only conclusion. This is an unusual case. The defendant possesses many fine qualities. There is nothing in his background to explain why he did this. It is beyond understanding.'' He sentenced Frank to eighteen years in Sheridan Reformatory, which meant that if all went well he could be up for parole in six years.

* * *

Another fifteen-year-old boy, Bobby Owens, stabbed his mother to death with a butcher knife in their frame home in a blue collar neighborhood.

An eighth-grader, he had played hooky that day, spending most of his time watching television at a girl friend's home. His mother worked. He arrived home before she did. He took a butcher knife with an eight-inch blade from a kitchen drawer and wrapped a washcloth around the handle. When his mother entered the kitchen door he stabbed her without a word. ''No, Bobby, no!'' she said. He took her car keys, a gasoline credit card, $2.57 from her purse, and fled. He abandoned the car. When arrested, he was playing ball on the school grounds. The only apparent incidents leading up to the killing were that he earlier had been reprimanded for truancy — by his father — and his mother would not permit him to use the car.

His father wanted Bobby to see his mother's body before she was buried and, although reluctant at first, the boy agreed to do so. As his attorney, I got permission from Chief Justice Cornelius J. Harrington, before whom we were to have the bench trial. The next morning the youth was taken in handcuffs to the funeral parlor to say his last farewell to the body of the woman who had borne him into the world and who had died by his hand fifteen years later.

I urged a finding of manslaughter, instead of murder as charged, but what set hard with Judge Harrington was Bobby's having wrapped the washcloth around the knife handle — an indication of premeditation. The judge found him guilty of murder and sentenced him to twenty years in prison, instead of twenty-five as the state had asked.

His father said he would stand by the boy. Apparently he did. Years later, I heard the boy was out, and living with his father.

* * *

Although he wasn't my youngest client, seventeen-year-old Philip Fordak was my smallest one. He was four feet, eleven inches tall and weighed, at the time of his trial, eighty-seven pounds.

He was on trial for murder, the fatal stabbing of a fourteen-year-old boy, and although the state was asking the death penalty, it must have been with tongue in cheek.

The jury trial was held in Judge Joseph A. Pope's court. Judge Pope, then in his late forties, was a very dear friend of mine. Small in stature, he was a big man in other ways, a precise and scholarly man whose main interest outside his profession was the classics, which he delighted in reading. He had worked his way through law school selling newspapers at his father's news stand at Madison and Wabash Avenues. A product of the First Ward Democratic organization on the Near West Side, Judge Pope had been an assistant state's attorney and then a lawyer in the city corporation counsel's office before his election to the Municipal Court and then, in the late fifties, to the Superior Court. He was a rare person in several ways; one was that he never owned a car — he always rode to work on the bus.

The issue in the trial was premeditation. Philip Fordak had killed Richard Valiak, fourteen, with a knife thrust to the abdomen. But had he done it with malice aforethought? At the trial, Fordak's story was that he had acted in self-defense.

The deceased boy was five feet, three inches tall and weighed between 130 and 140 pounds. He was a weight-lifter. His friend who was with him was also a weight-lifter and even taller than the Valiak boy; he testified that they had run into Fordak on the street, and that Valiak and Fordak had an argument. According to the friend, Valiak told Fordak they had been drinking, adding, "You couldn't drink a drop." More words were exchanged and Valiak said, "You think you're tough, you little runt." Fordak replied, "Do you want to fight?" The knifing had followed. The friend said he and Valiak actually had not been drinking liquor.

The defendant Fordak, the tips of his shoes barely touching the floor as they dangled from the witness chair, said he had met the two younger but larger boys in an alley accidentally. He said they told him they were drunk but had eaten toothpaste to cover their breaths. Valiak told him, he testified, "You can't drink, you little runt." As the argument grew, Fordak slapped Valiak and Valiak raised his arms and moved toward him while Valiak's friend came at him from the rear. He said he thought he was about to be beaten up. He stabbed Valiak.

Judge Pope charged the jury of six men and six women — ten of them parents — with instructions that allowed them to return a verdict of not guilty or a guilty verdict of either murder, voluntary manslaughter, or involuntary manslaughter. The jury deliberated four hours and five minutes. They found him guilty — of involuntary manslaughter. Judge Pope sentenced him to one-to-fourteen years.

Then a rare thing happened — a rare thing for public defenders. Philip Fordak stuck his hand at me and said, "I want to thank you, Mr. Getty." Then he left the courtroom with two bailiffs.

Few clients have ever thanked me, even when I won one's case. Usually when a guy gets a not guilty or his case is dismissed, that's the last I ever see or hear of him. I suppose he reasons, "Well, I was not guilty. What did he do for me?" The thanks, when there are any, come from those who don't go scot-free. Stephen Wola, who got life instead of death, had thanked me. And so did Philip Fordak.

* * *

No client of mine has ever gone to the electric chair, but there were some extremely close calls. The Filligan case was one of them. It also burned into my mind what can happen when you let a juror get by you during the pre-trial selection procedure.

Daniel Filligan, a door-to-door photographer who took babies' pictures by appointment, was on trial for his life in the murder of Mrs. Wanda Hull, a sixteen-year-old mother who had been beaten and stabbed seven times in the chest with a butcher knife. Mrs. Hull was found clad only in a bathrobe, panties, and slippers. Her six-month-old baby, unharmed, was nearby. Police found twenty-three-year-old Filligan's business card in the apartment. They traced Filligan, a husband and the father of two small children, and arrested him.

By the time I had been appointed in the case, Filligan had already given an incriminating statement and several articles of evidence, including his blood-stained shirt, had been seized by the police.

I attempted to suppress the statement and the seized articles of evidence, but Judge Pope, in whose court the jury trial was held, overruled me and allowed the evidence.

Filligan insisted he was not guilty because from his view it was self-defense and under the law self-defense is a defense to murder. He wanted his day in court. He also wanted a jury to determine his guilt or innocence. That was his right.

On the stand Filligan did not deny he had caused Wanda Hull's death. The only provocation for the fatal attack that he offered was that Mrs. Hull had tried to lure him into bed with her. Several buttons of her bathrobe were undone and her breast exposed and he could see that she only had on a pair of panties, he testified. He told her, "I have a wife," and he had an urge to hit her. Rejected, he said, she swore at him and struck him. He tripped and fell and she hit him twice with a sawed-off baseball bat he kept in his camera case to keep his flashbulbs from rattling. He then grabbed the bat and "blacked out" until he remembered, later, pulling the knife out of her body.

"Did you know you stabbed her?" I asked.

"I don't remember stabbing her at all," he said. "I remember trying to pull out the knife."

Filligan actually had no defense, and I couldn't get a psychiatric defense for him. I had two top psychiatrists examine him and they agreed he was sane. Even if, as he testified, she was "showing herself," which "made me want to hit her," that certainly was no defense for murder. But I did the best I could for him, collecting ten character witnesses to his good reputation, bringing his mother and his wife to the stand, and pointing out facts that lent some credence to Filligan's claim that she had made advances to him, and that when rejected, she struck him. I explored the possibilities of his not being responsible for his acts that morning, under our law, and that he might have stabbed her because of an irresistible impulse. Because with the evidence as it was, any such argument could only be ameliorative. Filligan had entered the apartment by direction of his employer because Mrs. Hull had called for an appointment: he never knew her or saw her before, yet forty-five minutes later he was a murderer. I gave my greatest attention, in closing, to an attack on the death penalty as "immoral, because no man or woman may play God," and as a symbol of terror that "brutalizes the state and its citizens." Everyone knew that Filligan might go to the chair.

In his closing, the prosecutor demanded death "for a cold-blooded murderer who deserves the electric chair." He told of Filligan's leaving the baby lying in its mother's blood, then calmly washing his hands, changing his shirt, and subsequently photographing the children of a dozen more customers that day. He waved the death knife in front of the jury and pounded a table with Filligan's sawed-off baseball bat, contending Filligan had killed Wanda Hull because she had resisted his sexual advances.

To no one's surprise, the jury brought back a verdict of guilty. He didn't get the chair, but he did get a long prison term — 299 years.

Why hadn't Filligan been given 199 years or possibly only sixty years? Because of one juror. He was of German ancestry and he had held out for death. He was a major in the Army

Reserves and, despite what I knew about jurors and backgrounds by then, I had let him slip by me during the selection. He had said he was in the reserves, but I hadn't enquired further, assuming he was of enlisted status. In the jury room, as I learned later, it had taken three and a half hours of arguing, and that sentence of 299 years helped to appease him. I later learned the other eleven jurors thought a sixty-year sentence was sufficient. After that day, I was even more cautious about selecting any juror of German descent — especially if he held a military officer's rank.

Anytime a term above sixty years is given, the judge or jury is playing the numbers game. Sometimes long terms are given out for newspaper consumption. Perhaps people believe they are safer on the streets if the term is many times longer than anyone's possible life expectancy. Yet, how long the convict remains in prison is entirely up to the parole board. Today, every convict, no matter what his sentence, appears before the parole board in at least eleven years, three months. Of course, the parole board could keep him imprisoned for one-half of his sentence. But it is all up to them, and in view of the unpredictability of human nature, it makes little difference whether the specified term is 199 or 299 years. But it did make a difference to that juror in the Filligan case.

* * *

In *The Golden Serpent,* Peruvian novelist Ciro Alegría had the outlaw say: "The poor man is respected only when he can kill." He might have added, "The poor woman, too," whose target is most likely to have been her man, after love has soured, as in Carlene Phipps' murder trial.

Carlene Phipps was charged with knifing to death her husband, Jasper Phipps, in Calumet City, one of Chicago's southern suburbs. Carlene was pretty, redhaired, and eighteen. Her husband Jasper was six years older. They had married the year before, she had borne his child, and they had lived together until he left her before the year was over. We had a hard-fought jury trial in Judge Samuel Epstein's court.

The fatal event had happened at three in the morning on the streets of Calumet City. It started, according to testimony of the state's witnesses, when Jasper Phipps, a small man who stood about five-eight and weighed 130 pounds, was in a booth at the Ozark Tavern around 11 P.M. (the witnesses disagreed as to time) and Carlene entered. Jasper was behind in his support payments. This issue quickly escalated into an argument, then a fight. But who walked up to whom first? It depended on which witness you asked. One said she had threatened Jasper before and had said in the tavern that he was no good and she was going to get rid of him. The witnesses from the tavern were mostly Jasper's men friends, and most of them offered testimony that pictured her viciously attacking Jasper and his not fighting back.

One witness, however, a construction worker who hadn't known either of them, gave a different version on cross-examination. Jasper hit Carlene, he testified, and struck her four or five times about the body. And, what was to be important later in the trial, this witness testified that he saw no weapon and nothing was thrown. In other words, she had no knife at that time. Carlene had told me that she had been given the knife by a stranger on the street outside, during a second altercation. The construction worker's account was laying the foundation for her claim.

The fatal knifing had occurred on the street and two cab dispatchers testified to hearing her utter, "I will kill you," but when had she said this? One testified, specifically, that it was *after* a knife had been taken from her; this would not prove intent at the time of the stabbing. The state contended she had taken the knife into the tavern for the purpose of killing her husband; she denied it, claiming that "a well-dressed stranger" had handed her the knife on the street outside while she and Jasper were struggling. The state was unable to prove that she did have the knife inside.

On the stand, I led her through her story up to the point of the scuffle when the stranger handed her the knife.

"Did you say at that time you were going to kill your husband?" I asked.

"No, I never said that," she replied.

"Then what happened?"

"The next thing I knew there was blood on his shirt. He said, 'Look what you done to me!' "

"Did you stab him?"

"I did not."

She insisted that Jasper had impaled himself on the knife by accident during the struggle.

The state had its bets hedged. Although Carlene was on trial for murder, a manslaughter count had also been thrown in, just for insurance. The jury of seven women and five men took six ballots and found her guilty of manslaughter, the lesser charge. The judge sentenced her to one to five years in the Dwight Reformatory for Women. She was released in eleven months.

* * *

The rejected woman did not always succeed in killing.

Joyce Bullard was an elevator operator in the Loop, charged with intent to commit murder. Twenty-two, she was on trial for shooting George Leon Gateford, thirty-eight and married. He was Miss Bullard's former gentleman friend. She had fired a pistol several times near him; one shot had creased his forehead.

The state's first witness was Gateford himself, still wearing a bandage on his head from the wound. He admitted he had had an affair with Miss Bullard but said that he had told her he was married. He told of her calling his home the night before the shooting, of her talking to his wife and then, the same evening, coming to his home and talking with his wife downstairs. But Miss Bullard left her spectacles there that night and the next day Gateford and his wife went to Miss Bullard's apartment house to return them. As he was putting her glasses in the mail slot,

Miss Bullard appeared in the vestibule with a small revolver, which she leveled at his head. He ducked. The gun went off. The bullet hit him, creasing his forehead. The gun kept shooting. He seized it and took it away from her.

He denied ever promising to marry her, but he admitted he was appearing reluctantly as a witness and that it was "partly my fault."

Miss Bullard, a petite brunette, was a superb actress when it came to getting sympathy. She told how Gateford had presented himself to her as a bachelor, had made love to her, and had promised to marry her. They had even set the date, she testified, on her birthday — which happened to be the day before she took the witness stand. What had she intended to wear at that wedding? I asked her. The new gray suit she had on, she said; she had bought it for her wedding dress.

Had Gateford planned to wear anything special for the occasion?

Yes.

What?

Like a consummate actress, she pointed out Gateford, sitting somewhat subdued in the courtroom.

"He is wearing the suit he was going to wear when he married me! We picked out the cloth and had it made just for our wedding."

Then, she testified, she told Gateford she was pregnant. What, if anything, had Gateford said?

"He told me to get an operation."

She began to cry. It was a very painful moment for her, and a tense one for others in the courtroom.

Once composed, she explained her purchase of the hand gun earlier, the day she had used it. She said she had intended to shoot herself with it, not Gateford. If so, I asked her, why had she taken it downstairs when he arrived?

"My real intention was to kill myself in front of him."

"Why?"

"He just gave me a dirty deal."

Joyce had been good for me on the stand. But when the assistant state's attorney began cross-examining her, it was as if another, very different woman had taken her place. Just like that, she changed, becoming a tigress, who snapped her answers back at the prosecutor. By the time she left the stand I was in doubt as to what the outcome would be.

In closing I emphasized to the jury the deep hurt and injustice she had suffered, and her mental state when she had shot him. Had she not said she really intended to kill herself instead? I bore down hard on the moral issues, Gateford's actions in the triangle: "Are you going to say that is the right thing to do?"

Joyce Bullard went free.

CHAPTER 15

Richard Speck and the Eight Slaughtered Nurses

HUNGRY JACK LAKE: cool blue shimmering waters loaded with bass and Northern walleyed pike. It was idyllic up there in Minnesota, a perfect retreat from the unrelenting pressures of the public defender's office and Chicago's muggy midsummer heat wave.

We fished all week. The three of us — my son Mike, his four-year-old son Mike, and I — were out on the lake every day. Young Mike stubbornly refused to miss a minute of the fun and was acting like a big fellow, as if he were a six-year-old. Poor kid, he had a hard time keeping up. Sometimes he'd fall asleep in the boat.

We were away from it all. No television or radio. No newspapers. No schedules. No worries. We had a cabin at a secluded fishing lodge operated by "Mother" Bunn and her son on the Gunflint Trail, right next to Canada. The air was fresh and cool. It was a quiet place, with all the solitude you could ask for, and the fishing was great. It was the perfect place on earth to relax and enjoy being with one's son and rambunctious grandson.

That interlude in July, 1966, is one I'll always cherish.

It took a day to drive up from Chicago, and a day to drive

home. During that week we were completely out of touch with the outside world, which was the way we wanted it. Good thing, too — for it would not have been the same restful vacation if I had known what was going on in Chicago at the time.

We started back to Illinois on July 16, a Saturday. The first up-to-date news we had was on the car radio, driving home. In Chicago, violence had erupted, with full-scale rioting in the black ghetto on the South Side. It was beginning to simmer down. Then we heard another ominous fragment of news, that eight nurses had been murdered. It had happened on Thursday, July 14 — two days before. It was shocking news. Next we learned that the murders had taken place somewhere in the Chicago area. We were listening to tail-end accounts of the news, amounting to scraps, and Mike and I pieced them together as best we could.

The next broadcast made it clear. It had happened on the South Side, right in the city of Chicago. By then I was hoping I didn't end up with the case.

We arrived home late that Saturday evening. The next morning I was called at home by two newspapermen. A suspect in the nurse murders, Richard Speck, had been arrested. What was my reaction to a statement made by Superintendent of Police Orlando Wilson over TV and in the newspapers and on radio, while holding up a picture of Speck, telling the entire world that Speck was the man who had committed the murders and that there was no doubt about it? My gut reaction was that it might very well be detrimental to the defense, imprinting the statement indelibly on the public mind so that the defendant might not receive a fair and impartial trial. I did not realize at the time that some months later I would be arguing that point.

I lived at Eighty-Fourth and Dante Avenue then, which was two and a half to three miles from the townhouse at 2319 East 100th Street where the young women had been killed. That Sunday afternoon I drove by the murder scene, to have a picture of it in my mind in case our office became involved in it. Sightseers were everywhere — people driving by, others standing on sidewalks and on lawns. Police were directing the steady flow of traffic. I drove on, not wishing to get into a traffic snarl, turned onto a side street, and headed home.

By this time I had tried more than four hundred jury cases while in the public defender's office, approximately one hundred of them murder cases. But now I was on the verge — without realizing it — of what was to be, without a doubt, the toughest case I was to handle in my entire career.

1. The Crime of the Century

That week in Chicago was like many another one in which a major crime has been committed. It was sweltering, over 90 degrees day after day, the kind of weather that saps energy and frays nerves.

It's hard to assess the effect such weather may have on persons capable of committing a vicious crime. In the black ghetto on the South Side, the heat had been a direct, precipitating factor in creating a climate of strife in which tempers had boiled over into the makings of a riot. On July 12, a Tuesday, a minor riot had begun when someone opened a fire hydrant at Roosevelt and Throop, in the predominantly black section between the University of Illinois Chicago campus and the Cook County Hospital. Policemen closed the hydrant. A black teenager opened it again. He was arrested. This triggered rioting in which stores were damaged, and some looted. More policemen were dispatched. The next day there were more incidents, and soon it had become a full-blown riot that, finally, placed every man on the Chicago police force on a twelve-hour day.

The violence became deadly. On the West Side, also in the black ghetto area, two persons — a fourteen-year-old girl and a twenty-eight-year-old man, both black — were shot and killed, apparently by stray bullets as policemen and snipers traded gunfire.

Mayor Daley asked Governor Otto Kerner for help in controlling the situation, and the governor called out the National

Guard, dispatching 3,000 guardsmen by trucks to the riot-stricken West Side of Chicago. Civil rights leader Dr. Martin Luther King, Jr., also entered the picture by demanding better recreational facilities in the black community. Mayor Daley acceded. Sprinklers were attached to a number of hydrants on the West and Northwest Sides to serve as showers for black children on hot days. By Thursday, July 14, the rioting was most intense, but it began to wane thereafter. In all, more than two hundred persons were arrested in the riots.

It was hot all that week in Chicago, but on Wednesday the 13th a cool front accompanying heavy thunderstorms moved into the southern portion of the city, bringing the temperature down slightly but raising the humidity. The high that day was 89 degrees.

That Wednesday night, at 2319 East 100th Street in the Jeffery Manor section of the South Side, a tragedy was shaping that would overnight eclipse the riots as far as headlines in Chicago, the nation, and the rest of the world were concerned. Jeffery Manor was a section that had been developed shortly after World War II by families from the older, crowded Chicago neighborhoods to the north. It was predominantly white-collar in makeup, with a large Jewish population, and was composed of row houses, small apartments, and two-story Georgian homes.

But the details of the mass murders inside the two-story brick townhouse on East 100th Street that night after midnight in the small hours of Thursday, July 14, were veiled from the outside world by the screen of night.

The first inkling that the outside world had of the horrors of that night came shortly after six o'clock that morning of Thursday, July 14, when neighbors heard a woman screaming.

"Help me!" she cried.

Soon afterward two women and a man hurriedly dressed and rushed toward the frantic outcries where they heard the same woman again.

"Help me! Help me! My friends are all dead! My friends are

all dead! I'm the only one alive! Oh, God! I'm the only one alive!

"Everyone is dead!

"Oh, God . . . he's killed them all . . ."

Just under the second-story window of the townhouse, on a ledge about a dozen feet from the ground, they saw a small, dark-haired young woman. She continued to scream hysterically.

The man ran into the street and hailed a police squad car that happened to be passing. One of the women, a nurse, recognized the woman on the ledge as Corazon Piezo Amurao, a twenty-three-year-old nurse from the Philippines. Miss Amurao was cautioned not to jump. The policeman, seeing Miss Amurao and realizing something was badly wrong, radioed to headquarters for assistance. Then he dashed toward the townhouse. Inside, he drew his revolver and entered the living room where his first shock came. He saw a nude body of a young woman on the couch with a strip of cloth around her neck. She had no pulse. Cold dead. He recognized her as Gloria Jean Davy, who e sister he had dated before he had married.

By then another policeman had arrived in a squad car and was talking to Miss Amurao outside on the ledge. He was summoned inside by the first policeman. The two of them, with pistols drawn, began searching the house. Upstairs they found an abattoir for which the corpse downstairs had scarcely prepared them. There were three bedrooms upstairs and bodies of young women were everywhere. Some had been strangled, some had been stabbed. Blood was splashed over the rooms. Everything was in disarray. Counting the body downstairs, there were eight victims.

Miss Amurao was pulled inside the window to safety and taken downstairs and to another townhouse two doors down where she began her long emotional recuperation from a night of death and terror. She was the lone survivor in the townhouse that had been rented by the South Chicago Community Hospital for its student nurses. All of the victims were student nurses, except two who, like Miss Amurao, were Filipino exchange graduate nurses.

The dead women were:

1. Gloria Jean Davy, twenty-two, of Dyer, Indiana, a well-liked young woman who in 1965 had been president of the Chicago Student Nurses Association; strangled with a strip of sheet, found on the first floor.

2. Suzanne Farris, twenty-one, of Chicago; multiple stab wounds in the chest and one in the chin; in the second floor hallway outside the bathroom.

3. Pamela Wilkening, twenty-two, of Lansing, Illinois, a South Side suburb; strangled with a strip of sheet and stabbed in the left breast; on a bed in the front east bedroom.

4. Patricia Matusek, twenty, of Chicago; strangled with a strip of sheet, wrists tied; in the same bedroom as Miss Wilkening.

5. Mary Ann Jordan, twenty, of Chicago; multiple stab wounds in the back, back of neck, and left eye; the same bedroom as Miss Wilkening and Miss Matusek. Miss Jordan was the only victim who did not live at the townhouse; she had been visiting as an overnight guest.

6. Nina Schmale, twenty-four, of Wheaton, Illinois, in nearby DuPage County; multiple stab wounds in the neck and strangled with a sheet, her hands tied and a gag in her mouth; on the floor in the west bedroom.

7. Merlita Gargullo, twenty-three, an exchange student from the Philippines; strangled with a strip of sheet and multiple stab wounds in the neck, her wrists tied behind her back; on the floor of the west bedroom.

8. Valentina Pasion, twenty-three, another Filipino exchange student; her neck slashed and jugular vein and trachea severed, with wrists and ankles tied; in the same west bedroom where the bodies of Miss Schmale and Miss Gargullo were found.

The two policemen at the death scene notified the central police headquarters at Eleventh and State. Within a very short time about a hundred or more detectives were dispatched to the area to begin a massive manhunt that immediately swept the ghetto rioting from the public mind and took over the news media's major spotlight. Within a matter of hours it was national, and international, news.

Soon after the initial discoveries of the bodies — which had not yet been officially identified — the first two policemen on the scene talked briefly to Miss Amurao, seeking a description of the person or persons responsible for the carnage. Her remarks, given in Filipino-accented English, as later recorded in the police bulletin revealed that she had seen one man, about twenty-five years of age, six feet tall, with short or crew-cut hair, no hat, wearing a black, waist-length jacket and dark pants. Several minutes later Miss Amurao was whisked away to the South Chicago Community Hospital in an unmarked police car.

A few hours after Miss Amurao's dramatic disclosure of the event, eight blue-and-white squadrols, with two policemen inside each one, pulled up. Each team took a stretcher inside and returned with a blanket-draped body, which was taken to the Cook County Morgue on the West Side. Throughout it all, the curious kept flocking to the area. The crowd soon grew so large that a kind of muted circus air characterized it, as newsboys hawked Loop newspapers blaring headlines of the murders and "good humor" trucks stopped to accommodate the throngs that came to talk and look.

The enormity of the crime was almost impossible to accept, an atrocity practically never seen except in war. Even veteran policemen could remember nothing to match it. Cook County Coroner Andrew J. Toman, clearly shaken by what he had seen, came outside the townhouse and told reporters, "There has never been anything like it that I have heard. It is the crime of the century. It is the worst crime I have ever seen."

Indeed, at least as far as Chicago was concerned, it was the crime of the century. The Bobby Franks murder in the Nineteen-Twenties was the only one, to my knowledge, that previously had been given that label. Everywhere, people talked about it, at work, on the street, at home, on trains and buses.

TV and newspaper reporters hurried to the scene and others were dispatched from other cities. The city in which a murder a day had come to be a normal statistic was shocked and horrified and, to a large extent, frightened. The killer was still at large.

* * *

Basically, Miss Amurao's story contained these essentials, as later corrected on details:

Around 11 P.M. as she and her roommate Merlita Gargullo were going to bed, she heard a rap on her door. Answering it, she discovered a man armed with a pistol. He forced her and her roommate to go with him to another bedroom, where he awakened the nurses who were there, and then to the third bedroom. There were six nurses in the townhouse at the time and three more arrived subsequently. In all, there eventually were nine women in the house. The man collected them in the large south bedroom and then cut bedsheets into strips. With these he tied the young women up and made them lie on the floor.

This done, he began to take them out of the room, one by one. After each absence he would return and take out another of the girls. During one of his trips from the room, Miss Amurao rolled under a bunk bed, where, because of her small size, she remained hidden. At last the house grew quiet. She stayed, tied, under the bed for hours. An alarm clock went off at five o'clock and finally ran down. She began to work loose her bonds. Having freed herself, she went to the front window, pushed out the screen, and began screaming for help.

Miss Amurao's account included that the intruder had been drinking and he had said he wouldn't hurt them, that he just wanted money. He said he wanted to go to New Orleans. He gathered their money before he took them from the room one at a time.

Although the apartment walls in the six-townhouse complex were known to be "paper thin," no one else had reported hearing any of the activities that went on that night at the death house. The residents of the apartment next door were on vacation at the time. No one had noticed anything unusual.

The salient facts of the case were soon clear and known to the world: eight nurses had been murdered, with the slayer or slayers at large; apparently none of the victims had been sexually molested. But in the wake of the nightmare killings, the details were not so precisely pinned down. Some of the data reported by the news media later turned out to be erroneous or slightly off. A good illustration is that of three Chicago newspaper versions of Miss Amurao's departure from the outside ledge of the townhouse: each one is different. In one story, a policeman led her out from the ledge; in another, she went through the bedrooms by herself; in the third, she jumped eight feet to the ground! Certainly at least two of them were in error. Although these were not necessarily significant deviations from the facts, they do illustrate how some details became garbled in the press, which later could have an influence on the public mind.

Chicago's *American* ran an eight-column, 96-point gothic capitals headline on page one — 8 STUDENT NURSES SLAIN — and the Chicago *Daily News* placed the multiple crimes in perspective with Cook County's violent past: "It was the worst single mass slaying in Chicago's history. The worst until now had been the St. Valentine's Day massacre in 1929 when seven men were shot down in a garage on North Clark Street."

Within a short time, the tone had been set. On a picture page depicting policemen removing the bodies, a distraught nurse weeping, scenes of the blood-splashed bedrooms, the headline at the top cried: WHERE FIEND MASSACRED 8 NURSES. Another story, about a psychiatrist's opinion, displayed this headline: ***ONLY A MONSTER COULD KILL 8: Psychiatrist.***

An occasional sentence was even more likely to create bias against some future defendant. Particularly if it were like this paragraph: "Meanwhile, technicians of the police crime laboratory, working under the direction of Capt. Daniel Dragel, had isolated 32 finger prints belonging, apparently, to the same person.'' Thirty-two prints had indeed been found, but there was never any evidence that they belonged to one person. It was a completely erroneous impression, yet many people accepted this as fact even after the trial was over the following year!

* * *

With public opinion immediately high and the police under tremendous pressure to make an arrest, the dragnet began hauling in suspects. One man was arrested in a hotel after attempting to buy a ticket to New Orleans. He was six inches shorter, seventy pounds lighter, and twenty-five years older than the killer was supposed to be, but he seemed to have blood on his shirt, acted nervous, and left without buying his ticket. After questioning, he was released. Other suspects were picked up on the Indiana Toll Road, at Kankakee, and at Pontiac, Illinois, and all were let go after a short while.

Meanwhile, the Federal Bureau of Investigation had offered the services of its crime laboratories and other divisions to Chicago's police superintendent, Orlando W. Wilson. By this time a number of fingerprints had been recorded from the townhouse and a man's sweat-soaked T-shirt had turned up on a desk in the downstairs living room.

The police by now were ringing doorbells and questioning everybody they could. Had they seen any suspicious persons? Because Miss Amurao said the man's breath smelled of alcohol, detectives combed the taverns within a two-mile radius of the townhouse. Hoping to facilitate the search, the police had an artist draw a sketch of the killer, based on an interview with Miss Amurao from her hospital bed where she was recovering from the ordeal, and this was printed on the front pages of the city's newspapers. The sketch portrayed a young, smooth-faced, crew-cut man.

On Saturday, July 16, two days after the murders, Police

Superintendent Wilson called reporters to his office at Eleventh and State. He made the first big announcement of the investigation. A murder warrant had been sworn out for Richard Franklin Speck. Holding up a photograph of Speck, Superintendent Wilson stated that Speck had been identified as the killer of the eight nurses, that there was no doubt of it, and that anyone who knew of Speck's whereabouts should notify the police immediately. Wilson's announcement was reported in the newspapers, complete with the pictures in which he showed Speck's photo, and it was also reported by television news programs. Wilson's announcement left no doubt in anyone's mind that the police superintendent, a man in a position of authority who was widely respected as the man who had reformed Chicago's police force following the Summerdale scandal, was positive that Speck was guilty.

Now, as I was to come to realize in the succeeding days, this was a damning indictment, as far as public opinion was concerned, of a suspect who hadn't even been arrested yet, much less tried. Why had Wilson expressed his opinion of Speck's guilt so forcibly? Well, his defense of the TV performance was that he was reassuring the people that the guilty man would be captured, in order to settle their fears. At the same time, perhaps this could have been done without saying positively that Speck was guilty. It was, after all, a judgment, and coming from a man who was head of this huge police department, it indicated that Speck was guilty beyond a reasonable doubt.

Speck's fingerprints were reported to have been found in the townhouse and a previous bad reputation was aired. The FBI issued a nationwide alert for Speck, who had become overnight the country's No. 1 most wanted man. One tattoo, on his upper left arm, identified him: "Born to Raise Hell." The massive manhunt designed to solve the "crime of the century" intensified now that it had a specific target.

The drama was not long in reaching a climax. Around midnight that Saturday, only hours after Wilson had fingered Speck as the wanted man, an inhabitant of a Skid Row hotel on Madison Street responded to knocks at the door of his room. A man stood in the hall, his left arm bleeding profusely; he asked for water. He was given water; then the night desk clerk was notified and he in turn called the police.

Because the bleeding man was in a room rented to "B. Brian," he was listed as that by the police when they came. (Actually, he had registered under another name, in another room, but the circumstances of his being in "B. Brian's" room were lost at that moment.) To the patrolmen, he was another of the daily attempted suicides and knife slashings that are common to night duty. One policeman made a tourniquet of his belt and a nightstick to halt the spilling of blood from the cut apparently made with a broken wine bottle. They sped to the emergency room of the Cook County Hospital.

In the trauma ward, Dr. Leroy Smith, a resident surgeon, began washing the blood off the patient's arm. The patient's face looked familiar to Dr. Smith. He had a nurse bring him the newspaper he had just put down, and he rubbed the blood from the left arm until he saw the letter B. He rubbed off more caked blood and read a tattoo — "Born to Raise Hell." Now the newspaper had come and he compared the picture on its front page with the man in front of him. He had the police called and the patient was put under arrest.

Preparing for surgery to close the deep cut, Dr. Smith asked, "What is your name?"

"Richard," the patient replied. Then he added, "Richard Speck."

He was given a blood transfusion and Dr. Smith closed the gash with five stitches. At 4:30 A.M. Speck began to come out from under the anesthetic; an hour after that, he was en route to the Cermak Memorial Hospital, within the Bridewell, which is the city jail. The manhunt was over, and that morning when the city awoke, everyone soon knew it.

How had Speck been singled out as the one who had killed the eight nurses?

While checking in the neighborhood, the police had gone to the National Maritime Union hiring hall, which stood at 2335 East 100th Street, only a number of yards from the nurses' home. They learned about Speck's job application as an apprentice seaman and obtained a passport-sized photo of him.

On Friday, this photo was shown to Miss Amurao, after she had already viewed more than 100 others. She thought it could be the man they were hunting. From this point on, the search narrowed to focus on one man — Richard Speck.

Ironically, Speck had been in the presence of policemen the day after the murders were committed and he had been left alone. The night of July 14 he had checked into the Raleigh Hotel on North Dearborn on the near North Side, and had taken a prostitute with him to his room. While he was still sleeping she slipped out and reported to the room clerk that the man she had been with had a gun. The police were called. Two policemen, not realizing Speck was a leading suspect, asked him his name and he told them truthfully. But the loaded .22 pistol, he said, belonged to the prostitute, not him. The patrolmen took the gun with them. It was not inventoried at the Chicago Avenue Police Station until sometime later. Speck went back to sleep in his room.

In a matter of hours, the world would know — from Orlando Wilson's mouth — that Speck was one of the most-sought men in history, and in a few more hours he would be one of the heaviest guarded prisoners in Chicago's annals.

This was the situation on my first day back in Chicago since my vacation. But who was Richard Speck?

Speck had been born the day before the Japanese attack on Pearl Harbor, on December 6, 1941, in Monmouth, Illinois, which is in the western part of the state about thirty miles from the Mississippi River and Iowa. He was the seventh of eight children and the youngest boy. The father died when Speck was young; the mother remarried and moved with her second husband, taking with them Richard and Richard's younger sister, to Dallas, Texas. After starting the first grade in Monmouth, Speck attended school in Dallas until he dropped out in the ninth grade.

He had worked as a laborer and truck driver and had had a long string of run-ins with the police, predominantly for juvenile and relatively minor reasons. However, in 1963 he was sent to the Texas penitentiary on a forgery in which he allegedly signed another man's name to a pay check. He was sentenced to three years in prison. He was released on parole in January, 1965. Soon afterward he was sentenced to the Dallas County Jail on an assault charge in which he allegedly had seized a woman from behind as she parked her car. However, first he was returned to the state prison as a parole violator and discharged not long afterward. Because of a communications mixup, Speck was not held for Dallas authorities and thus never served the jail term for assault.

Speck had married a fifteen-year-old girl in Dallas in 1962 and his wife had given birth to a daughter. But the marriage had gone rapidly on the rocks and early in 1966 it had ended in divorce. His former wife had remarried, and in March Speck returned to his birthplace of Monmouth, Illinois, where he had relatives. The older brother and sisters in the family had remained in Illinois and now had families of their own. In late April he left for Chicago, where a sister lived and where he hoped to land a job as a seaman.

Speck took a berth on the *C. B. Randall,* an ore boat, but in May appendicitis landed him in a hospital at Hancock, Michigan, for emergency surgery. Returning to his ship, he later went to Sault Sainte Marie, Michigan, and eventually returned to Chicago. Here, on June 30, his brother-in-law had taken him to the Maritime Union hiring hall on East 100th, close to the townhouse. Speck was not a union member, but under the law a nonmember had the same opportunity for a job as did a union member. After his application papers had been cleared by the government, he returned to the hiring hall on July 8 and on subsequent days. He was there the morning of July 13, less than twenty-four hours before the murders, and remained there until the afternoon preceding the deaths.

That, in brief, was the story of Richard Speck, who now lay hospitalized in the Bridewell, under police guard, waiting to be formally accused of murdering eight young women who had dedicated their lives to serving humanity.

By then he was despised by millions.

While the police continued its investigation, seeking any blood-stained clothing that the killer may have discarded and searching for the knife that had been used in the townhouse, State's Attorney Daniel P. Ward assigned a half-dozen assistants to start building a case against Speck. But Ward was moving cautiously. A former DePaul University law school professor who had been one of the new faces to brighten the Democratic ticket after the Summerdale disgrace, Ward was chary of violating one of the recent U.S. Supreme Court decisions restraining the police in questioning criminal suspects. One especially, the *Miranda* decision, ruled that a suspect was entitled to counsel when he was *about* to be accused of a crime.

Ward thought he had a strong case against Speck and he didn't want to blow it. Evidently with that in mind, he called early Monday morning — my first day back to work after my vacation — and asked to see me. I went to his office, where he told me that it looked very much as if Speck were an indigent person. He wanted to alert me that in all probability I would be appointed to defend the man and that he would like me to be present in the courtroom when the state presented information or made an accusation against Richard Speck.

Ward, as well as others, wanted to insure that Speck was represented immediately. Specifically because of the *Miranda* decision, he was concerned about what the courts might say later on.

Also on Monday I received a call from a relative of Richard Speck, indicating it was hoped by his family that I would represent him. Thus, by Monday morning it seemed to be a fact that I probably would be involved in the defense.

Not quite a fact, though. Dan Ward called me again. A lawyer, whom I will call Norton, had contended that he had been hired by Speck's relatives to represent the defendant. Ward and his assistant, Louis Garippo, suspected Norton was seeking publicity and in all probability would crawl out from under the burden later. (The case would last almost a year.)

The next day Norton sought to interview Speck and he was taken to Dan Ward's office on the second floor, where he was questioned with a court reporter present. I was in the room at the time. Mr. Norton wouldn't disclose who had hired him. Well, as a matter of fact, no one had. That afternoon as the state presented its information in Felony Court at the preliminary hearing, Norton bowed out. Speck didn't know Norton from a row of apples.

However, before I had been appointed counsel by the court and before I had yet seen Speck himself, another move had been taken by the police that would become a point of controversy at a later date. On Monday, about a day after Speck's arrest, the surviving nurse, Miss Amurao, was slipped into the Bridewell for the purpose of identifying Speck as the intruder in the townhouse. But Speck's condition prevented such a confrontation and Miss Amurao was returned to the South Chicago Community Hospital where she remained secluded. Then the following day, dressed in a nurse's uniform and accompanied by another nurse, two detectives, and the Bridewell's associate medical superintendent, Dr. William J. Norcross, she entered Speck's room in the Bridewell's Cermak Hospital, and took a look at the patient. Later she said, "He is the man."

He was never placed in any semblance of a lineup. To have made the identification properly, they should have waited until he had recovered and then placed him in a lineup. *People* v. *Wade* was in the U.S. Supreme Court and I knew of it, but it hadn't been decided at that time. *Wade* was to rule that a defendant had the right to counsel at the time of an identification and that the police had to place him in a situation where it would be a fair lineup. But the millions who read the newspapers and heard the TV reports of the confrontation very likely did not ponder this technical point concerning Speck's civil liberties, and the idea became firmly planted that Speck was, beyond a doubt, guilty.

By now I knew I was involved in a very, very tough case. Usually some lawyers will try to move in on the public defender in a big case, as Norton had tried to do, reasoning that the publicity will benefit them splendidly at a later date, but from that time on, there was never a lawyer in the country who wanted to get into this gigantic case. I had it to myself, it appeared, but the choice was certainly not my own. Most of all, this meant that from that point on I had to keep a free and open mind on the case, which I did. I did not intend to formulate any theory of the case, whether there might be one killer or more than one or any other specific angle, until I had seen the hard evidence first.

Soon after the confrontation, Dr. Norcross informed Judge Daniel J. Ryan of Felony Court that Speck apparently had suffered a heart attack. Subsequently, two court-appointed heart specialists diagnosed the medical problem as an inflammation of the sac surrounding the heart. Nonetheless, his condition was serious for some time.

* * *

The close relatives of Richard Speck — a brother and several sisters and their spouses — were all in Monmouth, Illinois, at this time. At 1:45 P.M. on the day of the preliminary hearing before Judge Ryan, I received a telegram from Monmouth.

It read: *"Please visit and see Richard Speck and advise him of his rights. It is our opinion that you should represent him."*

The names of his brother and several sisters followed.

At 2:30 P.M. at the hearing, which Speck was unable to attend because of his physical condition, Judge Ryan formally appointed me to represent Speck. He appointed me personally, so that the case would not fall to one of my young assistants. Both the state and the court wanted someone with a substantial trial background to represent Speck; then it couldn't be pointed out later that there was incompetence of counsel.

At this time, Speck was accused of one murder, that of Gloria Jean Davy, as a matter of technical procedure in order to hold him.

Naturally, I wanted to talk to the man I was appointed to

represent in order to fulfill my legal and moral responsibilities as his counsel. But Dr. Norcross appeared concerned about his condition and the effect such a conference might have on the patient. At that time he still believed Speck was suffering from a coronary and, of course, he had lost an amount of blood in the slashing incident. Dr. Norcross did not think it advisable for me to see him; he would let me know.

However, I soon insisted on talking to my new client; he needed all the advice he could get.

I took an assistant public defender, James Gramenos, with me to the Cermak Hospital, at Twenty-Seventh and California, just next door. I had decided early that I would need Gramenos to help me, for he had a vast investigative background. He had spent six years with the FBI, as part of an investigative team. He had also worked as an investigator of Internal Revenue Service personnel. He had given up all this so that he could become a trial lawyer, which had brought him to the public defender's office. Detroit-born, of Greek ancestry, handsome, dark wavy-haired Gramenos conveyed an air of deliberate action, as if he wouldn't move unless he was going to investigate with that move. He was diligent to the point of being a perfectionist. His application had been so impressive and voluminous that it was almost like reading a brief prepared for the Supreme Court. By the time of the nurse murders, Jim had been in the office about two years.

On a warm and beautiful day, Gramenos and I walked to the Bridewell over grounds swarming with representatives of the news media. TV cameramen and reporters, newspaper and radio reporters, photographers — the Bridewell was besieged by the news media. This had been, and was to continue to be, the pattern for any public move in any way connected with the Speck case, up to the end of the trial, and even afterward.

We were ushered to the second floor of the Cermak Hospital and down a long, glass-enclosed corridor that passed by many rooms in which there were hospital beds. Speck was in the last room. There was only his bed in it. Outside, four policemen stood guard. Dr. Norcross took us in and warned me that Speck had a bad heart condition. It was as if the state felt it might lose the defendant before he could be electrocuted.

Speck, six feet tall or taller, had long light brown hair combed straight back, a long nose and rather large ears and a pock-marked face. These were the only physical characteristics that I could see. It was a very small room and he was lying on the cot in it, wearing a white gown and stretched out under a sheet. His face was pale, and my impression was that he was weak and probably not very alert.

Afraid that the room might be bugged by the police, I asked Gramenos to look for any signs of an electronic listening or recording device. He did not spot one, although we were suspicious of the lighting fixture in the ceiling. But as a matter of caution I saw to it that everything was said in low voices. The police remained at the doorway, but they couldn't distinguish from there what we were saying. Norcross was in the room.

The interview only lasted for three or four minutes, and I did practically all of the talking. I introduced myself and asked Speck if he knew where he was. I told him I had been appointed to represent him and asked if he wanted me to do so, and he said he certainly did. His brother and his brother-in-law had by then made contact with me, but Speck said he did not want to see them. Which was understandable when interpreted to mean that he felt himself to be a failure in being accused of such a terrible crime. He told me his age, twenty-four, and that his mother lived in Dallas and that he had served time in the Texas prison at Huntsville for a "phony forgery." I had great difficulty making out what he said because of his thick Southern drawl. He didn't seem to open either his mouth or lips but just drawled it out. At times he seemed incoherent and I couldn't understand what he was saying.

I explained to him that he was under an extremely serious charge and that I would investigate the case and do what I could. I advised him of his rights and explained that he did not have to answer any questions. If anyone questioned him, he should ask for me. I cautioned him not to talk to anyone but me about the case, emphasizing that this included, especially, the police or any newspapermen. To this day he remembers this and has not done so.

That was it, just a brief converation. But I had one final question for him. His sister had asked her pastor to visit Speck and the minister had gone into the building with me. Now I asked Speck if he wished to see a clergyman.

"No," he drawled, "I don't want to see any minister."

So although I had taken the minister over to the Bridewell, he never went in to see Speck. Unfortunately, however, quite the opposite was reported in the press, that the minister did visit Speck — and Speck was quoted as having made an incriminating remark.

A TV reporter asked the minister, "Is Speck remorseful or not?" It was the traditional wife-beating question, but the minister, unprepared for the trick, replied, "Yes, I'm sure he is remorseful," not intending to imply guilt or that he had even seen Speck. In print, it became a damaging statement, and the minister apologized to me.

Later, when he felt better, Speck did want to see his sister, whom he was fond of, and I arranged for her to see him. She was a very respectable, very refined, church-going woman and she had had no idea of her brother's drinking habits until they had become a fact to every newspaper reader and TV watcher in America. When he had been in her home, she told me, he had been a perfect gentleman and had not drunk. You could hardly believe that she and Richard Speck were related, and there is no way to accurately measure the agony she and other relatives went through at this time.

The big question was, what had happened to Richard Speck on July 14, when the young nurses were being systematically slaughtered at the townhouse?

Getting his version of that night and the subsequent days became the goal of my follow-up interviews. The information came out in brief interviews on different days and some of it was unclear from time to time, partly because of his drawl and partly from the haziness with which he remembered. The second interview, on the following day, took a great deal of effort on both his and my part. Throughout our session, he had one arm attached to the bed by a manacle. Hospital authorities said they were afraid he would attempt suicide again.

He told of having met some sailors at the Shipyard Inn, a tavern and rooming house, on the evening in question. He did not remember their names but said they were either Canadians or had been on a Canadian ship. They were selling amphetamine pills that he called "redbirds" — a new term to me — for the price of three for twenty-five cents. He bought three and then they gave him three more.

He drank with them at a bar called Pete's Tap, in the same area, and then they returned to the Shipyard Inn, where he had already rented a room. He said he and the seamen went to his room where, about eight o'clock that evening, they all took intravenous injections of a drug, possibly morphine. He administered his shot himself, mainlining it into the vein.

As he talked he was not altogether coherent, but I jotted it all down as he mumbled.

After the injection, he didn't remember anything. The next thing he remembered was that he woke up Thursday, July 14, at ten-thirty in the morning. He had a gun, he said; he didn't know how he got it.

From that point on, it was a haze of alcohol as he told of being in the Raleigh Hotel and the prostitute there, and then of going to another hotel — the Starr — where he had cut himself with a razor blade. The next he remembered, he woke up in the hospital.

Actually, this second interview was not very factual, and this became characteristic of his cooperation throughout the case: he couldn't provide much information at all.

At a third brief interview a few days later, he told me of his former wife and their divorce, his daughter, and his employment at three businesses in Dallas. It was interesting to me that after he had left the penitentiary in Texas, he had done carpentry work in Dallas. It was far-fetched, but I began to wonder if it could at all be possible that the townhouse door had been made in the place where he had worked and, if so, if he had touched the door, leaving his prints after the door was put into use in Chicago. The fingerprints alleged to be his had been found on a door on the second floor. It was something to file for later.

I told him that fingerprints had been published in *Life* magazine that were alleged to be his, taken from the townhouse. In fact, this evidence had appeared in *Life* before the state's attorney had received them!

To this, Speck replied:

"If they have any prints, they aren't mine."

I tried to see if he might have been in the apartment at an earlier time, but he said he didn't know the house or any of the girls and he didn't recall ever being in it. Of course, if he could prove he had been in the townhouse at some time before the murders, this might have reasonably explained his fingerprints, if they were his, having been found there.

As he talked, he was confused on several dates, and he said he didn't remember anything during the crucial period. It was "like waking up from a nightmare."

None of which was much help to his lawyer.

In the hot days of late July, I prepared for Speck's arraignment. By the end of the month, there had been a record total of seventy-two murders committed in Cook County during July.

And on August 1, as if the summer would explode into endless horror, another mass killing was committed — the worst in U.S. history — when sniper Charles Whitman turned the University of Texas tower at Austin into his personal fortress and took the lives of sixteen persons, including an unborn child, and wounded thirty-one. That was the day on which Speck appeared before Alexander J. Napoli, the presiding judge of the Criminal Court.

The press was there in force. The courtroom was packed. Speck was under such heavy guard that he couldn't have moved if he had wanted to. Nor was the cordon of protection merely for show. There were valid fears that someone might try to finish him off when he appeared in court. The feeling was running that high.

''Are you Richard Franklin Speck?'' Judge Napoli asked when the case had been called. ''You will have to speak up now so I can hear you.''

''Yes,'' said Speck in a low voice.

State's Attorney Ward said, ''Let the record show the defendant indicated in the affirmative.''

''Now, Richard Speck,'' continued Judge Napoli, ''we have pending before this court eight indictments charging you with the crime of murder. Do you have your own counsel to represent you on these eight indictments?''

I said, ''He has indicated to me, your honor, that he has not employed counsel and he does not have funds with which to hire counsel.''

Probably the world knew by then that Speck was indigent, but the same formal questioning that other defendants faced was now necessary to establish this fact for the record.

Judge Napoli said, ''Richard Speck, will you look at the court, please, and just answer a few of my questions. Do you have any bank account of any kind? Will you answer?''

''No,'' said Speck.

''You do not? Do you own any real estate of any kind?''

''No.''

''Do you own any stocks or bonds of any kind?''

''No.''

''Do you have any finances of any kind or any assets?''

''No.''

''You are not in a financial position to hire a lawyer, your own counsel, is that correct?''

''Uh huh.''

Judge Napoli then appointed me in all eight cases.

''Let the record show that Mr. Gerald W. Getty, the public defender of Cook County, Illinois, is hereby appointed counsel for the defendant, Richard Speck.''

State's Attorney Ward said, ''And I think, your honor, under the circumstances, all of which have not been apparent, this court should disclose that Mr. Getty is the sole counsel representing the interest of the defendant, Richard Speck.''

"It's so ordered at this time," agreed Judge Napoli.

I entered pleas of innocent to the eight charges and I argued the point that publicity had been detrimental to the defense's receiving a fair trial. Speck was ordered held without bail and Judge Napoli assigned the case to Judge Herbert C. Paschen for trial.

In a normal year, the public defender is appointed in about one hundred murder cases. Some of the defendants plead guilty and others waive a jury and take a bench trial. But there are always those cases that must go to the people. Already it appeared that Speck would wind up before a jury. The indications were growing daily that there would probably be no simple solution. Because of this I knew that no other lawyer would ever want the case. It was too much to cope with.

The year before, I had stopped smoking. By the time of Speck's arraignment, I knew that if I got through this case without lighting up a cigar or cigarette I would be quit for good.

2. Building a Defense

How do you defend a man who doesn't remember where he was or what he was doing at the time the crimes were committed, yet denies any participation in the crimes?

A defendant's version is always the vital beginning point. So where do you begin when the defendant can't provide any answers for the crucial period of time?

There were other problems. Would the eight cases be tried one at a time, or would they be consolidated? There had never before been a trial in which one person faced eight murder charges simultaneously.

Hovering above it all was the shadow of the electric chair, which hadn't been used in Cook County since 1962. The state was sparing no effort in its campaign to burn Speck. There had never been a crime like this one before in Cook County.

The case was fast evolving into a lesson in the defense of the despised.

By early August, the roles had been cast in this struggle for a man's life and liberty. Speck, the defendant, would remain passive throughout. Young, hard-working William Martin, the assistant state's attorney, would prosecute. I would defend. Judge Herbert C. Paschen, a white-haired veteran of Cook County politics, would referee.

I

"I tell you there is no judge in Cook County immune from the pressures of this case!" Jim Doherty said.

"The reason I didn't petition for a change of venue to another judge is, you can't get a fair trial anywhere," I said.

Some of my assistants and I were discussing possible strategies. Like many of these conferences, it was a rambunctious, always open and lively session, against a background of police sirens and other traffic sounds endemic to the Criminal Court Building. As the assistants discussed murder cases they'd had with various judges — suggesting how that judge would perform in the Speck case — voices rose until frequently there was shouting. (Lawyers become dramatic even in informal settings!)

"I believe Paschen might slip many times along the line and cause error," I said. "I'm almost of the opinion to leave it there."

We talked about the problem of a psychiatric defense.

"In this case," said one of the assistants, "one psychiatrist won't help us, as it would in a wife murder."

"If the state's psychiatrist says he's healthy as you and me, as anyone walking the streets, and ours says he's kooky — then it's the electric chair!" said another.

"The best way is to get them together. It's like a jury or the Warren Commission."

I leaned toward the panel concept myself. Having read that psychiatrists disliked being pitted against one another in court, and that they preferred to present findings as a panel, I proposed that we aim at a panel of six eminent men — two psychiatrists and one psychologist proposed by us, and the same number by the state. The issues would be: Can he stand trial? What is his mental condition right now? What was it on July 13 and 14?

"We'd better have a panel," I said, "and we'd better trap them into taking a panel. Let's offer it in open court. If they reject it, then it's on record."

"He'll never see a jury," popped back a voice. "They'll send him down to the laughing academy and that's the end of it!"

II

Some of the mail was addressed only to "Spec's Lawyer" or "Getty, Chicago." It kept coming. Those who were virulently abusive seemed to have no conception of our Constitution. The mob impulse remained strong. The letters made any thoughtful person thankful that we had a safeguard like the Constitution to thwart the mob.

Many tried to be helpful. The letters from a housewife-mother in Canada, concerned with Speck's welfare, soon filled a folder. Others reported, even taped, prejudicial news comments.

It was soon evenly divided and this was an important straw in the wind if we went to a jury.

"Fifty percent don't think he did it," I said one day. "Some are praying for Speck. Fifty percent say what a bastard he is. What I'm saying is that, on a jury, you're going to get some of those people."

III

Personally, I liked Judge Paschen and I think he liked me. He was very congenial and I never hesitated to go see him in his chambers when I needed to do so. He called me "Jer" and it seemed that he felt "Ol' Jer" couldn't do much wrong — except for representing defendants. Despite these attributes, he was not a judge the defense would want in a bench trial. But in a jury trial I believed he would give me more leeway than would another judge. He would not stop you from saying what you wanted to say; at least, he never stopped me. But there was the other side, that he would almost invariably favor the state on any important objection from the defense.

Judge Paschen conducted court in a leisurely manner, but he had control at all times. He brooked no nonsense or outbursts or outlandish tactics. He made you feel you had to be on your best behavior before him. I think he wanted to give everyone a full and complete hearing, which he always did, but I think that, possibly because of his early training, he was handicapped by his being more or less inclined toward the side of the prosecution.

He was from a well-to-do, middle-class family. Three of his grandparents had come to Chicago from Germany. He had founded the Glencoe National Bank, of which he was board chairman, and his family was in the construction business, with large contracts with the city and state.

His political life had been full. In 1952 he had been Governor Adlai Stevenson's alternate to the Democratic National Convention; he, himself, was a candidate for lieutenant governor. Losing that race, he served as Cook County treasurer for one term and ran for governor in 1956. However, because of publicity over a "benefit fund" in the treasurer's office, which brought him immediate criticism, he withdrew from the race and was replaced by Judge Richard B. Austin. Democrat Austin narrowly lost to Republican William G. Stratton. A Chicago Bar Association investigation later cleared Paschen of any wrongdoing. Many observers thought that, had it not been for the adverse publicity and the late-hour withdrawal, Paschen would have become governor of Illinois.

He was elected to the bench in 1962.

Now at sixty-one Herbert C. Paschen looked more like a judge than anyone Hollywood could have produced. He was a tall, stately man with silvery hair and a kindly face. He combed his hair back neatly and wore black hornrimmed glasses. He had an excellent judicial temperament; he could sit and listen for hours. His cultured, well-modulated voice was one a President would have been proud of, and when he put on that black robe, you'd have thought St. Peter himself had entered the courtroom.

IV

Ordinarily, an inquest would have been held. None was. It was first delayed because of Speck's illness, then it was postponed indefinitely. The state wasn't ready. They would have had to produce the surviving nurse, and we would have had a statement from her. There would have been a deluge of publicity, which would have been wild.

An inquest, though, would have scotched some of the fantastic rumors that were sweeping the county. Word-of-mouth accounts — completely unfounded — spread tales of unspeakable atrocities, that all the victims' breasts had been cut off, that the bodies had been sliced up. None of it was true.

V

On the day of Speck's arraignment I had subpoenaed the protocols, or formal autopsy reports, of the eight dead women and in September several of us from the public defender's office viewed the evidence in the police department's crime lab, by order of the court.

We had to delay our final review of the evidence because the crime lab was so crowded. By mid-September, ours wasn't the only headline case in Chicago. Valerie Percy, daughter of United States Senator-to-be Charles H. Percy, had been murdered, and the lab staff was working overtime in its search for clues. It had been a violent, tragic summer.

In the Speck case, the police had seventy-four pieces of evidence. These ranged from fingerprints to photographs of the victims. The photographs were as shocking as any I had ever seen. Some were in gruesome color, others in black-and-white. One especially startled me. It was of one of the Filipino girls. Her throat had been slashed. It was a horrible, sickening sight. Others who had been stabbed did not suffer mutilation beyond the stab wounds.

Technicians had carefully taken vaginal, oral, and anal swabs of each of the victims. Only one specimen, from an anal swab of Gloria Jean Davy, had tested positive for semen. The only other foreign matter found on the person of a victim was a single strand of short, black hair found between the thumb and forefinger of Valentina Pasion. Technicians said it was "similar to the hair of Speck" but would go no further. Later I hired an expert on hair samples, who advised me that hair analysis is not an exact science although hair can be tested for specific content of certain metals; the state didn't use it in the trial.

A piece of evidence that could become cumulative was a BVD brand T-shirt found at the townhouse. The same type and size, 38-40, T-shirt had been found among his belongings at the hotel where he had stayed. A second T-shirt, of another brand, had been found in the townhouse a few days after the murders. They said this, too, was Speck's. Through the grapevine — strictly hearsay — I heard that some persons in the police department tried to reopen the investigation when the second T-shirt was discovered. They lost out. The one-killer theory remained the official one.

The only really damaging physical evidence consisted of three fingerprints they alleged were Speck's. These had been found on a door in the townhouse. The police contended they were identical with Speck's, but I had to keep an open mind and find out for myself. They could be wrong. After all, fingerprint identification was not an exact science. It was opinion evidence.

There now remained one other part of the state's case that I had not yet studied: the eyewitness, Corazon Amurao. Under the law I had a right to interview her. Since my knowledge of what she had seen had come from the newspapers and from hearsay, I didn't know how good a witness she really was. I did know she hadn't identified Speck out of a lineup. I had heard all sorts of things. One story had her saying, when taken to Speck's hospital room for the identification, "Is that him? I'm glad you've caught him." Another version was that she said, "That's him — thank God, you've got him." Obviously she had seen someone that terrible night. But how well did she remember him?

VI

After about a dozen interviews with Speck, I had nothing new to go on. If he did commit the murders, he told me, he was completely blank about it. He appeared to be honest about this. He said he had been shocked at hearing Police Superintendent Orlando Wilson's statement accusing him of the crime and learning of the $10,000 reward out for him; his heart almost stopped; he couldn't believe it. He had reacted by trying to kill himself.

There was the possibility that his memory failure could be the basis for his being declared incompetent to stand trial. He couldn't cooperate with counsel because he couldn't tell me what he did, if he had committed the crimes, and if he did, what weapons he had used. He couldn't tell me where he had acquired the gun taken from him at the Raleigh. He remembered that over a period of time he had carried a small three-inch knife, but he didn't know what had happened to it.

I couldn't believe that Speck had killed the eight women by himself. They had been trained nurses accustomed to psychiatric patients; they had known how to handle themselves. From the time Speck had told me of the three men with whom he had taken a mainline injection, I wondered if he had not been a guard that night instead of the lone murderer. But he could offer no details after the injection. He remembered only that he pulled the needle out of his arm and it "felt like a hundred locusts buzzing in my head." The men had told him which ship they were on, he said, but he couldn't remember it now. He finally recalled that one of the men was dark like a Puerto Rican and wore a black shirt. He couldn't go past that.

I tried to reason it out. What would happen to these men? Would they separate after the injection? Possibly. Or would they continue the relationship for the remainder of the evening? Probably. Then there was that second T-shirt in the townhouse. I couldn't imagine Speck wearing two T-shirts in that stuffy apartment in that hot, soupy weather. A long-sleeved coat and two T-shirts? It seemed unlikely. There had also been a lot of blood from the victims, but no bloody clothing had turned up among Speck's possessions. The strongest indication, to my mind, that others had been involved was the evidence of the twenty-nine fingerprints that the police had not identified as being Speck's. Did they belong to someone who had been in the townhouse that night? I suspected that some of them did. Had Speck been a guard who had conducted these girls to another man or other men? It seemed plausible.

Some details did clear up from our interviews. The police contended that Speck had slept in the park next to the townhouse, on the Tuesday night before the murders. He hadn't. He didn't know the park was there. On that particular night he had left his bags in a service station on 100th Street and had slept in an unfinished house just off 103rd Street. The next day he returned to the Maritime Union hiring hall where, later, his sister and his brother-in-law drove by and gave him twenty-five dollars. Shortly before noon he went to the Shipyard Inn, paid his rent in advance, and commenced drinking. The next day, after the murders, he said there had been a lot of police activity in the area of the Shipyard Inn and he feared that if he were picked up they would learn he was wanted in Dallas and he would have to return to serve his time there on an assault charge. So he took a cab north.

As far as he knew, he told me over and over, he positively did not kill anyone. When I read him the names of all the victims in the indictment he never once recognized a single one. And his memory never returned to fill in its lapse. I kept questioning him about the three men with whom he had had the injection. Once he blurted out, "I can't remember what happened even if they set me free!"

VII

The guards at the Bridewell, he said, kept telling him he was going to the chair. They taunted him by saying they were going to toast him and fry him. They'd tell him how they were going to dress him in a T-shirt and shorts, with a mask over his eyes, and just hold him in the electric chair.

He always gave them a stock reply.

"If I go, I go."

VIII

One of Speck's emotional problems was as much a part of him as the acne that scarred his face. Since he was a kid in grade school, he had had a fear of people staring at him. He wouldn't recite in front of a class or answer questions with others looking on. It made him nervous. He would play hooky to avoid facing it; finally he had dropped out of school.

Because of this, he told me one day, he wouldn't take the witness stand to testify in his own defense. No matter what.

IX

Speck learned to paint while in jail in Chicago. Dr. Marvin Ziporyn, the jail psychiatrist who visited him to prevent another attempt at suicide, first encouraged him. Speck used a paint-by-numbers set and later showed an aptitude for freehand sketching. To my distaste, he limited his subject matter to nudes and tigers, neither of which was likely to improve the public image of a man accused of murdering eight young women.

One day, when Speck proudly displayed his latest nudes and tigers, in a bit of pique I asked him, "Why can't you draw *Bambi?*"

A few days later he presented me with a gift — a painting of Walt Disney's gentle fawn!

As the months passed his faith in me grew; it was as if I were a kind of father figure he had not had. He had lost his own father at an early age and he had not got along with his stepfather at all. He had always been a loner and now he had somebody doing something for him: defending him, visiting him and talking about his case. He was completely trustful of me. He sometimes told me I was working too hard for him; he felt it was a lost cause. Instead of the case, he'd ask about what I had done over the weekend, how my family was doing, or he'd discuss a book he was reading or a card game with a guard. He liked to talk and seemed to be trying to establish a friendship that he could cling to.

A client readily discerns when you are doing your best for him. He respects you for it and in this way you instill confidence in a defendant without becoming what would be considered a personal friend. With Speck, I apparently succeeded in this, but I didn't realize until later how essential my relationship had become to him. During the trial one day the sheriff told me, "I have to assure him you're in the courtroom. He might explode if I take him to the courtroom and you're not there."

X

Speck's family were religious people. Although the first impulse of some was not to support him, they all decided that it was the Christian thing to do and they agreed to appear in court for him — an almost unbearable, wrenching thing for them to do, for it would publicly humiliate them in the communities where they lived.

Richard, though, never showed any indication of becoming religious in the same way. Despite his gregariousness, he never wanted to see a minister, he never wanted to attend church. People sent him stacks of religious information of all kinds. He did not read any of it.

Emotionally, he was far removed from the eight victims. He

never expressed a real sorrow for the families. It was as if he didn't realize he was accused of killing the girls. There were few toward whom he did show any deep, positive feelings. They were his mother, his child, and his sister and brother-in-law in Chicago. He disliked his former wife intensely.

XI

Thirty-five pre-trial motions were heard in chambers to avoid additional publicity. Speck seemed to actually enjoy these sessions. The same persons were always there and he didn't mind them after a while. The motions were heard in the jury room adjoining the courtroom. We all sat around the jury table, which resembled a directors' table. Judge Paschen was at the head, with the state on one side and the defense on the other, and with Speck at the foot. Speck acted as if he were a member of the board of directors at a monthly meeting.

Out in the courtroom, he was resentful of the spectators who were strangers. He didn't want to face them. Sometimes he would sit sideways with, figuratively, his head in the sand. Later, it became a large achievement to see that he faced the jury. He had to be watched or he would look off and stare into space. It was a problem. A defendant makes a better impression when he sits up straight and faces the jury.

XII

The state liked the idea of a competency examination by a court-appointed panel. That gave us six psychiatrists and two psychologists, plus Dr. Haines of the Cook County Behavior Clinic, whom Judge Paschen added as his appointed psychiatrist; he was not a member of the panel.

I had expected the panel to find Speck incompetent, which had been the reason for the motion. To my surprise, all the doctors found him mentally competent and concluded that on July 13 and 14 he was responsible for his acts. On top of this, despite Judge Paschen's admonition not to divulge this information, newspaper stories also came out about the findings, apparently supplied by one of the psychiatrists named by the state. Speck, the panel agreed, had a "psychopathic personality, [and exhibited] antisocial behavior with alcoholism." Although some of the doctors hinted at more serious defects, none would say so in the report. Dr. Roy R. Grinker, Sr., whom I had suggested, stated that it was "almost as if Speck is two personalities." One was his dull, normal one; the other one a violently hostile person. The second personality came out under the influence of alcohol. But the doctor saw no proof of organic illness or psychosis. Speck's EEG, or electroencephalograph, showed brief areas of slowing but was judged to be within normal limits. A neurologist said irregularities in the tracings were "consistent with the normal in a somewhat younger individual, perhaps of the age of twelve or thirteen years, and are not diagnostic of any neurologic disease." However, of interest to me were the slow transients on the occipital areas, on the right side — the area in which Speck complained of headaches.

One of the reports came from Dr. William Norcross, a surgeon-administrator with no psychiatric training who had treated Speck in the hospital. He had been named by the state, and his report contained incriminating matter. He quoted Speck: "I woke up with a pistol and with blood on my hands. Where did I get the gun, Doc?" Throughout it, Norcross indicated he assumed Speck was guilty. The claim of amnesia "appears to be spurious for some reason," Norcross wrote.

Norcross' anecdotal approach included Speck's attitude toward capital punishment. "The chair, say, that's a good way to straighten a fellow out!" he quoted Speck as saying. "Anybody who is opposed to capital punishment is silly — how else are you going to control people? They deserve the chair when they kill somebody." As for the argument that the chair did not deter, Speck said, "That's a joke. It sure stops the man that's electrocuted. He won't kill anybody again!"

Norcross wasn't the only one who apparently delved into matters of evidence as well as the mind. Dr. Haines left us this nugget:

"He was in the Boy Scouts for a period of a week but was not good on tying knots. He was not good on knots aboard ship."

XIII

Since the panel had found Speck competent, I saw no reason for a competency hearing before a jury. Judge Paschen disagreed — even though one psychiatrist had violated the court's order and stated to the press the panel's conclusion. I protested.

"The court does intend to have a competency hearing," he said, "from everything that has occurred in this case, from your requesting the appointment of a panel of psychiatrists and the statements in the press that your defense was going to be a defense of insanity."

He believed the news accounts. As it turned out I never had an insanity defense.

I denied that my motion for the panel had automatically argued for a competency hearing.

He stood firm. "The question having been raised in the record, Mr. Getty, there will be a competency hearing without further discussion."

"I sincerely hope that you are not guided by the newspapers as to what my defense will be in this case."

"No. But the question has been raised."

XIV

I had never tried a case with Bill Martin as an adversary before, but some of my assistants had. He was a hard worker, diligent, and methodical. Already I had observed that he didn't seem to have much of a sense of humor. He didn't joke around. This became evident to all, later, as he dealt with jurors and witnesses.

He was an honest and worthy opponent.

He also had nearly everything going for him. Eight deaths. An atrocious crime. Most of the facts.

XV

It was evident that the defense would have to rely heavily on in-fighting on the legal questions that would arise. I was determined to present a workman, scholarly approach to the case, a defense in the best tradition of the legal profession, devoid of the wrestling match type of trial that it could easily become. At times, that was not easy.

Before the competency hearing began, we discussed the ground rules with the judge. I suggested that the doctors say nothing about July 13, 14, and 15 because it might be incriminating.

"But, as far as early history," I said, "what they found out, things like that, which would not be incriminating, why — "

Judge Paschen said, "I don't want them to blurt out that he was in jail in such and such a place for something, either — "

"Well — "

" — because you're going to holler like holy hell."

"I have hollered like holy hell already," I said, "but I'm not going to ask him whether he was in jail elsewhere."

It began with the direct testimony of Dr. Vladimir Urse, who concluded that Speck was competent to stand trial, knew the extent of the charges and could cooperate with counsel. On cross-examination I questioned him about Speck's work after he had dropped out of school. Speck was fired from two jobs for drinking.

"You asked him when he started to drink hard liquor, didn't you?" I said.

"Yes."

"And about what age was that?"

"At a very early age. At twelve or thirteen."

"And where did he get this liquor?"

"He said he stole vodka from his stepfather."

"And then, to refresh your memory, did he drive a truck in Dallas for some time?"

"Yes. I believe that was with the Budweiser distributor."

"And how long was that?"

"That was not too many months."

"Why did he leave that employment?"

"He had been involved in some accidents, and the drinking was mentioned with respect to this period of employment."

Then we discussed drugs.

"Did he ever tell you that he used narcotics in conjunction with his drinking?"

"He, I believe, confused narcotics with barbiturics."

"Did he tell you that he used those?"

"He said that he used what he called 'redbirds.' "

"Yes?"

"And 'yellow jackets.' "

"And what effect does that have on one, Doctor?"

"Well, yellow jackets and redbirds are ordinarily Nembutal and Seconal, which are barbituric drugs. The effect of these is that they are hypnotic. They are used usually as sleep-inducing medicines, in general medicine and surgery, and in hospitals."

"Would you say that this man used alcohol to excess, from your examination?"

"I would say that he had an alcohol problem."

"Was one of your conclusions in this matter here that he suffered from alcoholism?"

"If one interprets alcoholism as an alcohol problem, then I presume the two gibe. I would say that he was a frequent user of alcohol, undoubtedly to some excess."

"And does alcohol have any effect on the mind?"

"Of course."

"Did he tell you that he used alcohol in conjunction with these barbiturates?"

"Yes. He mentioned that on occasion he would have both alcohol and barbiturates."

"And did he tell you, on these occasions, that he used alcohol to excess?"

"To produce a state of drunkenness, I presume this could be a reasonable thing for him."

"And at the same time he used barbiturates?"

"Yes."

"And alcohol coupled with barbiturates would have an effect on the mind and mental process?"

"Yes."

"If they were used to this excess, wouldn't this produce some hallucinations?"

"Ordinarily not."

"Well, could it?"

"I presume it could."

"And hallucinations is a mental disease, isn't it?"

"Hallucinations are not a mental disease. They are a symptom of mental disease."

"And if used to excess, he could have delusions, couldn't he?"

"Rather than delusions, he might have some misinterpretations of things going on about him."

"Misinterpretations?"

"Yes."

"And would he have, in this state, full control of his impulses?"

"Not necessarily so."

"So that he would lack control of his impulses?"

"He could lack control."

"He would lack control of knowing the difference between right and wrong?"

Martin jumped up. "Judge, I object to that as not being material."

"Sustained," shot back the judge.

"Well," I continued, "he would lack control of — he would lack the ability to control these impulses, wouldn't he?"

"The same objection," said Martin.

"Sustained," said Judge Paschen.

"Why, that's very important, your honor!" I said.

"We're merely on a competency hearing now," said the judge.

"A competency hearing? That's what I'm proceeding on, too."

We took our argument into the judge's chambers where, after

a generous exchange of words, Judge Paschen allowed me to ask if Speck drank on July 12 and 13.

"Did he tell you that he used barbiturates on July 13th, 1966?" I asked the psychiatrist.

"As I recall it," said Dr. Urse, "he said that he was looking for some redbirds."

"Did he tell you that he had some redbirds?"

"I do not recall at this time."

"To refresh your memory, did he tell you . . . Well, let me ask you this, did he tell you that on July 13th he had what he termed a fix?"

"Yes."

"And by this fix, did that indicate to you that he had used narcotics?"

"This is a term that is used by narcotic addicts to mean the use of a needle and a syringe, but it does not necessarily mean that the individual who is using this is necessarily using a narcotic preparation."

"Well, did he tell you this, that on July 13th he was drunk that day, and when he shot that junk he went blank?"

"Yes, this I recall his telling me."

"Now, tell me, Doctor, a person drinking and shooting this junk or narcotics, would that cause amnesia?"

"It could cause an amnesia, if the individual had been drinking and had in fact taken a shot of narcotics, so on and so on."

We then approached a medical classification.

"Would you say that from the drinking of Richard Speck here that he had developed chronic alcoholism?"

"I believe he would be classified as a chronic alcoholic, yes."

"Doctor, does excessive use of alcohol cause organic brain damage?"

"Yes."

"And would such damage impair an individual's judgment?"

"Yes."

"That's all."

On redirect by Martin, Dr. Urse testified that he did not

believe Speck had organic brain damage or that he suffered from hallucinations or delusions. Nor had he found Speck psychotic when he examined him.

Each doctor contributed a bit more, in a similar pattern. But each stated he believed Speck was competent and suffered no organic brain damage. In the cross-examination of Dr. Edward Kelleher, director of the Municipal Court's Psychiatric Institute, another factor was revealed: that the doctors had studied statements that apparently had to do with evidence in the case.

"Now," I asked him, "in your report you had the opportunity to see statements in the possession of the state's attorney's office, didn't you?"

"Yes, I did."

"And you read those statements?"

"Yes, I did."

"And how much time did you spend in the state's attorney's office?"

"On September the 20th, I spent roughly two hours looking over these reports in the state's attorney's office."

"Did you ever consult with me, Doctor?"

"No, I did not."

"You knew I represented Richard Speck, didn't you?"

"Yes, sir."

During the cross-examination of several witnesses, I had registered that some jurors were nodding with me when they noted the psychiatrists hedging. This, plus the fact that some aspects of mental disease had been brought out, encouraged me to believe I had a chance of the jury's ruling Speck incompetent.

As it turned out, the jury never did have a chance to consider a verdict.

In chambers, Martin asked Judge Paschen to direct a verdict of competency, "because there is no disputable issue of fact for a jury to decide." I vigorously objected.

But Judge Paschen said, "All stated he was competent, that he understood the charge against him, the nature of the proceedings, and he was capable of assisting his counsel in his defense. There's no proof to the contrary; and eminently qualified men testified that he was competent to stand trial. In the absence of any proof to the contrary, I will direct a verdict."

"Well," I said, "this is the saddest day in Cook County that the people cannot decide the competency or incompetency of a man who is placed on trial. This record is permeated with facts that now I agree with the court that there should have been and should be a competency hearing. It's the saddest day in this county when a verdict, in the light of this record, shall be directed. I'm ashamed."

"I will still direct it. There is no evidence to the contrary. Whenever you're ready, we will go out."

We returned to the courtroom.

Judge Paschen faced the jury. "There being no evidence adduced as to his incompetency, the court will direct you to sign a verdict finding the defendant Richard Franklin Speck competent."

"Object," I said. "And we enumerate that there was plenty of evidence adduced here by cross-examination that it should have been given to a jury to decide the issues by their verdict."

It was my opinion that the directing of a verdict was an invasion of the province of the jury. What if the jury had found that Speck was incompetent to stand trial? The ball game would have been over.

Had error now been committed in the record?

XVI

I had learned my lesson in the competency hearing. Psychiatrists are human beings just like the rest of us, no better than the people on a jury. Despite their marvelous training in the specialty of the mind, they have the same feelings as those who sit in the jury box and their minds are similarly affected by what they read, see, and hear in newspapers, on TV and on radio. And in one like the Speck case, I was convinced, a case separate and distinct from other murders because of its exceptional qualities, psychiatrists are affected by the gruesomeness of the crime and they look upon the person accused of it differently than they would one of their own patients.

They also viewed the gruesome photographs of the dead women's bodies. Here, illogically, we had psychiatrists, who were supposed to examine the defendant's mind and tell us if he had any mental disease, looking at the evidence! Studying the state's evidence would hardly help them decide a man's mental condition, but it would influence *their* minds.

As much as I wanted to think they were all strong men who couldn't be persuaded, I felt that one psychiatrist on the panel was the foreman, whether or not he was formally selected as a jury chooses one, and that he had a great deal to do with swaying the others.

The experience taught me to forget about panels in the future, and to forget about niceties when you are a partisan in the defense of a person. If you need psychiatric evidence, go find your own witnesses.

XVII

A lot of people thought Speck had confessed to me. He never did, nor to anyone else. Several times I was told, "Why don't you plead him guilty, because he is guilty? The evidence says he's guilty." With even psychiatrists indicating that they felt he was guilty, why wasn't a guilty plea entered?

In the first place, Speck never admitted any guilt to me. If he committed these crimes, he didn't remember. This meant that, under our Constitution, the state had to *prove* he was guilty beyond a reasonable doubt. I was his advocate, not his judge or jury, and having undertaken his defense I was in the words of the Chicago Bar Association's canon, "bound by all fair and honorable means, to present every defense that the law of the land permits, to the end that no person may be deprived of life and liberty but by due process of law."

XVIII

Late one afternoon in the latter part of November I wandered into Judge Paschen's chambers. As in any other case, I wanted to know what the judge was thinking.

I told Judge Paschen that I could not plead Speck guilty. But I asked him point-blank, man to man: If I found that I could plead Speck guilty, in good conscience and with the consent of his family, with or without any specific admissions of guilt, would he, Paschen, waive the death penalty?

He replied, "If it is submitted, I can't guarantee anything. If it's like I understand it is from the newspapers and TV, I'd have to give him the chair. I think I would give him the death penalty."

So from that moment on, I knew Speck had nothing to lose by going the whole route.

XIX

Several moves were being made simultaneously. While we were involved with the question of Speck's competency, we were also concerned with a motion for a change of venue from Cook County.

Actually, even though the crimes had been committed there and the feeling was high, Cook County was probably the best place in Illinois to hold the trial. Chicago was, after all, a sophisticated city; it might have been possible to secure enough open-minded jurors to give us a chance. But I had to seek a change of venue, because in cases where publicity would create prejudice the law dictates it. So I had to protect our record on appeal by seeking a change. It was a change I did not really want.

To support my petition, my staff served *subpoenas duces tecum* on Chicago's daily newspapers, TV and radio stations, and community and suburban papers. *Subpoena duces tecum* literally means "bring with you" and is served on a witness who has documents or printed matter that will be needed in a trial. We asked for copies of articles, tapes, and transcriptions mentioning Speck and the murders from July 14 to August 1, the critical period of adverse publicity.

Most of the news media cooperated; some sought to quash our subpoenas. We managed to work out agreements. Eventually, after Jerry Wexler, one of my assistants, had compiled the mountain of support for our motion, our exhibits included — to give an indication of Jerry's Herculean task — more than two dozen Chicago news outlets: *Daily News, Sun-Times, American, Tribune;* the Lerner papers; the *Southeast Economist,* the *Abendpost* (German language), the newspapers in the Polish, Lithuanian, and Czechoslovakian languages; the *Daily Defender,* the black newspaper; a group of detective magazines; *Life* magazine ("which probably had all the evidence that the state may attempt to present, even before the state's attorney's office," I told the court); radio scripts from WLS, WVON, WNUS, WIND, WGN, WBBM, WMAQ, and WCFL; and film from WGN-TV, WBBM-TV, WBKB-TV, and WMBQ-TV.

I argued that we might not be able to determine whether a juror carried in his mind something he had read about the defendant, something that we would never be allowed to hear in the courtroom. I cited the prejudicial statement from Police Superintendent Wilson, how he had called Speck the slayer, not a suspect. I displayed to the court Wilson's picture at that press conference. I noted one network news report that stated, "Thirty-two of Speck's fingerprints were found in the nurses' living quarters." We had an iceberg of support for our motion; these were but the tip.

The material filled a room. Judge Paschen received it, to read and ponder on.

Martin said he did not object to our motion, and the day after directing the verdict at the competency hearing, the judge granted our motion for a change of place of trial.

Three weeks later, the case was assigned to Peoria County in the Tenth Judicial Circuit. I asked Judge Paschen if he had known it was going to Peoria on Friday. He said no. On Saturday? He had had a good idea by then, he said.

"The reason I asked that, your honor, was that it appeared in the Sunday newspaper that it was going to be in Peoria," I said.

"That was a guess."

"And of course — "

"That was a guess."

"And, of course, as defense counsel, I felt a little bit hurt that the newspapers knew it before ol' Jer, you know?"

"The newspapers seem to know everything before me."

"Yes."

"I was not making any announcement ahead of time. I can't help what people guess. People guess a lot of things."

Undoubtedly many Democratic politicians relaxed a little when the trial was taken out of Chicago. The fall elections were over, but there were the city elections in the spring. With the eyes of the nation on the case, it helped to know the news reports of the trial would be datelined from another city.

XX

It was unprecedented in Illinois for a judge to go with the case when the place of trial was changed. But Judge John E. Richards, presiding over the Tenth Circuit, indicated there was a shortage of judges in Peoria and asked the Illinois Supreme Court to assign one. At the end of December, Chief Justice Ray I. Klingbiel assigned Paschen, temporarily transferring him to the Tenth Circuit.

By then we had already bought 160 back issues of the Peoria *Journal Star*, and found that the publicity there had been substantially the same as in Chicago. But of even more importance was the judge. Should we accept Paschen, or petition for another one?

"Who should we get if not Paschen?" I asked, as I talked it over one afternoon with several assistants. "There are some judges I wouldn't want in this case. At least I can get along with him. He doesn't give me ulcers. He says *I* give *him* ulcers."

"This is not a good judge." one assistant said. "He checks with the state."

"We have to get it away from Paschen," said another. "He'll box you in but without causing error."

The majority opinion and mine also were that we could not waive any rights, and we would be waiving if we didn't ask for a change.

"Whatever happens," said Doherty, "I think we may have an insurance policy already because of the directed verdict in the competency hearing."

"This is the one thing that changed my mind about Paschen," I said. "Without any motion by me or by the state, he ordered the competency hearing on his own. That resulted in considerable damage to my client. Then when I built up a pretty fair record and it looked like the jury might find him incompetent to stand trial, he directs the verdict!"

"Why don't we just bring Speck up in a net and let you argue competency?" suggested one wry-witted assistant.

The next day I filed a petition to remove Paschen as trial judge, asking for a substitute judge. I specifically referred to his directing the verdict of competency. He refused to disqualify himself, ruling that my motion had been filed too late. Martin and I argued over the ten-day time limit allowed for automatic substitution. I thought I was right. My reasoning was that even though he had been in this case when the trial was transferred to Peoria and he was reappointed as the judge he was as new to this case as if a trial judge in Peoria had been appointed, and therefore the motion was made within the statutory ten-day limit. Martin and the judge did not agree with me.

XXI

While waiting for the trial to begin, we checked out all the leads, farfetched or not. Some people claimed to have alibis for Speck. He was with them, instead of at the townhouse, at the time the murders were being committed. Or so they said.

A man who identified himself as "Jake" called Robert J. Seltzner, managing editor of the *Daily Calumet,* a South Side Chicago and suburban newspaper, and stated that he and Speck had been drinking with a nurse that night. He didn't remember her name. He said he and Speck took the nurse to her apartment at about 11 P.M. on July 13 and then left. "Jake" and Speck remained together for several hours more.

Seltzner had "Jake" get in touch with me. Two of my men brought him to my office. The first thing I noticed about him was that he had been drinking.

"He didn't do it. I swear to God he didn't do it." said "Jake."

He was reluctant to reveal his last name.

"I am here to help him," I said, "but I can't do it unless you cooperate."

He still wouldn't tell his surname.

"Well," I said, "why don't you help me out? What's your last name? I can't just keep saying 'Jake'!"

If Jake's story were true, this would place Speck way up on the North Side as late as 1:30 A.M. of July 14, miles from the townhouse.

The only thing is," I said, "they say they have his fingerprints in the house."

Jake turned out to be an ex-convict from Michigan who had run out on child support payments in Indiana. I verified his identification, which he finally gave me, from fingerprints taken from a coffee cup he handled in my office. But he grew less and less cooperative. Elements of his story didn't hold up.

One couple assured me that Speck had been in their home on the far North Side the night of the murder. But they were mistaken, I learned when I talked to them.

One woman from New Orleans appeared in my office, claiming Speck was not Speck, but someone else. She gave us a name. She said he was connected with stolen works of art. I obtained a picture of the man. Speck hadn't ever been to New Orleans. He didn't know the man he was supposed to be.

But even the kooks had to be listened to.

Then there was the letter from Buenos Aires. I had it translated from the Spanish. It was signed by a woman and claimed Speck was innocent. A doctor — unnamed — was said to have been involved in the crimes. We checked it out. The address was fictitious.

She became our "Argentine mystery lady."

XXII

We investigated everything. We tried to trace the door at the townhouse's south bedroom, to see if it had come from the particular lumberyard where Speck had once worked, and might have made fingerprint impressions. But the door had been on the house for a number of years.

We studied all of the official records, including those of Speck's incarceration. In the Bridewell, back in July, his keepers had jotted down every slightest move he had made, his sighs, his position. So thorough were the minutia-clogged notes that we suspected the orders had been given in hopes that Speck would make incriminating remarks.

"8:00 — 'That sure was some report you had last night,' said Speck still eating bread and milk.

"8:26 — Speck grunts."

One of the guards wrote down his own yawn as he fought drowsiness!

More interesting than the records, though, were the witnesses. In all, the state had a list of 210 witnesses. About ninety of them were policemen or persons connected with the police department, all of whom we interviewed in our efforts to find out how they had arrived at conclusions of guilt, how they had taken possession of certain articles, and the circumstances in which evidence was gathered. Articles of Speck's had been taken from the Raleigh. Had they had a search warrant, inasmuch as Speck had paid his rent to July 20? Then there was the .22 revolver and six cartridges taken from him the morning of July 15 at the Raleigh, without the policemen's realizing who he was. Speck was in bed and had not invited them in. Was the search and seizure legal? If not, we could move to suppress the gun as evidence.

A key police report was that of Patrolman Leonard J. Ponne of the Fourth District, one of the first on the murder scene. He had written in his report that Miss Amurao had described the killer as having "short or crew-cut hair" and as appearing in her doorway "with a gun in one hand and a knife in the other hand." If the killer had a crew cut, then it couldn't have been Speck, who had never had one in his life. Ponne was questioned. He remembered her describing the intruder with those terms. He and his partner had interviewed her while she was crying and in a hysterical state.

Police artist Otis Rathel was interviewed by Gramenos. Rathel didn't recall Miss Amurao's exact words as she described the killer to him and only vaguely recalled the substance of their conversation as he sketched the drawing. The killer, she told him, had a long, thin face and did not look like a man who would hurt anyone. "He looked just like a man," without explaining further, Rathel quoted her as saying. He quoted her as saying she saw the man at her door and it wasn't too light. He asked her how long the hair was and she said it was not long, he said. He asked if it was a crew cut. She didn't seem to understand. A nurse with her indicated with her fingers a crew cut and Miss Amurao, according to Rathel's interview, said, "Yes," but slightly longer. She had made no mention of a pocked face, he said. His sketch ran in the daily police bulletin of July 16.

Tom McCurrie and George Brobst were the busiest of our investigators on the case, but Gramenos and I also made inroads as we talked to witnesses in the vicinity of 100th Street where Speck had done much of his drinking. One day he and I talked with as many as thirty witnesses in the various taverns from 9:30 in the morning until 10 at night.

In this way we learned that he had taken a gun from an older woman he was drinking with on July 13. She had had it in her purse. Was this the same gun that the intruder had brandished in the townhouse? Who knows? The surviving nurse never described it and the pistol was illegally seized at the Raleigh.

XXIII

Four days before New Year's, 1967, Gramenos left for Texas, to check on Speck's life there. By then the state's attorney had dispatched a number of men to Dallas. They were the men in the white hats, representing society against all sin, and they immediately secured the cooperation of the police and other authorities. Characteristically, Gramenos had the public defender's work all to himself, much in the manner of the legendary Texas Ranger's "one riot, one Ranger" formula. But Gramenos distinguished himself.

Dr. Marvin Ziporyn, the jail psychiatrist, wanted to interview Speck's mother in Dallas. On the provision he did not use the material in a book — which I understood he was planning to write — he was permitted to talk to the mother and Speck's sister, in the presence of Gramenos.

We were particularly interested in Speck's medical background. Speck's mother told them that in 1942, three and a half months following his birth, Richard had suffered double pneumonia and had been hospitalized for four weeks and had been in an oxygen tent. Unconscious when taken to the hospital at Monmouth, Illinois, his fever between the third and tenth day had gone up to about 106 degrees. The mother was told that he might not survive, for children usually died from this type of fever and this condition. But if the baby lived, the doctor further warned, the illness and the oxygen tent treatment might affect his brain; he might not be able to learn as fast as other children.

Unlike her other children, Richard did have difficulty in learning. He would stumble and was awkward. He became accident prone. Even in the first grade he was a nervous child and couldn't concentrate on his work. He was particularly poor in English and arithmetic. Eventually his younger sister, an honor student, passed him in school. This made him feel bad.

When the boy was six years old, his father died. The mother remarried in 1950 and moved with her new husband and her two youngest children to Dallas. Richard was nine, his sister seven. He repeatedly failed English, a class in which he was supposed to stand before the class and recite. He refused to do so. At seventeen and a half, he dropped out of school.

His mother recalled that during the week, when he was not drinking, Richard complained of headaches. Often he said he felt dizzy. She told of his lapses of memory and his frequent head injuries. Much of it, his sister verified.

Interestingly, Richard did not use his true name, Speck, until he married in 1962. Before that, he called himself Richard Franklin Lindbergh, using his stepfather's surname.

In all, Gramenos interviewed thirty-six persons in Dallas. Speck's former wife told of their sometimes stormy life together. She told of his arriving home from work in the afternoons depressed, and how he would drop, as from exhaustion, when he arrived home, often crying around bedtime. He never struck her, she said, but he cried. When he was not drinking and taking pills, she considered him a nice fellow. Gramenos also checked all possible records at the Dallas Police Department, the county clerk's office, the juvenile department, school, and the companies where Speck had worked. He located some of Speck's old acquaintances, but none of them proved to be very helpful.

XXIV

By then there was one major state's witness we had not interviewed — the eyewitness, Corazon Amurao. Everything we knew about her had come from the newspapers, hearsay, and the transcript of a tape recording of her questioning by Chief of Detectives Michael Spiotto and two of his aides. A nurse for her was also present. The interview occurred shortly after the crimes.

In the tape they apparently were showing her some pictures.

"He seems to have a — with the hair sticking out," she said.

"Similar to that, but the hair is not the same," said Detective Byron Carlile.

"Is there, is there anything else that's different about it?" asked Spiotto.

"[inaudible] only the hair," said Miss Amurao.

"Only the hair," said Carlile.

"Only the hair," said Spiotto. "Everything else is like him, hmm?"

"What was different about the hair?" asked Carlile.

"Shorter," said Miss Amurao.

"It was shorter," said Carlile.

"It was something like this, but it was shorter," she said. As for his lips, she said he kept smiling. The man had worn a black suit coat, she said, but she didn't remember the color of his shirt. She told of a man who had passed by the house three times one night "only last week," but she was unable to say if he was the same man who had been in the apartment.

Sergeant John Griffith said, "Tell me this: If we were to just ride around the city, do you think you'd be able to recognize that man just walking down the street?"

According to the tape transcript, she replied, "[inaudible] because Americans have the same faces [inaudible]."

One of her interviewers, unidentified in the transcript, said, "It seems to me you heard that expression before, only it's reversed. Yes, we've used the expression ourselves. All American men look alike. Well, now, certainly this guy and I, we don't look alike, do we? Now he's good looking."

"Now he'll tell you, but I'm better," said Carlile.

It was an informal interrogation and it raised more questions than it answered. We had to know more about what she had seen.

XXV

On a Sunday afternoon in late January, we took Miss Amurao's deposition. It is very desolate around the Criminal Court Building and County Jail on a Sunday. It gave me a weary feeling. Miss Amurao, a small, black-haired young woman with big dark eyes, was brought into the second-floor room by state's attorney's policemen. She and Martin sat at one end of the long conference table and Gramenos and I at the other end.

Transcribed, the deposition came to 133 pages. I was to use it in my cross-examination of her later.

XXVI

Identification by an eyewitness is not as precise as many people may believe. If it was a major crime, the witness is likely to have been under great stress. Picking a suspect out of a police lineup is sometimes a hit-or-miss matter. Even plainclothes detectives, bearing no resemblance to the criminal in size, shape, or looks, have been fingered in such lineups.

XXVII

Consolidation of the eight cases into one trial was up to the discretion of the court, unless the state consolidated them. We couldn't demand it as a matter of right.

The advantage of consolidation was that we would have one trial — not eight. Everyone in the country knew there were eight murders. From the defense point of view, there seemed to be nothing we could gain by having eight trials.

XXVIII

There was the matter of suppression of the pistol. It had been seized from his room at the Raleigh, without a search warrant, without his consent.

"For all purposes," I said at one of our defense conferences, "he was in his home. He wasn't in a flophouse, he was in his castle. We have no criteria that you have to be in a $100,000 house. If you pay 90 cents a day it's your home just as much as a $300,000 bungalow, for constitutional purposes!"

Someone asked if Speck would take the stand to testify in our motions to suppress.

"Hell, no," I said. "He's not about to testify. He'd commit suicide before he'd take the stand!"

I filed a great number of motions, including one for an in-camera hearing on certain pre-trial motions and for an order impounding the motions, to preclude any publicity on evidence suppressed by the court so that prospective jurors would not know of it. Then in chambers I filed motions to suppress specific evidence taken from the Starr and Raleigh Hotels, including the pistol, and a knife recovered from the Calumet River. We did not know whose knife it was, but it had been dredged out with a magnet after one of the doctors at the hospital had obtained an incriminating admission about a knife from

Speck before counsel was appointed, thereby violating the *Miranda* rule. But Speck told me he never recalled saying he had thrown a knife away, nor did he recall throwing it away. The state agreed not to use it.

We were able to show that his room at the Raleigh had been searched and the gun seized while he was still a tenant, and before his rent period had expired. The state claimed a search warrant had been issued on July 20, but by then police had already been in and out as if the room were an auditorium.

In late January, as we were in the midst of these motions, the worst snowstorm in the history of Chicago dumped twenty-two inches on the city. I slept all night in my office with my overcoat on. So did Gramenos and my daughter Marie Therese, who was a legal secretary. Judge Paschen was snowed in too and slept in the jail along with some assistant state's attorneys. Nobody made it in that day. The streets were jammed. Cars were abandoned on the freeways. In court we waived the presence of Speck because there weren't enough jail personnel to go after him.

A few days later I made an all-out fight to suppress Corazon Amurao's testimony and identification of Speck. Because he did not have counsel at the time, her identification of him was unconstitutional and had tainted all of her testimony, I contended. Viewing his photo in advance had "planted" his likeness in her mind and, I argued, therefore she was familiar with his face from that photo. Also she had viewed him alone in a hospital room, not in a lineup. The *Wade* case, which was to be decided by the U.S. Supreme Court about a year later, turned on this very point and was to be reversed. We also argued our motion for a change of place of trial. But the court didn't see it our way.

XXIX

"My theory of the defense from the first week has been prove him guilty beyond a reasonable doubt. If they find him not guilty, that's one thing. If they find him guilty, then there is more to it. That's when we bring up the mental defect,'' I said to some of my assistants one day.

After all the investigative and psychiatric testing, the result was the same. I truly did not have a psychiatric defense. Coupled with this, Speck could never say that he was involved in the crimes, if pushed to the point of admitting guilt. In any event, an insanity defense is tantamount to pleading guilty. What the defendant is really saying in such a defense is, ''If I did it then I had a mental disease that would not permit me to control my actions.''

A voice broke in. ''If they see these pictures [of the dead nurses] they won't be satisfied with the electric chair!''

XXX

Some days were worse than others.

One morning in early February, Judge Joseph A. Power of the executive committee of the Circuit Court requested that I meet him in Judge Paschen's chambers. When I arrived at the seventh floor office, Paschen was behind his desk and Power at his side. Martin was standing. Acting State's Attorney John Stamos and Lou Garippo, an assistant, were sitting on a couch. There was a court reporter.

Judge Power asked if I had a contract with Richard Speck to write a book.

''No,'' I said. ''I am not an author.''

Did I talk to any author about writing a book? No. Did Speck have a contract to sell his story to a writer or publishing company and was I a party to that contract? No, I said, but there were persons known to me who had had Speck sign a document that would allow them to write articles. These were doctors who wanted to write medical articles. I had considered writing legal articles, but that would be some time after the final disposition of the case. Newspapermen had asked me to write articles or a book, and magazines had approached me concerning not Speck's, but my own life, and I had turned them all down.

Judge Power explained that there had been an emergency

meeting of the executive committee of judges about a report that I intended to write a book. Some of the judges — but presumably not he — were concerned that I might be more interested in writing a book than in defending Speck!

It turned out to be an error in data. Apparently Chief Judge John S. Boyle had heard, via the grapevine, which I interpreted to mean the warden of the county jail, that I was going to write a book about the case and that this was the only reason I was representing Speck. Boyle, as chief judge of the Cook County Circuit Court, directed all the other judges or assigned them. So Boyle sent word to Judge Power, a friend of mine, and Stamos to grill me.

Judge Boyle had his information mixed up. He should have called instead on Dr. Ziporyn, the jail psychiatrist, who did write a book while the case was pending in the appellate stage.

XXXI

Dr. Ziporyn contended that he spent more than one hundred hours with Speck. Since the entire competency panel had been with Speck around 10 percent of that time, I thought this should be impressive. If Speck had any mental illness, Dr. Ziporyn should know of it.

As it turned out, I didn't use Dr. Ziporyn. He was willing to testify that Speck had a mental illness only in certain instances: when he was under the influence of alcohol, barbiturates, or narcotics. To substantiate the use of these, I would have to elicit it from the mouth of Speck himself, and he wouldn't take the stand.

"Do you think we can put Speck on the stand?" I asked.

"No," said Dr. Ziporyn, "I don't think he'll go on the stand. He told me, 'I can't go out there with all those people looking at me and saying, Killer, killer, killer. I couldn't talk in front of 'em. Look how long it took me to talk to you.' "

Dr. Ziporyn reported one anecdote involving Speck and one of his guards.

"How much alcohol can you take?" the guard asked.

"About a pint," replied Speck.

"You take redballs?"

"You mean redbirds," corrected Speck.

"What if you take redbirds and a pint together, what do you get?"

"Eight murders and the electric chair."

Dr. Ziporyn concluded, "It's a good thing he's not on his own jury." Then he spoke of other physical and mental aspects of Speck. "I don't know if he did it or not, but he was certainly capable of doing it." He was particularly impressed by the good coordination of Speck's hands and cited how he had drawn, freehand, a picture of the Walt Disney character, Pluto.

But if he had committed the crimes, I still didn't understand how he had done it alone.

"When you think of it," I said, "imagine killing eight people with your hands! You know, I'm talking to him and we get to a certain point, and he said, 'I did it!' 'Well,' I said, 'why didn't you tell me that before?' 'Well, I don't know if I did or not,' he said. So I told him he'd better straighten up. 'Those psychiatrists are going to believe you!' "

Dr. Ziporyn noted that adults, like Speck, who had been compared with hyperactive children also had an intolerance to alcohol and drugs. "Hyperactive people can't tolerate drugs."

I had considered calling Ziporyn as a witness to counteract the panel's testimony, if I went with a psychiatric defense. But I soon learned he would be cautious about refuting them.

"It isn't easy to look at this panel's opinion and go in there and oppose them," he said. "It's like arguing against the whole Supreme Court. To go against these guys and say they're wrong takes an arrogance I don't possess."

Dr. Ziporyn saw Speck as an obsessive-compulsive personality and diagnosed "an organic brain defect, chronic brain syndrome associated with cerebral trauma." He ruled out a sociopathic personality disorder because Speck expressed guilt, shame, anxiety, and adhered to a belief in codes of conduct plus morality. He considered the defect characterized by an intolerance to drugs and alcohol, which caused him to lose control over impulsive behavior. Dr. Ziporyn speculated that early pneumonia, shortly after birth, had prevented Speck from having enough oxygen for his young brain. Anybody with brain damage has trouble controlling behavior, he said.

I wondered about Dr. Ziporyn's classifying Speck as "religious."

"Do you think he believes in a Supreme Being?" I asked.

"Sure. He is very moralistic."

"Think we can get him probation?"

All of us chuckled at that.

"Well," I said, "we need to have a laugh or two, once in a while."

XXXII

As a result of my successful motion before Judge Paschen, Dr. Ner Littner was allowed to examine Speck as a psychiatrist for the defense in February. Dr. Littner, a psychoanalyst, was medical director of the Child Therapy Training Program of the Chicago Institute of Psychoanalysis. He had published widely in professional journals.

Depending on what Dr. Littner found, his testimony might be used in the trial. Or, if Speck were found guilty, we could use it later in a mitigation hearing before sentencing.

Dr. Littner thoroughly explored Speck's history and interviewed him. He concluded with this evaluation:

"Although he does not appear to be psychotic, the degree of his mental disease seems to be of pre-psychotic proportions. Even if he is not guilty of the crimes with which he is charged, I believe that he is in need of intensive and prolonged mental treatment as, according to the evidence currently available, he seems to me to be a danger both to himself as well as to the community.

"I believe that his mental disease has been present in overt form since at least the age of thirteen years and that it has been growing steadily worse ever since. There are some signs suggestive of its presence since the age of six years."

At last, a psychiatric view that laid it out without hedging.

XXXIII

Two days after we took Corazon Amurao's deposition, in late January, we turned up two alibi witnesses for Speck!

They were Elliott and Sophie Dufrayer. They worked at Kay's Pilot House on East 100th Street, in the vicinity of the Shipyard Inn. They were the kind of people you'd want for alibi witnesses: trusted employees who enjoyed a good reputation in the community.

They had told their story to the police, back in July, but had been told they must be mistaken. We had secured their names when the state, belatedly, added them to a supplemental list of state's witnesses, which we received in late January.

Gramenos and I talked to them, one at a time. Speck, they said, had been in Kay's Pilot House just before midnight and had left after midnight on the night of the murders.

The murderer had entered the townhouse, a mile and a half away, at 11 P.M., the police had by then definitely established.

A person cannot be in two places at one time.

The Dufrayers were positive they had seen Speck at that particular time. They had nothing to gain from telling us and had, in fact, already lost time from work because of questioning from the state's attorney's office. Their only desire was to tell the truth, no matter whom it helped.

3. Eight Verdicts in Peoria

A cold, raw wind swept across the Corn Belt and tore at your face that February day that Speck went on trial in Peoria.

Except for the freezing temperatures and the wind-stripped trees, it was a lovely, but incongruous, setting for this deadly legal struggle that would unveil a story of violent death multiplied by eight and climax in a decision on a man's liberty — life or death. The new, modern courthouse had been dedicated by Mrs. Lyndon B. Johnson. She had called Peoria "one of the prettiest cities in America" and I agreed. It had once been a tough town, with a bad reputation; now it was cleaned up. At the courthouse square, other history still lingered. In 1854, Abraham Lincoln and Stephen B. Douglas had debated here. A Civil War monument stood a few feet away. Now Speck was in the county jail across the street. He had been driven the 158 miles from Chicago in a convoy of deputies armed with shotguns and machine guns.

Newsmen from newspapers, magazines, television, and radio swarmed onto the city and into Courtroom A, where the eighty-five seats were soon filled by those involved in the trial, by newsmen, and by the lucky spectators who held tickets.

I felt at home in Peoria. ''Basically,'' I told a reporter, ''I use a small-town style in the big city. I guess you could call it a let's-not-get-excited-about-anything style.''

But I soon had plenty to get excited about.

I

The trial began with the *voir dire* — the Latin term for ''to tell the truth'' — process of selecting a jury. Judge Paschen had ordered the eight cases consolidated, over the objection of the prosecution; there would be only one trial. In essence, we were trying eight murder cases simultaneously. This meant the twenty peremptory challenges that each side had would be multiplied by eight. I had 160 challenges; so did Martin.

The judge laid down strict, but reasonable, rules for the press. They could report only what was actually said, or what occurred, in open court. He allowed no cameras or recording devices, and no drawing or sketching could be done in the courtroom. All observers were searched, and no one could come or go while a session was in progress.

Martin took a four-man prosecution team with him to Peoria. I took Gramenos on a full-time basis, with Doherty coming down from time to time. George Brobst, one of our top investigators, was in Peoria much of the time. When the trial got under way, the defense's case still had not jelled completely.

But I had worked out a long series of questions for the veniremen, emphasizing the presumption of innocence, laying the groundwork for later questioning of fingerprint evidence, insuring that, if the defendant were found guilty, the veniremen would keep an open mind as to punishment, considering imprisonment as an alternative to death. And as we studied the jury lists a day in advance, two prominent Peoria residents — Elmo Koos, an attorney, and Mitch Maloof, a real estate man — advised us on the local situation and the prospective jurors. Of course, the state with their investigators, and the assistance of the Peoria state's attorney's office, was investigating almost every prospective juror.

Naturally, the state was qualifying the jury for the death penalty. The first venireman didn't believe in capital punishment. He was excused for cause. And so it went. We were on our way.

It was a tedious, nerve-fraying experience that stretched from February 20 until the end of March. Martin, in an emotionless voice, would snap out his questions coldly and businesslike as he sought tight-lipped, strict, law-and-order types. I tried to engage them in conversation, as if we were chatting over the backyard fence, always looking for the warm-hearted and scarred, preferably older persons, ones who could be expected to sympathize with another in life's darker days. When one didn't hesitate in replying to scruples on the death penalty, it suggested an inflexibility that wasn't hopeful for the defense. One woman said she had no scruples against the death penalty, but I noted in my trial book that she "hung her head" as she said it. The state excused her. A man also said he had no scruples. "No hesitation," I noted. I excused him. Another woman said she would vote for death in a proper case, but she responded painfully, it seemed to me. The state excused her. And the state excused one medical technician who perhaps could have best understood their scientific evidence and explained it to other jurors. Every gesture, every nuance, every expression of each venireman was scrutinized by both sides.

It was a grind, sometimes characterized by flaring tempers on both sides, but it also had its moments of levity. While I was examining a laborer as a possible juror, I asked him if he could be fair.

"Well, I don't know," he said. "I might fall asleep."

"Martin might put you to sleep, but I won't," I promised him.

Martin asked one elderly man if the fact that the trial might last six weeks would influence him as a juror.

"I'm not going any place," replied the man.

Speck, seated at the defense table, chuckled and turned to me. "Neither am I."

Another time, after Judge Paschen had again excused a venireman for cause, Speck asked me, "Say, do you think the judge will excuse me for cause?"

Another venireman, a woman, said she was nervous.

"Please relax," I said. "After all, this is your home. You live here." I paused a moment. "Now, the state's attorney, he's from Chicago."

We all laughed, including Judge Paschen, Martin, and Speck.

Then Judge Paschen, still smiling, asked, "And where are you from?"

"I'm from a little town," I said. "A little town just outside the city of Chicago." (Dolton, in the suburbs.)

The most difficult chore, from the defense's point of view, was weeding out those who had been influenced by what they had read in the newspapers or heard on TV or radio. I could never be certain I had plumbed the depth of unconscious prejudice in a person. Sometimes, after insisting he could be fair, a person would blurt out that he couldn't give Speck anything but death. "If I had to find him not guilty, I couldn't go home," several said. Two thought Speck had confessed to the crime!

After we had questioned more than one hundred prospects, Martin let his aides, John Glenville and George Murtaugh, help in the questioning. Later I had Gramenos take over for the defense for a while. But that didn't last long. Neither the state nor the judge would give him an inch. They overlooked what I did. I finally took over again, even though my throat was sore.

During the voir dire, the Chicago *Tribune* filed suit against Judge Paschen, seeking to countermand the press rules he had imposed. The defense joined the suit as a friend of the court. We liked his rules on publicity; they helped us get a fairer trial, we thought. The case went to the Illinois Supreme Court, which ordered the ground rules revised to a certain extent. Newsmen were allowed to purchase transcripts each day from the official court reporter; events in open court could be reported, except for the names of jurors until they had either been excused or sworn and sequestered.

Juries in Illinois are selected by panels of four. Each panel must be accepted by both state and defense before those four are sworn and sequestered. It was March 2 before we agreed on our first panel; by mid-March, we had the second panel; at the end of the month, the third. We had questioned about six hundred veniremen to acquire a jury of six men and six women, plus two alternates, a man and a woman.

Who were they? Two elderly men, one of whom had once lived in Chicago, two housewives, two women who worked (one of them middle-aged), three workingmen (one middle-aged), a young divorcee, a former Marine officer, and a Bradley University professor who had completed most of his Ph.D. work. One of the alternates was a grandmother, the other a machine operator. One of the older men was a retired businessman whose nurse granddaughter had known one of the murder victims. But I thought he would be all right. His age was one thing, and I just sensed that he was okay. Accepting the ex-Marine was more complicated. I was certain Martin wanted him, because of his background; by accepting him, I got the three others in that panel that I was willing to accept. But I did not count the ex-Marine officer out entirely; he seemed forceful and I reasoned that if I could sell him a good case, he could influence the rest of the jury. With the professor I reasoned similarly. He was a man with a gentle background and a gentle manner. He also seemed to have a gift for persuasion; if the ex-Marine got out of hand, perhaps the professor could hang the jury.

II

Even after the trial had started, we continued our investigation. While we were selecting a jury in Peoria, a new lead popped up in Chicago — a suspect other than Speck. Fred Cohn and Leo Ranachowski went to work on it. But the man was found to have been in the state hospital for the mentally ill during the pertinent July, 1966, dates.

Later, an inmate of the Cook County Jail reported to our office that he knew a man who "looks more like Speck than Speck does." He described the man as having a tattoo on his right arm labeled, "Born to Raise Hell," with short, crew-cut hair. He told of an incident in a tavern two days after the murders in which one man had thrust a newspaper in front of the Speck-like suspect. On the front page was the artist's sketch of the murderer. "This looks like you," the man was told. He got up and left.

Our informant didn't know the man's last name or where he worked. We checked it as far as we could. We couldn't locate him. Another lead gone bad.

III

Paschen was a "union judge." Court began exactly at 9:30, adjourned at 12 noon, reconvened at 1:30, and stopped right on the minute at 5 P.M.

There wasn't any court on Saturdays and Sundays, so Speck kept bugging me for a weekend pass.

"I promise to be back by Sunday night," he said.

Gramenos heard him. During lunch hour one day, Jim jokingly typed the appropriate words on a sheet of paper.

2/23/67

TO: *Sheriff of Peoria County*
THIS WILL AUTHORIZE RICHARD FRANKLIN SPECK TO BE ALLOWED A WEEKEND PASS WITH THE CONDITION THAT HE RETURN TO THIS COURTROOM ON MONDAY, FEBRUARY 27, 1967.

Judge Herbert Paschen
Circuit Court of Peoria County

The gregarious judge was very likeable and easy to get along with. He used to attend the same church service as I did at eleven o'clock in Peoria, and afterward he and his gracious wife would invite me up to their apartment. He was very hospitable to both the state and the defense. Any time I suggested a legal paper needed signing he was likely to take my word for it and sign with scarcely a glance at it.

One afternoon during a respite from court, someone asked Paschen to sign an autograph and I took it as a ripe opportunity.

"Say, Judge, Mr. Speck wants you to autograph this."

I proffered the "pass." He was about to sign it, when I suggested he might want to read it first. He did, and he burst into uncontrollable laughter. Martin was close by. He did not laugh.

As the trial got under way, surprisingly, Speck relaxed and displayed a striking sense of humor. In fact, he became my most humorous client — in the grimmest case. Certainly I had not joked with him and always remained serious in dealing with him. By then he seemed to have complete faith in me. I conferred with him briefly after each court session and he apparently realized I was doing all I could for him. Possibly this feeling had released his humor.

As quips went, his was mostly gallows humor. One venireman said he couldn't stand being cooped up. Speck said he couldn't either. One guard told Speck, "You're getting fat as a pig," to which Speck replied, "Yeah, they're fattening me up for the kill." He added, "I am getting fat. I have to exercise. I lifted a candy bar wrapper last night and sprained two fingers."

Speck tore a cartoon from a magazine and relabeled it to fit what he considered his situation. In it a lawyer and his client stood before the bar of justice. The black-robed judge leaned over the bench, emptying a huge pistol's bullets into the defendant, destroying him. Speck labeled the judge "Paschon," the defendant "Speck," and the lawyer "Getty." He changed the name in the punchline to cause the bailiff to say, "Judge Paschon has yet to have a decision reversed."

To us at the defense table he would provide gibes at the other side. "That prosecutor would mess up a two-car funeral," he said once. Other times he would turn serious, but what he said would be so incongruous with his situation that it, too, was almost funny. Asked if he believed in capital punishment, he said, "Hell, yes." He meant it. But he didn't want life in prison if he were convicted. "I would rather have the chair than 100 years to 100 and a day."

You never knew when a *bon mot* would pop out of his mouth. During the jury selection he turned to me and said, "I always knew I'd get a big charge out of life, but I never thought it would be anything like this!" Later, as the evidence started piling up against him, he observed, "This is sure a bad case — well, you can't win them all."

This was the unseen, unknown side to Speck the drifter, drinker, and accused murderer. And as the trial progressed, he continued to develop his skill at sketching and painting that he had not known he possessed before his arrest and his sessions with Dr. Ziporyn. By now he had progressed to freehand work in oils. One day he presented me with an oil painting of a horse's head. In the corner he had inscribed:

"To Gerald Getty, the Greatest Man I Know."

It was a thank-you note in a class by itself, as far as my clients were concerned. It wasn't a bad painting, either.

IV

Gramenos and Doherty were "night people." I told them they could do anything they wished in Peoria, with two exceptions. "Don't charge any bar bills to me and don't call me after ten-thirty at night, for I'm in bed by then."

Gramenos liked to work at night. Many times he hadn't made a start on the summaries of the day's testimony by the time I went to bed. But by morning he would have it all summarized. He hit his stride after midnight.

V

Bill Martin, the chief prosecutor, was a devastating lawyer. Although only thirty, the stocky, bespectacled, close-cropped Martin was like a machine in putting a case together. He was an adversary to be respected.

Now he stood erect before the jury in Courtroom A and, hardly moving at all, he poured out the prosecution's version of the murders in his opening address to the jury.

"The evidence will show that at approximately 11 P.M. last July 13, Miss Amurao was awakened by a knocking at her bedroom door. She noted that the light was still on in the bedroom, the ceiling light. She got up and went to the door and unlocked it and opened it. There she saw the defendant, Richard Franklin Speck, standing in her doorway, with a small, black revolver pointed at her."

In strict order, Martin recited how, by the state's version, Speck had rounded up the six young women then in the townhouse and, at gunpoint, had them sit in a circle on the floor while they offered him the money they had. He then took a knife and sliced a bedsheet into strips and tied up the six girls. Then Miss Davy arrived home and she was made the seventh captive. At 12:35 A.M. Miss Jordan and Miss Farris arrived. They were among the first killed, taken from the room where the others were. Martin charged that Speck sexually assaulted Miss Davy, the last one killed. On his last trip into the room, he didn't detect Miss Amurao, hiding under a bed, and subsequently he left.

I had prepared my opening statement in anticipation of securing a jury. Now as I followed Martin to open my defense of

Speck, I told the jury, "The theory of the defense is that Speck, this defendant, is not the perpetrator of this crime. The state will have to prove this beyond a reasonable doubt." Then I went into the state's evidence. I emphasized that the police had sought a suspect with a crew cut, that Miss Amurao at first had identified Speck's picture as being "more similar" rather than saying, "That's the man!", that the fingerprint evidence was inexact and incomplete, that Speck was identified by circumstances of his being close to the murder scene, and that Miss Amurao's identification was made under difficult conditions as far as lighting was concerned. Her identification was not convincing and the fingerprint testimony was punctuated with doubt — the only two pieces of evidence that coupled the defendant with the crime.

Then Martin opened the state's case by calling to the witness stand a cartographer who had supervised the making of three maps of the particular area of the South Side we would be concerned with. On cross-examination, he increased the distance from the Shipyard Inn at 101st Street and Avenue N to the nurses' residence. Instead of a mile and a third, he remeasured it and called it closer to a mile and a half. The struggle had begun.

Martin's first several witnesses established Speck's whereabouts during the three days prior to the crimes. One seaman played cards with Speck at the maritime union office on East 100th, near the townhouse, on July 11 and then saw him again on July 12, on which day he drove Speck to a job on the Sinclair ship, *Great Lakes*. But when they reached the docks, another man had already been given the job and the mix-up sent Speck back to the union hiring hall. On the morning of July 13, the seaman saw Speck again. Martin asked him if he had heard Speck mention any other cities. Over my objection, Judge Paschen allowed him to reply. "He said maybe he was going to New Orleans," said the witness. (Miss Amurao was to testify that the intruder had said he needed money to go to New Orleans.) On cross, I established that New Orleans was one of several ports a man could ship out of easily.

The parade of witnesses continued. A construction worker had met Speck the evening of July 13 in the Shipyard Inn tavern on Avenue N. He testified to seeing Speck with a pistol in one of the booths. Speck talked to this man and the man's bride-to-be. Speck told them of his former wife and daughter and spoke of his ex-spouse in derogatory terms. They last saw Speck between 9:30 and 9:45 P.M. when they left the tavern. Another patron of that bar told of hearing something drop to the floor and saw Speck bend over and pick up a pocketknife. He said he left the tavern at 10 P.M., which was the last time he saw Speck.

On cross, I brought out the environment in which the witness had "heard" the "knife" dropped.

"Was the juke box playing, also?"

"Yes, it was."

"Of course, people were talking in there."

"Yes, sir, I imagine."

"What kind of music was being played?"

"I heard mostly rock and roll."

The service station attendant where Speck had left his bags on the night of July 12 testified that Speck had picked up the bags the next morning, July 13. Then Speck breakfasted there on a candy bar and a bottle of pop.

On cross I asked him, "And then you noticed his hair — his hair was long and it was combed back?"

"Yes, sir."

"In other words, not a crew cut?"

"No."

"Did you notice anything about his face?"

"There was pockmarks, complexion was pitted."

"On the 14th the police came there — this is Thursday?"

"Yes."

"And did they ask you about a man with a crew cut, dark hair, didn't they?"

"No, they said a crew cut and I believe it was a dark jacket or dark pants, I am not sure."

"And they emphasized a crew cut?"

"Yes."

"And they never said anything about a man with brown long hair, combed back, did they?"

"No."

"And they never said anything about a man with acne on his face or marks on his face?"

"I don't recall."

With each witness, I established on cross-examination the fact of Speck's pocked face, his long hair. From time to time I questioned them about what Speck had worn, each time showing that he had not been dressed in black on that particular occasion. The manager of the Shipyard Inn, a woman, testified that Speck walked into her bar about 11 A.M. on July 13 — twelve hours before Miss Amurao was surprised in her room at the townhouse. He drank a glass of beer and rented a room from her upstairs, paying the $10 week's rent in advance with a twenty-dollar bill and paying another dollar for key deposit. He drank more during the day. In the evening he was in the Shipyard Inn. She last saw him around 10:10 or 10:15 P.M. that evening. On cross, I elicited from her that he was wearing a red knit shirt, and it was established that there was no bus line on 100th Street, the most direct route to the townhouse. The state's testimony so far had Speck disappearing shortly after 10 P.M., so I asked her:

"He very well could have gone upstairs, as far as you know?"

"I wouldn't know."

After the murders, the police had found an empty beer can in Speck's room. I asked her about other features of the room.

"Were the covers pulled back?"

"No. The bed was used."

"You would say the bed had been slept in?"

"That's right."

I asked her if a lake ship, which I named, was in the shipyard nearby that night and she said she thought so.

As I had with the others, I asked her, "And would you tell us one thing you noticed about his face?"

"Well, how can you miss it?"

"Yes, how can you? Tell us."

"I noticed he had the marks on his face."

"Pockmarks?"

"Pockmarks."

The young man who had dated Miss Davy that night testified that they had arrived at the townhouse at 11:30 P.M. A few minutes later, between 11:35 and 11:40 P.M. she had gone into the house. This fixed the time perfectly and, as was to be seen, corroborated Miss Amurao as to time.

In my opening statement I had admitted the deaths of the eight young women. This meant, as far as the defense was concerned, the state didn't have to prove they were dead. When Martin began to call life-and-death witnesses, a formality, I objected. Judge Paschen heard our arguments in chambers, out of earshot of the jury. I argued that such testimony was superfluous and could only be presented for the purpose of inflaming the jury as they heard close relatives or parents tell of seeing the bodies for the first time. The judge overruled me. Seven such witnesses — three fathers, a mother, a brother, a sister, and a hospital official for the Filipino girls — filed through the courtroom, each telling of seeing the victim alive and then answering Martin's question, "When did you last see her?" The replies came: "July 14 in the Chicago morgue," "Dead in her coffin," and then, in a hushed courtroom, it was over. I did not cross-examine any of them.

VI

Tuesday, April 4 — the second day of testimony in the trial — was election day in Chicago. Mayor Daley won an unprecedented fourth term, carrying every ward in the city, and swamping Republican John L. Waner with a 516,000 vote plurality. "The most dynamic four years in Chicago's history" lay ahead, the Mayor promised.

The same day, as a reminder that my administrative duties never slackened, I received a copy of the payroll and notes on other matters from Mary O'Brien, my secretary who had been in the office since 1947. She reminded me that, even as we were trying the Speck case, there was never to be a respite from pressure-filled cases for the public defender and his staff.

''Howard Abrams told me we were appointed in three headline cases in Felony Court today,'' she wrote, and she listed them: ''An insurance hoax case, a laborer under $100,000 bond in a little girl kidnapping case, and the case of a woman who killed a policeman.''

VII

My daughters Muriel and Marie Therese came down for part of the trial. By then the weather had changed. We had moved from the blizzards of winter to the warmth of spring. The pressures of the trial had mounted so that the easiest way to visit with my family was for them to join me in Peoria. Muriel was continuing to help unofficially by clipping all of the news stories about the case that appeared in the Chicago papers. With four daily sources, that was no small chore.

I saw that they received tickets to watch the trial while they were in Peoria. The judge had prohibited those under twenty-one from entering the courtroom. This meant obtaining special permission for Marie Therese. She was eighteen.

VIII

Dark-eyed and tiny, about four feet ten, Corazon Amurao took the stand as the state's star witness. Pretty and petite, her face by then was known over the world as the sole survivor of that night of terror. Her appearance became a climactic moment in the trial.

To prepare for her testimony, Martin's aides wheeled in a large scale model of the townhouse that had been built by the FBI. It was 30 inches high, 3 feet wide, and 4 feet long. It took four bailiffs to lift the two-story ''dollhouse.''

Martin guided Miss Amurao through her preliminary testimony, as she told of her background in the Philippines and how she had come to Chicago with Miss Gargullo and Miss Pasion and had commenced working at the South Chicago Community Hospital in May, 1966. Using the dollhouse as the model, she explained to Martin where each nurse's bed had been situated in the house. She told of her day's routine on Wednesday, July 13. She answered Martin's questions in slow, deliberate speech and good English that you could readily understand. Then she neared the central event as she told of writing a letter and going upstairs at about 10:30 P.M. When she got to her room, Merlita Gargullo had already preceded her. In the large, or south, bedroom she had noted that Valentina Pasion, Patricia Matusek, and Pamela Wilkening were lying on their beds. She locked the room shared by Miss Gargullo and herself. Miss Gargullo asked her to leave the light on; she was going to say her prayers. Then Miss Amurao went to bed and to sleep.

"Did you wake up at any time later, Wednesday night, July 13th?" asked Martin.

"Yes."

"And would you tell the court and jury how you happened to wake up?"

"I heard a knock in our bedroom. It was about four knocks and the knocking was done in a normal manner."

"When you woke up, was the ceiling light on or off?"

"It was still on."

"Do you know approximately what time it was when you heard the four knocks at your bedroom door?"

"It's about eleven o'clock."

"How did you know the time?"

"There was a clock right there on our dresser in our bedroom."

"Did you look at it?"

"I looked at it."

"What did you do after you heard the four knocks at the door?"

"Then I got up and I answered the one who is knocking on our door."

"And will you describe what happened when you went to the door?"

"I went up to the — I went to the door and I unlocked it and I started to open it and at once there's somebody who is pushing the door."

"What happened next?"

"Well, then I saw a man. . . ." She broke down and wept. For more than a minute as she pressed a handkerchief to her face, there was a deep silence in the courtroom. Judge Paschen offered her water. I suggested a recess, but she declined. She was soon under control. "I saw a man standing on the center of our door with a gun in his right hand pointed toward me and I noticed that he had marks on his face, the clothes was dark from the shoulder to the foot and his hair was blond, hair combed toward the back, and some hair in the front."

She told of staring at the man for one to two minutes.

"Did he say anything or did you say anything?" asked Martin.

"He asked me, 'Where are your companions?' and then he grabbed my forearm."

"Now, Miss Amurao, if you see that same man in the courtroom today, who came to your bedroom door on Wednesday night, July 13, would you please step down and point him out, please."

The bailiff opened the gate to the witness box. She stepped down and walked to within a few feet of Speck, pointed him out with her black eyes straight upon him.

"This is the man," she said, and then returned to the stand.

"Identifying for the record the defendant, Richard Franklin Speck," intoned Martin.

It was the dramatic confrontation many had been waiting for, and a large number of newsmen immediately rushed out of the courtroom, to phone in the latest development and beat the competition and make a deadline.

"You will not all get up and disturb this proceeding!" said the judge, but they kept going.

I asked for a private conference. We left the courtroom. In chambers I said, "I want the record to reflect that when she dramatically left the witness stand and walked and pointed at this defendant and said, 'This is the man,' that there was a commotion in the rear of the courtroom and many people left. I do not know how many left the courtroom and those people are from the press."

"I object to the description given by defense counsel," said Martin.

"Well, you describe it," I retorted.

"We will ask the court to describe it," said Martin.

Judge Paschen said, "She walked over here, she was asked to step out and point out a man. She walked over to him and pointed to him and said, 'This is the man.' The press did then start to leave and the court cautioned them about leaving noisily."

"But they did leave noisily."

"They did leave," said the judge.

"About twenty of them."

"I object to 'twenty,' " said Martin.

"I wouldn't say twenty, I would say ten to twelve," said the judge. "Because it only holds about thirty back there and there are more than twenty left."

"May I say something here?" asked Doherty, who was in court that day.

"Yes," said the judge.

"This is as a result of an unusual procedure of, instead of asking someone to point from the witness stand — and there have been numerous witnesses here — this is the only one that they went through this ostentatious display for the sole purpose of prejudicing the jury, to which we object."

"Well, it is difficult for her to see where she is there," said Judge Paschen.

"Of course, on account of this, I move for a mistrial," I said.

"Mistrial denied," said the judge.

We returned to the courtroom. Martin resumed direct examination.

"Miss Amurao, except for his clothing, does the man that you pointed out in the courtroom today look any different than he did when you first saw him on Wednesday night, July 13th?"

"He is just the same."

"After he grabbed you by the arm, what did you do?"

She told of going to the rear or south bedroom, which was larger than the other bedrooms. She and the other two Filipino nurses rushed into a closet there and held the door. They were there about five minutes when a woman's voice told them to come out, that the man was not going to harm them. When they came out, the light was off. Miss Matusek and Miss Schmale were standing nearby. Speck, she said, was holding Miss Wilkening at the waist, with a gun still in his right hand. When all the other women walked over toward him, he released Miss Wilkening and made all six of them sit together on the floor.

"Did either he say anything at that time or did any other girls?" asked Martin.

"One of the girls asked Speck, 'What do you want?' And then Speck answered, 'I want money, I'm going to New Orleans,' " she said.

Later, she said, one of the women told the man, "We are going to give you some money." He asked, "How much do you have?" Various answers came from his captives: "I have five dollars." "I have six." "I have fifteen." Miss Amurao said, "I have ten dollars." Miss Matusek asked to get up to get her purse. She was allowed to go to her bed for her purse, from which she gave money to him. Then, serially, he obtained money in the same manner from Misses Wilkening, Pasion, and Schmale. He forced all of them to go together with him to Miss Schmale's room; then they returned to the south bedroom. During this time all lights were off, except for the one in the bathroom.

Once again, they all sat down.

"What did Speck do at that time?" asked Martin.

"Then Speck counted at us, by pointing the gun, and he said, 'One, two, three, four, five, six.' "

"After Speck had counted you and the other five girls, what did he do?"

"Then, after we were sitting down, after he had counted us, we heard a female voice downstairs."

Shortly afterward, Miss Davy entered the room. The man opened the door for her.

"Miss Davy was surprised and she scream in a low voice," said Miss Amurao. "And then Speck thrust the gun close towards Davy, Davy's body."

Miss Davy was told to sit down. She was asked if she had money. She gave him two dollars. Five minutes later, the man she identified as Speck stood up and took a bedsheet from a nearby bed. He sliced it into strips with a small knife "about three to four inches." This was the first time she had seen a knife. He draped the strips around his neck. At this time the pistol was on a bunk near him. Then he began tying up the girls. First he tied Miss Wilkening's ankles, then her wrists. Then he tied Miss Davy and placed her in one of the bunks. He repeated the procedure with Miss Schmale and Miss Pasion, leaving her sitting.

"Did you hear Speck say anything, during the time that he was tying these girls?" asked Martin.

"When he was tying one of the girls, he told us, 'Don't be afraid, I'm not going to kill you.' "

He was tying Miss Matusek when the doorbell rang. The man took Miss Amurao and Miss Gargullo downstairs to the door. He kept a pistol on them. At the front door, with the gun in her back, Miss Amurao announced that no one was there. The person who rang the bell had gone. They returned to the south bedroom upstairs, and he continued tying Miss Matusek.

He began tying Miss Amurao.

"How far was Speck's face from your face at the time he tied your ankles?" Martin asked.

"One to two feet away from me."

"Did you notice anything about him at that time?"

"When he was tying my ankles, I smelled alcohol on his breath."

Next he tied Miss Gargullo, the last of the seven nurses. After a while he untied Miss Wilkening's ankles and led her out of the big south bedroom, the gun pointed at her. The door was left partially open. "After about one minute, I heard Miss Wilkening say, 'Ah.' It was like a sigh." Then they heard nothing. Several minutes later Miss Jordan and Miss Farris entered the south bedroom, dressed in Bermuda shorts. The man she said was Speck reappeared behind the new arrivals. "You two come here," she quoted him as saying. He pointed the pistol at them. He ordered them again in a louder voice. He took them out of the room and closed the door.

Martin asked her if she had then heard anything.

"I heard a noise as if Miss Jordan and Miss Farris were resisting." She said it was "as if they were yelling but in low voices." Later, she heard water running in the bathroom. The man returned to the south bedroom, untied Miss Schmale's ankles with the knife and took her from the room.

"After about one minute, I heard Nina Schmale said 'Ah,' just the same like Miss Wilkening."

"Did you hear any noise after that?"

"No."

It was during this absence that four nurses — the three Filipinos and Miss Matusek — changed their positions in efforts to elude the man. Miss Davy remained tied on the bed. Miss Amurao wriggled under Miss Pasion's bed. She heard the water running in the bathroom; then the man returned. He dragged Miss Pasion out without untying her. A few minutes later she heard Miss Pasion say, "Ah." Then he came and carried out Miss Gargullo, still tied.

"Then after about five minutes, I heard Miss Gargullo said 'Masikit.' "

"Could you tell the court and jury what 'Masikit' means in your native language?"

"It means 'It hurts.' "

" 'It hurts?' "

"Yes."

Thirty minutes later he returned for Miss Matusek, and took her out of the room. When he came back thirty to forty minutes later, he sat on the bed where Miss Davy lay.

"What did you see?" asked Martin.

"I saw Speck was pulling off Miss Davy's jeans." She broke down again and Judge Paschen called a brief recess. She then described what, from her vantage point, was a sexual attack. She looked away and when she next looked up the room was empty. She took this opportunity to crawl from her position to another one under Miss Davy's bed. She managed to conceal her entire body under the lower bunk bed. A blanket draped down from the bed to the floor, further concealing her.

"Then I heard — after I crawled from the bottom bunk of Miss Davy's bed it was — then I heard the man going. I heard the footsteps, it entered in the south bedroom, and I saw that it was Speck."

"What happened then?"

"Then I heard the coins jingling in the purse."

"What happened after that?"

"Then Speck left and he leave the entrance door open, and he turn off the light. When he came in he turned on the light but when he left he turned off the light."

The rest of the time, she said, the light had been off, although there was light coming in from outside.

She remained under the bed until the alarm clock went off in the south bedroom. It was then 5:00 A.M. She started to untie her wrists, then her ankles. Another alarm went off at 5:30.

"Then I crawled towards Miss Wilkening's bed, under Wilkening's bed, and I looked out and I saw that there was nobody moving.

"What did you do then?"

"Then I stand up and I went to my bedroom and on my way to my bedroom I saw a body lying in the bathroom, but I don't know who was there. And then my bedroom door was widely open and I saw three bodies lying with blood and I only recognized Miss Jordan and Miss Wilkening."

"What did you do when you went into your bedroom, the front, east bedroom after you had seen the bodies there?"

"After I saw the three bodies lying down on the floor with blood, I closed the — my bedroom door because I was afraid Speck might still be there, and then I went up to my bed and I opened the glass window and I screamed for help."

It was several minutes later and she was on the ledge before help came.

During the testimony I frequently objected to Martin's leading the witness. Each time I was overruled. I also objected to Martin's using wooden figurines that resembled coffins to represent each of the nurses as he placed them in the model "dollhouse" in line with Miss Amurao's testimony. I asked for a conference in chambers. But it had no effect on the judge.

As I listened to the survivor's story, I had the impression that she was better informed than when her statement was taken in January. This led me to suspect she had been well-coached in her testimony.

Her direct examination ended at twenty minutes to five and so Judge Paschen adjourned court for the day, so as not to split up my cross-examination. The next morning — the fourth day of testimony — I opened my cross-examination of Corazon Amurao.

IX

My greatest problem was not to seem rough with her. She had the sympathy of everyone in the courtroom for the terrible ordeal she had gone through. She had my sympathy. But I had to use all my faculties in the best defense possible for my client. This meant I had to surface any flaw in her testimony that I could find. I had to get rough with her in a nice way, if it could be done. Particularly, I had to try to bring out that she frankly did *not* know the identity of the man in the apartment. I bent over backwards to avoid any behavior that might hint of my being harsh to her. Periodically, I kept asking her if she would like a recess or a drink of water.

"Good morning, Miss Amurao," I began.

"Good morning," she said.

"Is that the correct pronunciation — Amurao?"

"Yes, sir."

"And you recall that I was present when you were talked to on January 22, 1967, is that right?"

"Yes, you were present there."

I swiftly, but gently, moved to the townhouse that evening before the gun-wielding stranger entered it. I inquired about lighting and time. The apartment was not air-conditioned, except for the west bedroom where Miss Schmale slept. Was the air conditioner on there? She didn't recall. I emphasized the lighting after the stranger came and took them all into the south bedroom.

"Now," I said, "so we will understand, when you came out of the clothes closet, the light in the south bedroom was off?"

"Yes, sir," she said.

"That light was never turned on, while you were seated there on the floor with the rest of the girls?"

"No, sir."

"In fact, the only time, as I understand it, the light was turned on was when you were under the bed."

"When I am under the bed and when I am about to enter the south closet."

"Yes. Was that after all the girls were out of there? Or was the light ever turned on while all the girls were seated there at any time?"

"No, sir."

"And, of course, that was for several hours, wasn't it?"

"Yes."

I brought out that the light was also off in Miss Schmale's room, and in Miss Amurao's room, the east bedroom. The only light came from the bathroom.

I carefully skipped questioning her about any aspect of the murders themselves, which would make it impossible for Martin to draw any further attention to the scene of horror on redirect examination after I was through with her. But I paid careful attention to her description of the killer and her subsequent identification of Speck.

''Well, to any of these policemen, did you describe the man that had been upstairs?''

''Yes, I described to them.''

''You described. And were they writing down?''

''Yes, they are.''

''And was that the description that you gave to Officer Leonard J. Ponne, 'a man, twenty-five years of age, six feet tall, short or crew-cut hair, no hat, wearing a black, waist-length jacket, dark pants'?''

''I did not say the 'crew cut,' sir.''

''So if Officer Ponne wrote that down, he's incorrect about that?''

''I did not say that, sir.''

''You didn't?''

''I did not.''

''Now you never told Officer Ponne that this man had marks on his face, did you?''

''I told him he have marks on his face.''

''And if he didn't write it down, he should have, is that correct?''

''I don't know if he wrote it down.''

She told of being given, later in the hospital, a book of pictures by the police.

''Well, now, tell me this. Did you see any pictures in that book that you commented upon?''

''I saw one picture that was similar to Speck.''

''You saw a picture in there?''

''Just one in that book.''

''Did you comment to the officer that this picture was similar to the man that was in the apartment?''

"Yes, I told them. I show it and I told them that it is similar to the man, to Speck."

"You said, 'This picture is similar?' "

"Yes, sir."

"And then he looked at the picture, didn't he?"

"Yes, the officer looked at the picture."

"Did you point out any other pictures that were similar?"

"No. They just gave me a picture that was loose. It was not in the book."

"Right. And then the police officer looked at the picture and the man that had been showing them to you, didn't he?"

"Yes, he did."

"Did the police artist look at the picture? Did the other policeman look at it?"

"I can't recall if he looked at the picture."

Then I questioned her about the loose picture she had viewed subsequently. This was the picture of Speck.

"You said this picture was more similar. Is that what you said?"

"It is more similar, the same as Speck."

"You said 'more similar,' isn't that right?"

"Yes."

"You didn't know Speck's name at that time, did you?"

"I don't know his name at the time."

I had to emphasize, through her testimony, that she had said the picture of Speck was "more similar" to the man she had seen the night before and that an identification had not been made on the basis of the picture. In other words, the defense had to attempt to reconstruct the precise scene at the time she was looking at the pictures.

"You never said to the artist, 'This is the man that was in the apartment,' did you?" I asked.

"I can't recall that I say that."

"You said that picture was more similar."

"The loose picture? Yes, it is more similar than the picture that was in the book."

"Sure. And you never said that was the man that was in the apartment?"

"I did not say that to the artist."

Further, on cross-examination, she told me she had told the policemen the killer had worn "black clothes" rather than a "black suit" as the police bulletin had it. She also stated that the police artist, who was already sketching from her description, did look at the picture that was shown her. But I also asked her about the artist himself, as a kind of memory test.

"Now the police artist that was sitting there drawing in a chair alongside of your bed, was he a white man or a colored man?"

"I don't know, sir, whether he was a white man or not. I can't recall."

She testified that she knew what a crew cut was, that she had emphasized to the artist that the hair was combed back and had not said a crew cut, but that "he just draw it like that." She said she had also told him about marks on the man's face. All the other description, she said, she didn't recall. Whether the artist had asked her about other facial details, she didn't remember.

"When you say, 'I can't recall,' does this mean you can't recall telling the artist or you can't recall about the man?"

"I can't recall about the man, about his ears, about his nose, or about his eyes, I can't recall."

"You can't recall anything of that, about the man that was in the apartment. Miss Amurao, you can't recall anything about the man that was in the apartment relative to his eyes, size of his eyes, or eyebrows?"

"No."

"Or you can't recall the man that was in the apartment, anything about his lips?"

"No, sir."

"And you can't recall anything about the man that was in the apartment, as to the shape or size of his ears or whether they were away from his head or close to his head?"

"I can't recall, sir."

I thought the points had been made and any further hammering them home could only result in an emotional backlash. But the questions had to be asked. There were no shortcuts to defending a man on trial for his life. After a recess, I discussed her first visit to Cermak Hospital, when she had not been allowed to view Speck.

"No one told you why you were there, what you had come there for, and no one told you why you had to leave?"

"When I am still there in the office somebody told me that the man was not yet ready."

"Well, did you have any idea then what you were there for?"

"I have an idea, sir. I have an idea that I am going to see somebody."

"To identify somebody?"

"Yes, to identify somebody, but nobody told me."

The next day she returned to the Cermak and was informed by Dr. Norcross that he would take her to one room. She was dressed in a nurse's uniform.

"Did he tell you that there would be one man in that bed, in that room?"

"He did not tell me there is one man or what. He just told me that I would — I just act like a nurse and don't excite that man because he has pericarditis."

She entered the room behind Dr. Norcross. She stood near the foot of the bed.

"And this man that was in bed, was there a sheet over him, were his legs or body covered with a sheet?"

"I can't recall whether his legs was covered with a sheet."

"And how long did you remain in the room?"

"I can't recall how long."

"Well, there weren't any other patients in any other beds, were there?"

"There is only one bed there and one patient."

"Well, then you went downstairs and they talked to you further downstairs?"

"Yes, sir."

"Dr. Norcross's office?"

"Yes. I just told them that is the man."

"As a matter of fact, wasn't it until you got downstairs that you told them that that was the man, in Dr. Norcross's office?"

"No, I was still upstairs when I told Mr. Wallenda that that is the man."

"You were outside the room?"

"Yes, I'm outside the room."

A few minutes later I ended it with, "All right. Thank you." I had avoided any reference to the rooms where the murders had been committed. Since Martin could cover on redirect only the material I had touched on in cross-examination, he excused her with "No further questions" and we recessed for lunch. I had tried to conduct the cross-examination more in the manner of a friendly conversation and to scrupulously avoid giving an impression that I was badgering her. But I felt I had brought forth some points that would be helpful to the jury in deciding the validity of the identification.

X

The most devastating move by the state came next when Martin introduced seven black-and-white photographs in evidence. Taken soon after the murders had been discovered, the pictures depicted the positions and conditions of the eight bodies. Immediately after Martin's move, I asked to be heard in chambers, where I argued heatedly for an hour and a half over the pictures. The photographs were grisly. There was one of a nude body of a strangled woman, and there was that particularly horrible one of a Filipino with her throat slit. You could see portions of the voice box hanging out. They were enough to make anyone shudder and I insisted they would be inflammatory and prejudicial to Speck's cause, without any other function. Judge Paschen overruled my objections.

Back in the courtroom, Martin handed the photos to the jury. Some of the jurors appeared to control their emotions with difficulty as they looked at them. The exhibits clearly made a deep emotional impact.

The pictures were introduced as part of the testimony of Detective Jack Wallenda. Wallenda described in detail how the bodies were found, their wounds, how they were bound or strangled. Following the viewing of the pictures, it became especially memorable testimony. The next day a pathologist, Dr. Eugene Tapia, provided detailed testimony of the cause of death for each of the eight victims. He counted thirty-three stab wounds on six of the women; one had been stabbed eighteen times. Four had been both strangled and stabbed; two died from stab wounds only, two from strangulation only. No physical findings of rape or sexual assault were offered in evidence. I did not cross-examine Dr. Tapia.

The state followed this with witnesses designed to trace Speck's movements from the morning of July 14 until his arrest two days later. A seaman told of meeting Speck in a bar at 11 A.M. on July 14 and going with him to the Shipyard Inn. He didn't recall seeing any blood on Speck's clothing at any time. The witness was "pretty well loaded" and Speck let him use his room. He testified that the bed had been slept in. They left together when Speck received a phone call about a job vacancy on the tanker docked in East Chicago, Indiana, which was near.

Rapidly, the witnesses testified to various aspects of Speck's movements in Chicago, as drinking partners, cab drivers, a dispatcher, citizens, and policemen took turns at the witness box. The state in this way traced Speck to room 806 of the Raleigh Hotel on North Dearborn. At this point, legal fireworks erupted again as Martin attempted to present evidence related to Speck's stay at the Raleigh: the pistol confiscation and evidence of Speck's having registered under another name. Judge Paschen earlier had ordered the pistol suppressed as evidence because it was seized without a search warrant. I also tried to suppress the state's questioning of the clerk at the Raleigh; Martin's purpose was to introduce evidence that Speck registered under an alias. I argued that the illegal police entry into

Speck's room rendered this testimony improper. But Judge Paschen overruled me. The clerk testified.

From there, Speck was traced to the Starr Hotel where he drank some more and met an alcoholic resident, who now appeared as a witness. Next came the policeman who had retrieved the bleeding Speck from the Starr in response to a 12:05 A.M., July 17 call. He said Speck had been slashed with a broken wine bottle. He took Speck to the hospital without realizing who he was. Then the hospital personnel testified.

XI

The state wound up its case with fingerprint evidence. These witnesses became the climax of the state's case and time and again Martin and I clashed in our forensic struggle over evidence. At one point while I was cross-examining one of the police crime lab technicians, Martin jumped to his feet and pounded his table as he objected to my approach. There were other moments when we both shouted at each other. Our arguments were not subdued even when Judge Paschen declared recesses to hear us in his chambers, as we did when I objected to admitting in evidence a fingerprint card on Speck that had been taken during his hospitalization.

One technician testified to finding three fingerprints on the door to the master bedroom of the townhouse, where the victims had been bound. Two prints were near the door knob; another was found the next day toward the bottom of the door. Over my objections, the actual door was brought into the courtroom and the technician, William Scanlon, used it to demonstrate to the jury how he looked for prints.

On cross-examination I brought out through Scanlon that, in all, a total of thirty-four palm and fingerprints had been found in the townhouse. There were a total of thirty-two fingerprints. Prints had been found on a water glass, a file box on a first floor desk, a window frame in the kitchen, another bedroom door, and a towel rack downstairs. There were fine clear prints from the same hand on the water glass.

Scanlon's testimony was the state's first step in presenting the three fingerprints alleged to be Speck's. But I was able to make clear that twenty-nine other fingerprints and two palm prints had also been found. Later, it would be made clear, these definitely did not belong to Speck or any known persons who had entered that house.

Lieutenant Emil G. Giese took the stand. He was from the police department's fingerprint identification section.

On direct examination Giese explained the basic principles of identification through fingerprints and that he had never known of duplication. He compared the three prints found on the door to prints taken from Speck in the hospital and from Speck's Coast Guard card.

"Do you have an opinion on whether the same person made the latent prints, and those on the card?" Martin asked.

"Yes. My opinion is they are identical with the digits I have indicated and therefore were made by the same individual."

He stated that the fingers making the prints had been the middle and index fingers of the right hand and the middle finger of the left hand. Two of the prints, he said, had seventeen points of similarity and one of them had ten. In no case, he testified, would more than twelve points of identity be required for positive identification in comparing them. He called the three prints "identical" with Speck's.

It was established, through Giese, that the police had not identified the remaining twenty-nine fingerprints. It was suggested that the three fingerprints alleged to be Speck's could have belonged to Miss Farris and Miss Davy. Giese admitted that the flow of ridges on one of Miss Davy's fingerprints ran in the same direction as those on a print taken from the door.

"But if you mean the same ridge characteristics, my answer is no," Giese said.

Giese could not be shaken.

Giese was an expert on fingerprint identification. Burton Behrke was also an expert. But Behrke never appeared as the concluding expert witness for the state. Instead, they called a surprise witness to the stand — Andre Moenssens.

I was shocked. Moenssens, a fingerprint expert from Chicago's Institute of Applied Sciences, was to have been a witness for the defense! He was to have been my own fingerprint expert.

Immediately I approached the bench and requested a recess. The attorneys and Judge Paschen retreated to the judge's chambers to argue it out. Already the court had ruled that Martin was to provide the defense with a list of witnesses. Moenssens, of course, was not on any list that the state had given me. There had been no indication that he would be called as a prosecution witness.

Moenssens had, in effect, given me a short course in fingerprinting and I intended to call him to the stand to ask only one question. I had paid him fifty dollars for his time, but this was a mere token, considering the time he had given me and the quality of his instruction. But after I had paid him for his services I considered the state's subpoenaing him to be an underhanded deed that should not be permitted legally.

The judge allowed him to testify, but Judge Paschen did stand up for the defense on the one occasion when the state wanted to ask Moenssens if he had consulted with me. Judge Paschen ruled that they could not couple the witness with me.

Martin gave Moenssens a card containing Speck's fingerprints. His attack was to be on the defense contention that one of the prints could have been left by one of the nurses, Miss Farris, instead of Speck. We had claimed the print was smudged at the core and was insufficient for identification.

"Did you make a comparison between that card and the latent print found near the bottom of the door?" asked Martin.

"Yes, I did," said Moenssens.

"What did you determine?"

"I determined that the latent print on the door was identical with the Number Eight [middle finger, left hand] print on this card."

In reply to a question, Moenssens said he had studied the prints during the noon hour. The opposition wanted me to ask him, on cross, how he had learned so much in such a short time.

Of course, he would have had to reveal that he had seen the prints before, as my tutor. I'd have been a fool to have asked that. I had been hit in the head a lot in my early trials by asking questions when I didn't know the answers. I had learned that lesson long ago.

On cross, I did what I could regarding the print.

''It doesn't have a delta, does it?''

''The core area is smudged, yes,'' he said. A core is the inner loop of a fingerprint, and a delta is a sort of V-mark made where two lines come together.

Then I asked him the one question I had planned to ask him as a witness for the defense.

''And if there were one unexplained point of dissimilarity, then it would be disqualified, wouldn't it?''

''Yes, sir.''

''And the core can't be seen where it is smudged, can it?''

''It cannot.''

''It is a partial print, right?''

''It is.''

So if, under the smudge, a point of dissimilarity should be found, the entire print would be thrown out. But who could tell what lay in the smudge?

On redirect, Martin asked, ''You didn't find any point of dissimilarity, is that right?'' Moenssens hadn't. He agreed with Martin that the two prints — the one on the card and the one on the door — were identical.

''And you don't need a full print to make an identification?''

''No, sir.''

''Partial print is sufficient?''

''Yes, sir.''

Hours later, after we had completed a series of arguments in chambers, we returned to the courtroom and Martin said, ''May it please the court, ladies and gentlemen of the jury, the state will rest its case.''

There had been forty-one witnesses and more than one hundred exhibits placed in evidence for the prosecution. You had to acknowledge it as an extremely strong case, particularly if you believed the eyewitness identification and the infallibility of the fingerprint experts.

XII

"I've never seen anybody like him, which makes him a little kookie," I told members of Speck's family. "He's not worried a bit! He made me promise I'd either get him the electric chair or, as he called it, the nuthouse. I told him I couldn't try for the electric chair, there are too many others trying to get the chair for him.

"He says, 'I must have done it 'cause the girl says I did and they have these fingerprints, so I must have.' But he doesn't remember and he can't tell me he did it.

"It's a bad case. The multiple accusations and the wide publicity alone are enough to make it that."

XIII

Speck absolutely would not take the stand in his own defense. There was no way I could induce him to do so. It traced back to his old phobia of reciting or being in front of people and having them stare at him. It was no exaggeration that he feared the witness chair more than the electric chair.

In his defense I called eight members of his family: his mother, five sisters, a brother, and a brother-in-law. For one thing I wanted the jury to see that he came from a decent family. Their appearances were brief. Two of the sisters cried. His mother blew Speck a kiss and waved a small handkerchief at him as she left.

His sister and brother-in-law in Chicago told of giving Speck money and of helping him in various ways. She said that policemen had come to their home on July 15, seeking Speck, and one had asked if he had a crew cut. No, she had said. "Well, he does now," she quoted the officer as saying. Her husband told of giving Speck some of his T-shirts. Most of them, he said, were Fruit-o'-the-Loom and BVD brands. (Of the three T-shirts in evidence — two found at the townhouse, one taken off Speck at the hospital — two were BVD and one was Hanes and all three were size 38-40.)

The first nonfamily witness for the defense was a welder who had shot pool with Speck at the Shipyard Inn on the night of July 13. This had been several minutes before 9 P.M. He testified he had not seen Speck in any of the booths and that Speck was wearing a red shirt and brown boots. Neither color, the jurors would remember, had been associated with the man in the townhouse.

XIV

"Somebody's going to get Speck."

The person didn't identify himself. He called the courthouse and then hung up. The word was passed on to the sheriff. It was interpreted as a threat on Speck's life and possible danger to others in the courtroom.

Without explaining what had happened, everyone in the courtroom was told to file out in an orderly manner. All were searched again, as they had been each time they entered. The courtroom was searched. No weapon was found. Court resumed.

XV

Speck's fingerprints were scarred. But the fingerprint experts had failed to show these scars on the prints found in the townhouse. I introduced thirteen exhibits, mostly of the unidentified fingerprints, but also the prints of two of the victims, and a police drawing of the suspect as originally depicted. I wanted the jurors to be given magnifying glasses with which to examine the fingerprints already identified as being Speck's. But Judge Paschen sustained the state's objections. You can't compare prints without a magnifying glass. I had hoped to show smudges in key areas that would indicate how defective was the state's evidence. Instead, now they would be taking Lieutenant Giese's word for it — jurors who were supposed to be triers of the facts.

Doherty, Gramenos, and I spent three hours in the law library, looking for a precedent. We didn't find one acceptable to the court. We reconvened.

XVI

I called Elliott Dufrayer to the stand.

Dufrayer was a lean, soft-spoken man who tended bar at Kay's Pilot House, a mile and a half from the townhouse.

"Calling your attention to July 13, 1966, did you see Richard Speck?" I asked him after a few preliminaries.

"Yes, I did, at Kay's Pilot House."

"And what time was that?"

"Well, the first time was around eight o'clock."

"And did you have any conversation with him?"

"Not the first time, except he ordered a drink and I fixed it for him."

"What kind of a drink did he order?"

"He drank VO and Coke."

"And where did he sit?"

"He sat in the first booth as you come in the door."

"Could you describe how he was dressed?"

"Yes, sir. He had on a red shirt."

After one drink, Dufrayer said, Speck took the glass back to the bar where he had picked it up and said, "I'll see you." It was 8:30 P.M. or later.

Dufrayer had described Speck's pock-marked face and said, "I thought at first he was a German sailor. I don't know why, but that's what I thought." As for his paying attention to Speck's identification, Dufrayer said, "It was very slow that night. We usually are very busy, but not on that night."

"On July 13, a Wednesday, did you see him at any other time?" I asked.

"Yes, sir, I did."

"What time did you see him?"

"It was very close to midnight."

On the second visit, he said, Speck asked for a hamburger and chips with it. Dufrayer explained that chips went with the order. "He sat at the first stool at the lunch counter and stayed quite a while." The bartender supplied a rather precise description. "I noticed a tattoo on his right arm that contained the word 'Shirley.' It was a crude mark."

Dufrayer said he put the hamburger patty on the grill for Speck but that his wife served it.

"And how did you fix the time that he was in there?" I asked.

"At twelve o'clock, Arco Door Company has their break, and they were in for about ten minutes and they drink as much as they can in that time. I put a hamburger down for him and I had to get the wife to finish it."

"Now, can you tell us how long — what time he left?"

"Well, I fix the time at between 12:15 and 12:30."

He said the police had returned, after a preliminary interview of him, and had talked to him again, telling him, "Well, you must be wrong, because the killer entered there at 11." Dufrayer testified, "So I said, 'You must have the wrong man and the murderer is still walking around.' "

I asked him, "And you're sure that that was the man that was in Kay's Pilot House on those dates at that time?"

"I would stake my life on it."

Martin cross-examined gingerly. He limited his emphasis to whether or not Dufrayer was certain about the time. But the body of Dufrayer's testimony he left intact. Dufrayer was an impressive witness and told his story with obvious honesty without a trace of personal interest in it.

Mrs. Sophie Dufrayer, the bartender's wife and a mother of four, substantiated her husband's testimony next as a defense witness. She was the waitress and short order cook. She told of Speck's being in the tavern twice that night, the first time between 8 and 8:30 P.M.

"Did you see Richard Speck any other time that evening?"

"Yes, he returned."

"What time was that?"

"It was after 11:30."

"And how do you set the time?"

"Well, usually it is a routine that I have with the workers coming in; I usually try to wash the dishes between 11:30 and 12 at night."

"When you saw Richard Speck there, did he have anything to eat or drink, the second time he came in?"

"Yes, I served him a hamburger and he drank a glass of ice water."

"Now the second time that he was in there, what time did he leave?"

"Well, the workers left at ten after twelve, and he must have stayed ten or fifteen minutes after they left."

I also established that the Dufrayers had first refused to talk with me when I was searching for witnesses whose testimony might benefit Speck. It also came out that she and her husband had talked with policemen and state's attorney's investigators about the time of Speck's second trip to the Pilot House. Weeks after the crimes, she said, Assistant State's Attorney John F. Glenville visited them at their work. "He wanted to know were we sure of the time," she said. "We said we were definitely sure of the time. He asked if we could be mistaken — was it before that time? We said no."

I asked her if she was positive that Speck was in the tavern after midnight.

"I am sure that's the man."

"On cross-examination, Martin asked, "You recall, Mrs. Dufrayer, that you told Mr. Glenville on Friday, July 22, that the defendant came in sometime between 8:45 and 9 and left between 9:15 and 9:30."

"No," she said, "he assumed maybe he could have come in at that time."

"You never made the statement that he came in sometime between 8:45 and 9 and left sometime — "

"I told him — when I told him it was around 7:30 to 8:30 he said, 'Well, give or take, could it have been 8:30 to 9:30?' and I never answered him."

He asked about her looking at a clock and she replied that she did so to determine when she should go to the kitchen to wash dishes before the large group of workers would be due. The time for this would be after 11, around 11:30 P.M.

On redirect, I referred to her interrogators' checking of the tavern's clock for accuracy on the day she and her husband were taken to the state's attorney's office.

"We told him the clock was six minutes fast," she said, "and he called and he said the clock was seven minutes fast."

On recross, Martin asked if she had studied the clock that night and she said, in substance, no, but that she had to watch the clock to be ready for the workers, who sometimes would call orders in ahead of time. And she also usually watched the clock around the time she would have to go to the kitchen and clean it up.

Mrs. Dufrayer stepped down from the witness chair. I introduced two pictures of Speck's tattooed arms, to corroborate the couple's testimony. Then I returned to my place at the defense counsel's table. It was almost five o'clock that Thursday afternoon. It had been a long day.

"The defense rests."

I didn't have anything else. It was as simple as that.

XVII

Much of my mail during the Speck case was revolting. Many writers had sadistic plans for the defendant — and for me. A few made direct threats that they were "going to take care" of me. They didn't have the guts to sign their letters. But as the trial started in Peoria, an interesting thing happened. I began receiving more nice letters than nasty ones. People were beginning to realize, "Well, gee, there is some equality in our laws." Some letters said, "Now that we see and now that we hear this evidence, and know what it is, we don't believe Richard Speck is guilty.'' Others wrote from foreign countries. They were amazed at how a man who had no funds could have such an extensive trial. Those were from nations where they don't have jury trials. I think some of them were smuggled out.

When we received our mail at the courthouse in Peoria, I would open mine there in the judge's chambers with the opposing lawyers present. Some letters were actually signed with verdicts: Not Guilty, or Guilty. I would open them and read the decisions aloud. ''Not Guilty.'' Then, ''Guilty.'' I never saw any evidence that it contributed to the opposition's mental health.

XVIII

Judge Paschen recessed the next day, which was a Friday, so that he and the opposing attorneys could discuss the instructions he would give the jury on Saturday. If we lawyers couldn't agree on specific instructions, then he would rule. We had no problems. It was as if the state's attorneys knew they had a winner. They seemed willing to agree to anything, short of ordering a not guilty verdict.

XIX

Slender, intense George Murtaugh, one of Martin's assistants, opened for the state in the final argument. He rapidly strode into a bitter denunciation of Speck as one with ''the face, the mind, the heart of a murderer.'' He verbally, and emotionally, reenacted the horrible crimes, comparing Speck to a wolf among sheep, a hawk among chickens. As for the fingerprints, he said, ''Speck may just as well have signed his name.'' He referred to Miss Amurao and her testimony. ''She has a life that will be left indelibly marked by that man's face and that man's talk.'' It was ''the most enormous heinous crime this world has ever seen and I hope to God never sees again.'' Going over Miss Amurao's testimony he emphasized the merciless way in which the victims had died, naming each of them. Then he said,

"Remove this cancer! Remove it like you would remove a bad tooth!"

At one point Speck muttered, "I'd like to get George out in the hall." You could hear it while Murtaugh was speaking. Judge Paschen whispered to a deputy to quiet the defendant.

XX

Days before we made our final arguments to the jury, I had begun making notes in my trial book for my closing argument to the jury. I knew the strongest part of the state's case was the fingerprints. So I carefully went over much of the testimony concerning the prints, in order to highlight the incompleteness of the prints alleged to be Speck's.

As I began, I emphasized that the jury must adhere to the principle of presuming innocence until the defendant had been proved guilty — and beyond a reasonable doubt — not in the headlines but by the evidence produced in that courtroom.

"I'm relying on the evidence in this case. I'm not relying on pointing my finger at a stranger and calling him a murderer, as has my young colleague on the other side of the table. You know, sometimes young men think lightly of taking a man's life." As for capital punishment, I admonished, "You can't just look at a man and do it for revenge at the urging of an assistant state's attorney who does it to make a reputation."

I began reviewing the state's case. The identification. Definitely the murderer was in the apartment at 11 P.M. That was accepted by everyone. The man initially appeared at Miss Amurao's door and led her out. "From that moment on there were no lights in that room. The only light was in the bathroom, but when they went to and fro, the man was behind them. Now I don't want to say anything about that little girl, but I'm defending a man for his life." I questioned how well she was able to see him in that lighting and atmosphere.

As for Speck's money, which was purported to be from the victims, I reminded the jurors that a total of fifty dollars had been given him by his sister and brother-in-law.

I delved further into the identification, how the police had first sought a man with crew-cut hair, without marks on his face. The artist's sketch had portrayed the suspect thusly.

"Those marks are the most identifying marks a person can have. But it doesn't appear on the drawing. Yet she says she told the police artist that he had pockmarks and had long hair. But did the police artist take the stand? He was not called by the state. The policeman was not on the stand. They're not going to perjure themselves."

There was a haste to judgment, I insisted, brought about by "the higher-ups in the Chicago Police Department."

"All your lives you will have to wonder about that description. I don't want to say anything about that little girl. But I have a job to do. I asked her, Do you recall his lips? Do you recall his nose? Do you recall his ears? And she can't recall. 'You can't recall if you told that to the artist?' 'I can't recall.' Is that the type of identification you want? 'I can't recall the man.' "

I pointed out some discrepancies in witnesses' testimony and then I reached the fingerprint evidence, the three latent prints found on the south bedroom door. "I told you at the outset they were smudged prints. I think this has been established by state's witnesses." I also reminded them of other prints found in the townhouse, and how I had asked an expert if the prints of Miss Farris had the same ridge patterns as Richard Speck's and he had said yes. "And I asked him, 'If there were one point of dissimilarity on this smudged area, what would you do — discard it?' '*Yes! Yes!*'

"What about the twenty-nine unidentified prints and the two palm prints? They were matched with those who lived in the house and they're still unidentified. And on that glass there were five prints, possibly six. And where was that glass found? Downstairs, on that desk. And where was that BVD shirt found? Downstairs, on that desk. And where were these prints? On that box on the desk. And these they don't want to talk about. It seems that some killers are loose.

"How many were there? They want you to believe Richard Speck wore two T-shirts on a hot day. They also want you to believe he also wore a black jacket over two T-shirts in 95 degrees of heat."

I discussed Speck's flight. I described how the superintendent of Chicago's police, in his haste to judgment, had Speck's name and picture in the newspapers and on television. "What would you have done?" I asked the jurors. "You might have attempted to run, or if you're desperate you might try to kill yourself, and it just might have some effect on your mind — your name blaring out of every TV and newspaper."

I paused a moment. "Now after I am through speaking, I won't be able to talk to you again. But Mr. Martin has lived with this case, and Mr. Martin wants a conviction and so do the police department higher-ups want a conviction.

"Now that's the state's case. Do you want to kill somebody on *that?* Do you want to find somebody guilty on that evidence? I think not.

"But there are one or two other things in this case and that's Mr. and Mrs. Dufrayer's testimony. I've defended thousands of indigents. I've defended in more than four hundred jury trials. Now, when you say alibi witnesses, they are the best alibi witnesses I have ever seen — because of the way they came to Jerry Getty. I learned of them through the state because they had to give their list of witnesses to me."

I went over, in some detail, how the police had first discovered the Dufrayers and then wouldn't believe them. I emphasized how positive the couple had been. " 'I'd stake my life on it! ' Mr. Dufrayer said. A man who is the father of four sons, and his wife, a mother, a housewife and employed by her husband part time. Are you going to wonder about that? Are you ever going to wonder about that? That's where Richard Speck was. That's why there was a rush to judgment."

I asked them to "weigh the opinions — that's all it is. Test the identification. Why the two T-shirts? Why all the unidentified finger and palm prints?" Then there was Mr. and

Mrs. Dufrayer's testimony. "The state knew of them long before I did. They tried to shake 'em." Returning to the two T-shirts, I reminded them that the men who wore them "had been in there an hour and a half before Richard Speck left Kay's Pilot House." I urged them to make a proper decision.

I had considered dwelling more on arguments against the death penalty, perhaps putting the fear of God into some of the women jurors. But that tactic was fraught with risk. If I overdid it, they might think I thought my client was guilty — and then they'd have to give him death. So throughout my closing I concentrated on the evidence, which I by now hoped the professor or possibly two or three of the women would analyze as I had viewed it.

XXI

Bill Martin, in his rebuttal, described the death of each nurse while pointing at Speck. "He who would kick, slash, and strangle [he inserted a victim's name], he did not have the strength to take his own life. He knew there could be only one penalty for the crime."

He countered all my arguments.

"The defense's case boils down to Elliott and Sophie Dufrayer. They need be wrong but an hour and a half to put this man one and one-third miles away in a black shirt. You know the human mind is not a stopwatch. How long can you remember a certain time?" He described the scene as a busy bar with customers going in and out. "How can they know the exact time? But Corazon Amurao could never erase that face from her mind. She got up before man and God and took an oath" — he began shouting — "and before man and God she stood up and walked over and said, 'That's the man!' "

As for the crew cut on the artist's sketch, he said Miss Amurao's emotional state and her knowledge of English probably led to a misunderstanding. "All the defense talked about was a crew cut, crew cut, crew cut," he added softly. He dwelled on the fingerprint evidence and replied to a portion of my closing, "Two T-shirts are not so unusual for a man who is used to changing his shirts several times a day. Maybe he had his small bag with him."

He ended, "To live with your conscience for the rest of your life, you must sign a verdict of guilty and fix his punishment at death! Write that verdict not in vengeance, not in animosity, but write it in truth, because it is a proper verdict.

"Don't let it be said that you fled from your responsibility. Don't do the easy thing by just giving him a guilty verdict. Sign the verdict finding his punishment at death!"

XXII

"Members of the jury," began Judge Paschen in his well-modulated voice, "the evidence in this case has been completed, and I will now instruct you as to the law. The law applicable to this case is stated in these instructions and it is your duty to follow all of them. You must not single out certain instructions and disregard others.

"It is your duty to determine the facts, and to determine them only from the evidence in this case. You are to apply the law to the facts and in this way decide the case."

XXIII

Some friends I hadn't seen for years would drive to Peoria to sit in on sessions of the trial. And a lot of friends came from Dolton. For Gracia, who was later to become my second wife, the Speck trial was the first one she had ever seen and she found it to be "just like the movies."

Whatever the jury was thinking, I had convinced Gracia. She was so certain the defense had won the case that now she began worrying about Speck's safety. She was afraid that, once he was freed, somebody would immediately kill him! Many others sent in letters stating that he was not guilty.

XXIV

You always entertain the idea that there might be an acquittal, although I knew Speck had been convicted by the news media before he ever went to trial. If there had been no publicity, and if it had been one murder and not eight, on the basis of the testimony I would have expected a not guilty verdict. But I had been around criminal courtrooms long enough to know that it would take two miracles for them to find him not guilty and I expected them to reason, "If we can't give him the death penalty in this case where eight were killed, in what case can you ever give anybody the death penalty?"

The jury deliberated for forty-nine minutes. Then they returned to the courtroom and the foreman announced that a verdict had been reached.

Court Clerk Paul Trompeter read the first verdict.

"We, the jury, find the defendant, Richard Franklin Speck, guilty of the murder of Gloria Jean Davy, in the manner and form charged in the indictment and fix his punishment at death."

He repeated the sentence, changing only the name, seven times.

Speck didn't display any emotion. He had been expecting it. But he immediately suggested to me that maybe an appellate court would reverse it.

And, of course, the jury's recommendation of death was not binding on the judge. Later, after a mitigation hearing, he could make it consecutive life sentences — or any other penalty — if he wished.

The story that came out later was that the jury had agreed unanimously on Speck's guilt on the first ballot. But on the first two ballots, one man had refused to go along with the death sentence recommendation, without which the state could not execute the defendant. On the third, the holdout juror gave in.

XXV

Reporter Ray Brennan of the Chicago *Sun-Times* had hired two boys to hold open a first-floor pay telephone line to his newsroom in Chicago. When the verdicts were announced, a couple of hundred people waiting outside the courtroom, who hadn't been able to gain entrance, roared their approval. By the time the sheriff had quieted them, Brennan ran to the railing outside our second-floor courtroom and called down to a fellow *Sun-Times* reporter who had taken over the phone from the two boys.

"Guilty!" Brennan yelled. "Death — on each and every count."

This precipitated another roar.

XXVI

After so many years of trying cases, it was a personal shock to me to hear a death penalty verdict for the first time. Although a person might believe the evidence, incomplete as it was, I couldn't see how twelve persons could agree to send a man to his death on it. How could they be sure? I couldn't have been, had I been in their shoes. A conviction, maybe, but death, no. And yet as I thought about the pressures on the jury and the kind of case it was, perhaps the worst case a lawyer or twelve people can have, I couldn't say it was much of a surprise. But emotionally I was shocked by it.

Sometime later Jim Doherty reported to me that Federal Judge Alex Napoli, a veteran prosecutor and a former chief justice of the Criminal Court, had told him:

"Nobody could have won that case."

4. The Fight Against Death

Despite what he had told me on that autumn afternoon months before, I still had a glimmer of hope that Judge Paschen wouldn't give Speck death. Under Illinois law, the jury's recommendation of death was not binding. The judge could do as he pleased.The jury had not heard psychiatric evidence as to Speck's mental condition. At the hearing prior to formal sentencing, Judge Paschen would have information that the jury had not known.

Judge Paschen understood life and psychiatry. He realized that the majority of the American people did not think the death penalty was doing the country any good.

Because any hope for mitigation was only a glimmer, I was prepared to carry the appeal as far as might be necessary to save the defendant's life. I have never believed in capital punishment. How can society justifiably take a life? Only one can take life, I believe, and that is the one who gives life, God himself.

Thus, following Speck's conviction, the case went into a new stage. First, I would seek to prevent his being sentenced to death. That failing, I would appeal the convictions and sentences, asking for a new trial or reduction of sentence.

My motion for a new trial alleged fifty-five errors, ranging from the court's allowing photographs of the victims to be shown the jury to the judge's overruling various defense objections. It was a Herculean task to analyze the trial record, which amounted to nearly 10,000 pages, including the pre-trial motions. But after lengthy argument Judge Paschen denied the motion.

The next hearing was held by mutual consent in Cook County. On the basis of this hearing the judge would pass sentences.

Jim Doherty and Fred Cohn assisted me. Before the hearing proper was under way, we attempted to obtain further tests. Our first witness was Dr. Frederic Andrew Gibbs, professor of neurology at the University of Illinois School of Medicine. Dr. Gibbs was in charge of the electroencephalography laboratories there.

Doherty asked him if Speck's EEG, recorded months before, was absolutely normal.

"No," responded Dr. Gibbs, "this is not a perfectly normal electroencephalogram."

"Can you tell us why, Doctor?"

"Because it contains some suspicious features, some slow

waves, particularly in the frontal and parietal areas, and some spoke-like patterns."

The doctor wouldn't say there was organic damage; he would want a more complete test before expressing an opinion. At first Judge Paschen seemed to have agreed to a further test, a 10-channel EEG test which was expected to be more thorough than the previous 8-channel one. We already had a hospital in Des Plaines where we could hold the examination.

Martin objected strenuously. Judge Paschen changed his mind. There would be no new test.

In the formal hearing that followed, Martin called Dr. Vladimir G. Urse to the stand.

"Dr. Urse," asked Martin, "were you, in effect, the chairman of a panel of five psychiatrists and one surgeon which was appointed by Judge Paschen to examine the defendant Richard Franklin Speck?"

He replied, "I hate to think of it as a chairman. I'm inclined to think more of it as a workhorse of the group trying to get things together and put them together and contact the various and sundry people in the times that it became necessary to contact them. They, in a sense, shall I say, elected me or, shall I say, foisted upon me this job."

It was this point that led me to believe that the panel had performed much like a jury, even to the similarity of electing a foreman.

Under direct examination by Martin, Dr. Urse stated that he considered the previous EEG "adequate medically" to support the medical verdicts that had been given.

Dr. Urse did not believe an epileptic furor had been a factor in the eight slayings. He cited Dr. Grinker's opinion that "it was not an epileptic furor and it could not be lasting four hours." The defense had brought up the possibility of Speck's having been in an epileptic furor on the night of the murders, and we were trying to have the court order sound sleep and alcohol provocative tests, which we thought might turn up evidence that would give the judge a broader view of the case. But an electroencephalographer and neurologist who followed Dr. Urse to the stand both testified that they didn't think deep sleep or alcohol tests would prove useful in the Speck case.

Judge Paschen said, "As interesting as it might be for scientific study, I am not interested in that at this time. I am not interested in making Richard Franklin Speck a guinea pig for history — "

"Well — " I began.

" — As far as I'm concerned," he finished.

"I never intended that he be a guinea pig," I said.

"I'm not saying that you did. I'm only interested in any mitigation, and I don't see where it can be of any value. After considering it, after hearing from members of the panel, I therefore sustain the state's objection and deny your motion."

I then called to the stand Dr. Ner Littner of the Institute of Psychoanalysis and medical director of its child therapy training program. Dr. Littner had examined Speck in February, before the trial.

I asked him, "Well, Doctor, on the basis of your examination, would you say that this defendant here, Richard Franklin Speck, is suffering from any mental disease or that there was anything wrong with his mind?"

"I consider that he, at the time that I examined him, was suffering from a serious mental disease," replied Dr. Littner.

We then examined the sociopathic, or psychopathic, personality classification that other psychiatrists had assigned Speck. The term sociopathic referred to "an individual who handles excessive anxiety and tension in his mind basically by criminal behavior or antisocial behavior," Dr. Littner said.

I asked, "Now, the sociopathic personality, does that type of person have less control than a person that was normal or not termed that? Let's say, less control of his emotions, his acts?"

"It would depend upon the kind of situation in which he is," said Dr. Littner. "If he is in a situation where tension is not being stirred up in his mind, then he would have normal control of his behavior. If, however, he is in a situation which, because he is particularly vulnerable to some aspect of that situation, if that situation stirs up in his mind a great deal of tension and anxiety and conflict, then the resulting behavior would not be under his control."

"Would he be able to control his acts in accordance with law?" I asked.

Dr. Littner replied, "Even though he could be completely aware of the requirements of the law, the tension within him, which automatically triggers the behavior, would cause him to commit antisocial behavior and he would not have any control of that antisocial behavior, even though he knows that it is antisocial. It's similar to someone who is in acute panic who might do things that are completely uncontrollable and which, if he were not in a panic, he would never do."

"Now," I said, "I also note in this combined report, where it is stated or after it is stated 'sociopathic personality,' there is a comma and it states, 'antisocial behavior with alcoholism.' Now, would a person that is a sociopathic personality, [with] antisocial behavior, if he had alcohol, what effect would that have?"

"You appreciate that this is an attempt to pigeonhole the various symptoms that the individual has, and people who have sociopathic personalities can have different kinds of behavior, so this is merely specific elaboration of this. And what is being referred to in this is a person who, when he is in a pressure cooker situation that stirs up all kinds of tension in his mind, uses a variety of ways for discharging or dealing with this tension. He uses alcoholism as a way of dealing with this tension, he uses antisocial behavior as a way of dealing with this tension, so that if it is a pressure cooker situation, as I said, he will not have control over the resulting behavior. Then one gets a secondary problem. If he is using alcoholism as a way of dealing with internal tension, the alcoholism itself can, secondarily, cause difficulties with control of behavior, so that there then would be a double problem with controlling impulses."

"Now, you previously told us, Doctor, that, from your examination, Richard Franklin Speck was suffering from a mental disease at the time of your examination. Now, how long would you say that this mental disease had been present?"

"Using as clues to the presence of the mental disease evidences of excessive anxiety or tension or ways of handling anxiety and tension, in my opinion he has been suffering from this disease at least since the age of thirteen. And there is present in his history evidence that the roots of his disease existed at least back to the age of six. I have no history of Mr. Speck's development prior to the age of six and so am unable to say whether there were evidences of the beginnings of the disease before six."

He discussed symptoms that included Speck's headaches, blurring vision, dizzy spells. There was a series of self-destructive acts that went back to the age of five. Then there was his problem of relating to others, his deviating from his family's pattern, and his trouble-proneness.

"The final series of clues that I would use to judge the presence of this mental disease has to do with his whole life pattern. He has tried, he has tried many times. He tried to manage school, he has tried to work at jobs, he has tried a marriage. He has not been successful in any of them. He has never been able to manage these steps of growing up and becoming a man. And this attempt to try, or the failure to succeed, I would consider evidence of a serious mental disease in his mind."

As a focal point, Dr. Littner described the job that shortly before the murders Speck had been offered but had lost to another man.

"I would see the expectation of getting the job and then being told at the last minute that a man with greater seniority had gotten it as being a straw that would really stir up this whole sense of jealousy. Once more another man had gotten something that he wanted and it would stir up the more basic problem, which is the anger of the women whom he thinks really prefer other men to him."

This brought us to July 13, 1966.

Dr. Littner continued, "There is some evidence that suggests that that particular Wednesday he was living in a pressure cooker in his mind. This evidence has to do with the fact that he drank all day, one of the typical methods for relieving tension. He took a lot of pills, apparently; and, apparently, he got from some stranger he met an intravenous injection which he knew nothing about. Then he describes the situation where he was involved with a prostitute and he was unable to be potent with her. Having paid for her services, he then turned her over to some other men whom he had been drinking with, if they wished to avail themselves of her services. I would see this whole patterning of that Wednesday as indications of an overwhelming amount of tension in his mind that he was trying to stop up by all of these various devices."

"Now, Doctor," I said, "if these special situations existed in this period prior to July 13, and if they triggered antisocial behavior in Richard Speck, would you say that this resulting antisocial behavior was under his control?"

"I would consider that this antisocial behavior, that would be a part of his typical pattern of reacting to overwhelming tension, would not be under his control at all. He would have no ability to control it."

"Could he control himself in accordance with the law?"

"Under those special pressure cooker situations, even though he might be completely aware of the dictates of the law, I do not think he would be able to control his behavior."

"Now, Doctor, if such a mental disease, as you have described was present in Richard Speck when you examined him — do you think that it is still present? If so, what mental treatment would you recommend and why?"

"I'm unaware of anything that has happened to Mr. Speck since that time in February when I saw him that could have helped him correct this mental disease, so that I would say that, as of now, I think he is still suffering from this serious mental disease. Speaking as a psychiatrist, in terms of the question of what can be done for a person with this kind of mental disease, if I may say so, it would seem to me that if we kill Mr. Speck, we have gained nothing. We haven't solved anything, we prevent nothing. If, instead, he is confined and there is made available to him intensive psychoanalytic treatment, there is a possibility that all of us may gain something. Perhaps he can get somewhat more peace of mind and perhaps we can learn a little bit more, so that we can do something about preventing or diagnosing or treating the Richard Specks of tomorrow."

When Dr. Littner had completed his testimony and Martin had cross-examined, I summarized the defense's case. I explained to the court that I had been unable to have a psychiatric defense, for that would be tantamount to pleading my client guilty and I could not have done that because Speck had not told me he was guilty. Thus I had been forced to wait until the day of mitigation to present my psychiatric evidence.

Then I talked about the death penalty. I argued it was not a deterrent to crime. I pointed out that when the death penalty is abolished, the murder rate declines, and that surveys showed that states without the death penalty have fewer murders.

"A deterrent? Within one hour after the verdict in this case — and it was all over radio and TV — in the very city of of Peoria, there was a murder that took place in the course of a holdup."

There was one other point.

"Your honor didn't want to make Mr. Speck a guinea pig by letting three other doctors examine him, but if the death penalty is given in this case, he will be a legal guinea pig. He will be through all the courts in the land, if it's not reversed in our Illinois Supreme Court. Lord knows how long this will go on."

It didn't do any good. In Peoria several days later, on June 5, 1967, Judge Paschen pronounced the death penalty and read the execution order.

Speck was to die on September 1, 1967.

5. A Case Is Closed

When I first returned to Chicago after the trial had finished, I felt years older. I had dark shadows under my eyes and I was tired. It had taken a lot out of me. After the formal sentencing in June, 1967, I felt I deserved a vacation and I flew to Hawaii for a week of swimming, sunning, and relaxing. It was the first respite I had had since learning of the case in July, 1966.

There was one small personal gain — I knew I would never smoke again. I had come close to smoking a few times during those stress-filled days, but I hadn't. I had quit for good.

With the sentencing done, the longest phase of the case began, with our primary goal being to save the defendant's life. In death cases, appeal to the Illinois Supreme Court was automatic. The law required it. The state might finally electrocute Speck, but it would be long after the date set by Judge Paschen.

Speck himself was very much aware of the importance of our appeal and, although he had once indicated he preferred the chair to a life in prison, he obviously had changed his mind by September when I received a letter from him in Stateville Prison.

Hello Mr. Getty,

Well hear I am at last, and how are you doing, just fine I hope. By all mean's dont get sick and die on me ok. If you should feel a cold coming on by all mean's stop what you are doing and go see a doctor you hear. Because the day you go, more likely I will go right after you, so stay in good health. . . . Well Mr Getty I got to let you go for now it is time for the officer to give me a Rub down and tuck me in bed and read me a bed time story befor I go to sleep ha ha.

In a case like Speck's, appeal involved a mountain of work. After all, it had taken six weeks to get a jury and two weeks to try the case. In all, I had made thirty-five motions by the time the trial was over, and had researched the law. Of those thirty-five motions, twenty had been granted, fifteen denied. Doherty, Gramenos, Marshall J. Hartman, and I had to analyze the entire record. It easily could have become a full-time task, yet Speck was but one of the 10,000 clients under indictment whom my office represented in a year.

The defense presented twenty-two distinct points of argument. Alleged errors included the denial of a change of venue from Peoria, the court's refusal to allow the jury to use magnifying glasses while examining fingerprints, admission of photographs of the victims "whose sole purpose could only be to inflame the jury," the state's calling of *my* fingerprint witness, denying substitution of judges, improperly directing of a verdict of competency, denying of a bifurcated trial, and refusing to allow a complete EEG. We knew the photographs had made deep impressions on the jury; we had interviewed several jurors and they had admitted it.

In June, 1968, while we were still working on the appeal, the U.S. Supreme Court ruled that a "hanging jury" that had automatically excluded veniremen opposed to capital punishment could not constitutionally impose the death penalty. This decision came from the appeal of William C. Witherspoon, who had been on Cook County's Death Row since 1960 for the murder of a Chicago policeman. In the Speck case, I had asked Judge Paschen to rule against qualifying jurors for the death penalty. Citing the Witherspoon decision, I now noted that more than 250 veniremen had been excused because of their conscientious or religious scruples against capital punishment.

Our deadline for mailing our appeal to the Illinois Supreme Court was July 22, 1968, more than a year after sentencing. Because of the importance of the case and the number of our points, our brief came to 193 printed pages. Appeal briefs were limited to seventy-five pages. In order to obtain a waiver of the rule on length I had to appear before Justice Thomas E. Kluczynski. He granted it.

That September, Doherty, Gramenos, and I argued the case before the Illinois Supreme Court. In November the court affirmed the lower court's decision and sentence. Speck remained under a death order. The next step became the U.S. Supreme Court.

Like many other condemned Americans, Speck's life was extended by an indefinite stay of execution that became a part of the U.S. Supreme Court's "moratorium" on executions. In June, 1972, this highest court in the land had virtually abolished capital punishment. The Speck appeal was sent back to the Illinois Supreme Court, citing the Witherspoon decision. In

October, 1972, the Illinois Supreme Court directed the trial court to resentence Speck to "a sentence other than death."

In the meantime, Judge Paschen had died and Cook County Judge Richard J. Fitzgerald was assigned to replace him in the case. The resentencing was to be held in Peoria, because the trial had been held there. The state flew Speck down in the governor's plane, for security reasons.

I was now in private practice, no longer the Public Defender, and had a great number of cases ready for trial. Since I had represented Speck all the way, I continued to do so without fee, at his request, in what was apparently to be his last court appearance. He still didn't remember what had happened to him on the night of July 14, 1966, he told me, and he was unable to take the stand to make a personal plea for clemency. That old phobia that had kept him mute even in the earlier mitigation hearing now still governed him.

"Are you going to lock him up? Sure — for a long time. But are we going to do it without any hopes, without any chance of his rehabilitating himself?" I asked in closing. "All our religions teach us charity, and charity is love, and this means that no man in the eyes of God, no man is beyond rehabilitation.

"Leave it up to professionals to determine when he should be rehabilitated — if ever. There should be some escape hatch. I'm not asking for the impossible, but I'm asking what the philosophy of our law is. We know of many prisoners who, after they are sentenced, do become responsible citizens — and this man should have that opportunity."

Judge Fitzgerald didn't see it my way. Although he cut down the sentence considerably from the state's recommendation, he sentenced Speck to eight consecutive terms of 50 to 150 years in the penitentiary. Put another way, it amounted to from 400 to 1,200 years. Speck would die in prison, but not in the electric chair.

It was November 21, 1972. More than six years had elapsed since I was appointed in the case. It had been a long, hard fight against death. Now it was over. The case was closed.

CHAPTER 16

Making Law in the Higher Courts

THE DEFENDANT may be innocent — or guilty. Nonetheless, he deserves a fair and impartial trial. It is the job of the public defender to ensure that he gets one, even if it means appealing to higher courts. A fair trial might have no influence in changing a guilty verdict, but there are times when it could mean the difference between life and death, as in the case of Lawrence Brzeska.

Brzeska was a tall, slender youth, nineteen at the time he was charged with the murder of Policeman Webster Simard in one of the villages out in the county. The state's case was that Brzeska had come out shooting when Simard and his partner had stopped to inspect a parked car around two o'clock one morning. Simard had been mortally wounded; his partner, seriously wounded. The partner had later identified Brzeska. Other evidence, including a footprint cast and Brzeska's statement, was introduced.

Charlie Bellows, as private counsel, represented Brzeska. He admittedly had a tough case. Any cop-killing is. The case was further complicated by the prosecutor's approach in his closing argument to the jury, a particularly searing statement that was aimed at clinching a death verdict.

The prosecutor minced no words. "Are you going to allow this defendant to go back to the county jail and tell the other inmates he had a lawyer that hoodwinked the jury into saving his life?"

But the heart of the state's closing was an unusual plea designed to strap Brzeska into the electric chair.

"I believe that any man who wilfully takes away the life of another, as this man took away Webster Simard's life — that his life should be forfeited. And if you have any qualms about taking his life, put it on me; I will take it. I will take it any day in the week. I will take full responsibility for his life, and if you give him the death penalty, blame me, because there never was a case like this in the criminal court, where a defendant deserves the death penalty more than this man deserves it. . . . There is only one verdict in this case, ladies and gentlemen, and as I said before, that if you have any feelings that you should not give the death penalty, give the responsibility to me. I will take it, because no case ever deserved it like this one."

The jury gave Brzeska the chair.

Bellows appealed the case, and won, saving his client from the chair. The Illinois Supreme Court reversed it primarily on the basis of the prosecutor's statements and conduct before the jury. "Every defendant, whether he be good or bad, guilty or innocent, has the right to a trial by jury and not by a reviewing court," the state supreme court justices noted.

As for the closing argument by the state, the Supreme Court noted:

"It is beyond the scope of proper argument to suggest that the responsibility for a verdict of guilty or a death penalty may be placed upon the state's attorney. The jury may not avoid the duty to form its own conclusion by taking the word of the prosecution on the matter of defendant's guilt, or by resolving any doubts it may have by considering the state's attorney's willingness to assume responsibility. Statements suggesting or inducing it to do so are clearly improper and prejudicial."

By this time, Brzeska and his father were out of money and

the defendant faced a new trial for murder of the policeman. This brought him to the public defender's office. I was appointed to represent him.

It remained a tough case. It was extremely difficult to select a jury. At one point we had agreed on seven jurors and had gone through seventy-nine veniremen when I was questioning a prospective juror.

"Do you have an open and free mind? You haven't formed an opinion as to his guilt or innocence, have you?" I asked him.

Instead of saying no or yes, he blurted out, "I think he's guilty!"

This, of course, could have had an influence on the seven jurors already in the box. A mistrial was declared by the judge and we started all over. A new venire was empaneled. This time we went through 115 veniremen before getting our jury.

It was a long, hard trial with the state and defense going all out with everything we had.

The jury found Brzeska guilty again. But this time, the verdict was 199 years. A lot of difference.

* * *

Justice Felix Frankfurter said in a 1945 U.S. Supreme Court opinion, "The history of American freedom is, in no small measure, the history of procedure."[1] That is very often what an appeal is all about. Did the trial court proceed in accordance with the law? Was the defendant accorded *all* of his constitutional rights?

Procedure may sometimes take precedence over the issue of guilt or innocence. In other words, the law must be complied with first. In some cases this may seem an overly technical approach to justice, but if you don't comply with the law in every single case, why have the law? When the law is not uniformly applied to every person and to every case, there can be no justice.

[1]*Molinski* v. *New York,* 324 U.S. 401, 414.

Two of my clients charged with murder were released without a trial because the law was not complied with by the state's attorney's office. Illinois had what is called the Fourth Term Act. The new Criminal Code that became law in 1964 states that a defendant not on bond and who has not asked for a postponement must be brought to trial within four terms of court; if he isn't, and the trial has not been delayed through any fault of his, he is entitled to a discharge, meaning he is as free of the charge as if he had been found not guilty.

In the late fifties and early sixties, the state lost a number of cases under the Fourth Term rule. It was not spelled out in the law then if four terms of court meant 120 days, or 121, or 123. In one of the murder cases I handled in which this happened, the defendant and I had been ready for trial and had not asked for a continuance. But the state had had a continuance. Soon the defendant had been in the county jail for 121 days. So I made a motion to release him under the Fourth Term Act.

Trying to salvage the case, the state's attorney argued that he had one more day, but Judge Matthew D. Hartigan disagreed, discharging the prisoner. The state sought to prevent his action by claiming he had no authority to do what he had done, and I ended up, in effect, defending the judge's action in the Illinois Supreme Court.

It was the only time I ever heard of the Illinois Supreme Court's deciding a matter without getting off the bench. The seven black-robed justices huddled right there on the bench and forthwith rendered a unanimous decision supporting Judge Hartigan.

* * *

One of my early appeals was a test case on the Drunkometer in Illinois. A lawyer who was head of the traffic institute at Northwestern University picked the case and Public Defender McCurrie assigned it to me. I told McCurrie it wasn't the best case for appeal, in my opinion, but he said, "Let's appeal it anyway.'' The police had deeper motives than we for an appeal because they hoped to gain legal status for the Drunkometer machine's findings.

In the Drunkometer test, the defendant had to blow into a balloon. His captured breath would be passed over a chemical substance. If the chemicals changed in color, like litmus paper, that would indicate the presence of alcohol. This machine was less sophisticated than those in use today, such as the Breatholizer.

A police chemist and the department's Drunkometer expert testified that samples of Michael Hlasko's breath, following an accident, had placed the blood alcohol concentration in excess of 30 percent. Solely on the basis of Drunkometer evidence, the judge had fined Hlasko $100. Hlasko claimed he drank only two glasses of beer before his arrest. Police contended that a reading of 15 percent alcohol in the bloodstream was sufficient to consider the driver unsafe.

My job was to prove that the Drunkometer could not be used without violating a citizen's legal rights. However, from a defense point of view, I felt they had picked a weak case. If I had been the original trial lawyer I would have brought in experts. This hadn't been done. Moreover, it couldn't now be done on appeal. But there were experts who would have said that the best test is a blood test; other experts would say the only sure way to determine the effect of alcohol on a person is to cut open the brain and examine it — not a very practical technique unless the person had been killed in a crash. At any rate, this meant I had less to work with than I might have, but I dutifully prepared my briefs and motions.

Our appeal was before the three justices of the Illinois Appellate Court, First District, who sat in Chicago. I argued that the testing device had not received general scientific recognition and did not provide an accurate index of the amount of alcohol in the bloodstream. But the big thrust of my argument was that you cannot cross-examine a machine, and our theory of American law was that you should be able to cross-examine witnesses to see if they are telling the truth and can be relied on. If you take only the results of a machine, you can't cross-examine.

The Appellate Court, however, noted that thirty-eight other states had the Drunkometer in use and that it had been ruled legal by the Texas Court of Criminal Appeals. It further noted the Northwestern University study, used by my opposition, which showed that the amount of alcohol exhaled from the lungs is the same as the amount found in the blood. The court, in effect, allowed it to be used as evidence, but not conclusive evidence. Its admission as evidence would be subject to the cross-examination of the machine's operator. Was he qualified? Was he able? Was the machine operating in perfect order?

Apparently the decision was of value and was justified by the slaughter on the highways in the early fifties, which the police was trying to curtail. But the only ones now qualified to operate the similar machines that have succeeded the Drunkometer are policemen who have taken courses on it and have received certificates from the Illinois Department of Welfare.

As recently as 1972 I was able to employ those earlier guidelines while defending a client charged with driving while intoxicated. On cross-examination, I asked the arresting policeman who had tested my client one question: Was he qualified to operate the machine? He wasn't. The defendant was found not guilty. You can't cross-examine a machine, but you can the man behind it.

* * *

Appeals usually involve much more than a $100 fine. Sometimes a man's life is at stake. Hugh Strevney's case aptly explains what I mean.

Strevney was accused, nineteen months after the crime, of the murder of a ten-year-old girl, whose body had been found in a ditch in the vicinity of what is now O'Hare International Airport. It was one of the big murder stories in Chicago. Strevney, a Cicero truck driver in his thirties and the father of three children, was held three days incommunicado. He finally — after his interrogator had repeatedly told him the facts of the case — "confessed." At five o'clock in the morning he was taken to the murder scene to re-enact the crime with an audience of 150, including reporters and photographers. The case had been cracked!

Irwin Bloch and Robert Harrington, both from the public defender's office, represented Strevney. During the investigation it was learned, through police sources, of a confession that had been made of the same murder by another man. But the same night he had confessed, the other man had hanged himself in his cell. This had happened in Hammond, Indiana, and in my opinion it was a better confession, as to time and other factors, than was Strevney's. Bloch had tried to introduce evidence about the other confession in the original trial, but it wasn't allowed.

The jury found Strevney guilty and sentenced him to death in the electric chair.

On appeal, Bloch, Harrington, and McCurrie hammered away at the other confession's not being considered, at the limiting of cross-examination of state's witnesses, and prejudicial remarks of the state's attorney. In 1952 the Illinois Supreme Court reversed and remanded the case on just these points, pointing out that there was "not a scintilla of evidence to connect him with that crime except his repudiated confession, taken by police officials after he had been held incommunicado for more than sixty hours." The other confession remained hearsay, and hearsay would generally be inadmissible, but in this particular case — said the court — the jury should have been given the opportunity to consider it.

Although I hadn't been the lawyer in the case at the trial or on appeal, I had aided in the appeal by helping prepare briefs and in the process I became very familiar with it. When it came time for a new trial, Bloch and Harrington had left the public defender's office and that left me to retry the case, but I had very little to do. The state's attorney appeared and said that he was going to drop the case. There wasn't sufficient evidence and he had "very grave doubt" of the defendant's guilt. It was over. An innocent man had been cleared, he was not to die in the electric chair.

* * *

When I was an assistant public defender, and for several years after I became head of the office, appeals were made at the discretion of the public defender. In those years we initiated from ten to fifteen appeals a year, or less.

In the late fifties, with *Griffin* v. *Illinois,* the state had been directed to provide transcripts of trials in felony convictions. Thus, the defendant himself had access to a free transcript and appeal was up to him. Then around 1963 with the arrival of the U.S. Supreme Court decision of *Douglas* v. *California,* appeals for the indigent were automatically provided for, if the defendants so wished. Naturally, they often did, and the public defender was appointed in their cases. This, of course, increased the workload for our office and in time produced a large backlog, for the county didn't supply us with the personnel to take care of the services that the Supreme Court had ruled the indigent were entitled to. There was a gap between law and reality. We simply couldn't do everything our new laws said we should do.

In the earlier days, we would travel to the state capital at Springfield by train. Both the Illinois Central and the Gulf, Mobile & Ohio ran through Springfield. The Gulf, Mobile & Ohio had a popular train that left Chicago about 9 P.M. It arrived in Springfield about 3 A.M. and a car was placed on a siding, allowing the passengers to get up at 7:30, dress, have breakfast, and go about their business. The special car was mainly for the legislators, but it was quite handy for us lawyers too.

In later years when Route 66 and other roads had improved, when trains had become fewer and fewer, we drove down.

Whenever I went I took an assistant. Either he had worked on the brief with me or maybe he had tried the case originally. Sometimes he would participate with me in argument, for experience, at the high court. Jim Doherty was with me on several occasions. When my son Mike was in law school, later, I took him with me several times to see how it all operated. Bill Fitzpatrick, now an associate judge, went with me when he was an assistant public defender. Invariably, a session of the Illinois Supreme Court was a learning experience.

* * *

Frequently, an appeal is based on the way the state acquired its evidence, and the rules should be the same for all of us who end up in court, whether we are innocent or guilty. It is the only fair way of proving guilt or innocence and maintaining the rights of all of us.

An abortion case in the middle fifties involved these basic constitutional guarantees and I fought the appeal for my client, Howard B. Haywoody, to the state's pinnacle, the Illinois Supreme Court.

The facts were these:

The defendants, Frank Miecio and Howard B. Haywoody, had been indicted together for abortion by the grand jury. Each defendant made a motion to suppress certain evidence taken by policemen: Haywoody, some articles taken from his home in his absence and without a search warrant; Miecio, certain papers taken from his person when he was arrested. Both motions were denied.

According to the trial record, Sadie Jarrett had had sexual relations with an unnamed man in June that year and had missed her next menstrual period. Her physician told her she was pregnant. In early October, through a friend, she made a telephone contact with a man named "Frankie," whom she later met. She identified him as the defendant Frank Miecio. Miecio made a phone call and they drove to see "Doc" on South Giles Street.

She was advised she would have to pay $300, of which she paid $200 then and was told to pay $100 later. When they arrived at the two-story brick house they went upstairs to the second floor where they met "Doc," a black man whom she identified as the defendant Haywoody. The front room, which they entered, had a daybed, two chairs, a dresser, and a desk. Haywoody asked her how far gone she was; she told him three months.

Haywoody had her take off her undergarments and soon afterward she felt a cold metal object, then a spreading sensation in her vagina, followed by a sharp cutting. She was packed with cotton. The metal object was taken out. She dressed and Haywoody gave her a glass of a milky-looking substance that she drank, and three pills to take later. She was to return in three days; Miecio told her to bring the $100 with her.

She returned as stipulated, this time experiencing some pain.

On October 10, her waterbag broke, followed by great cramping pains, fever, and nausea. She was taken to the emergency room of a hospital. Her uterus was enlarged, with a purulent, odoriferous discharge. She was given antibiotics, ice packs, and bed rest. Her pains continued. She expelled the fetus and placental tissue, which were preserved for pathological study. The pathologist, viewing a section under the microscope, reported cocci and bacilli infection in the tissue and in some areas of the fetus.

The police entered the case and Miss Jarrett described Miecio and Haywoody, whom she did not know by name at that point, and "John Doe" warrants were issued for their arrests. The next day a policewoman and a policeman, both in plain clothing, appeared at Haywoody's home, according to their testimony, and he apparently assumed they were there for an abortion. After a period of conversation in which Haywoody allegedly assured the policewoman he would help her "get rid of it somehow," and after he had cited several jobs he had done, the police officer produced his badge and the warrant. They took Haywoody to the police station, where he was identified by Sadie Jarrett; he denied ever having seen her before.

Meanwhile, a third policeman had remained at Haywoody's home; subsequently two officers searched the room and in a closet they seized a porcelain pan, a vaginal speculum, a stick about twelve inches long wrapped in tape and twine, a dilator, and a sponge forceps; from the room they took a flashlight and a roll of cotton.

These were the objects that were the subject of the motion to suppress that had been denied. They were to be entered in evidence against Haywoody.

A few days later, Miecio was arrested at a tavern on West Madison Street. Officers had him empty his pockets; a card was found and later introduced in evidence that had written on it Haywoody's name, address, phone number, and the word "Abortion."

Although it was a joint trial, the card was not to be used against Haywoody, and the objects seized at Haywoody's place were not to be used against Miecio.

The only witness for the defense was an obstetrician and gynecologist at a Chicago medical school who, in reply to a hypothetical question based on most of the medical facts in the case, said the expulsion of the fetus had been caused by spontaneous abortion, which meant it had happened by a force of nature, not by medication or instruments.

The jury, however, did not agree with the defense's theory. In separate verdicts, the jury found each defendant guilty. The court sentenced Miecio to one to two years in the penitentiary. Haywoody received a two to seven year term.

Then our appeals began. Miecio was represented by private counsel. As public defender I represented Haywoody, who had once been a peddler of patent medicines before he became more ambitious.

To a large extent, the appeal of a case is dry and somewhat lacking in the spontaneous drama that may appear at any moment in a courtroom trial. An abstract is prepared from the transcript of the trial — which consists of all the questions and answers and arguments taken by the court reporters. The abstract is a condensed running story of the trial. Then there is the brief citing the cases in your favor, and the points of error and then argument to support your legal issues. The state files a brief in opposition to your contentions. The transcript, abstract, and briefs are filed with the clerk of the Illinois Supreme Court. The case is placed on the court's docket, to be argued on a certain date.

The Illinois Supreme Court is housed in an impressive white-stone building, a smaller version of the U.S. Supreme Court Building. You take ten steps up to the main entrance, then turn to your right down a corridor to the clerk's office. When your case is up for oral argument, as it was in the Haywoody-Miecio case, you register in the clerk's office by 8:45 A.M. Then you go up another stairway to the second floor, where the courtroom is situated.

As you come off the stairway on the second floor, there is a large double doorway for the spectators to enter. However, the lawyers scheduled to argue that day turn to the left into a room with a large conference table and quite a few chairs in it where they can sit and talk or review their notes and briefs. There are not many seats in the courtroom for spectators, but then not many spectators attend.

When your case is called you merely move up to the counsel table where you face the bench of the Supreme Court justices. The clerk of the court sits at a special desk on one side of the room and the bailiff is at the other side. There is no court reporter present. Everything is taken down on a tape recording device. If one of the justices should have to leave during proceedings, he can still hear the arguments later on tape.

Court convenes at 10 A.M. After a noon adjournment they return in the afternoon. Each side is allotted thirty minutes for oral argument. When there is an appeal, the one who has initiated the appeal will proceed first, pointing out the trial errors, and then the other side, in our case the state, will answer.

Although unlawful search and seizure was an issue in both Haywoody and Miecio cases, the circumstances were different in each case, and the objects seized and used in evidence were different. In my own oral argument for Haywoody, I pointed out that his office was also his home and that, in effect, the police had entered and searched the room and seized the articles from it without first taking the proper legal steps of obtaining a search warrant.

One black-robed justice from the corner of my field of vision asked me, "This was his office?"

"Yes, your honor," I said. Haywoody's place of residence was a run-down room with an attached bathroom; this was supposed to be his place of business.

"Well, Counsel," continued the justice, "it wouldn't matter whether he had a fine mansion or not, it was his home?"

"That's right, your honor," I replied. "This constituted an illegal search."

When its opinion was filed, the Illinois Supreme Court found that Miecio's search of his person was legal and the evidence seized was admissible. His conviction was affirmed. He served his sentence.

But the court acknowledged that Haywoody's case presented a different question.

"The search and seizure were made without a search warrant and without his consent. . . . This search of Haywoody's home, in his absence, without a search warrant, and without his consent, was clearly illegal and in violation of his rights, guaranteed by the Fourth Amendment to the Constitution of the United States and section 6 of article II of the Constitution of Illinois. The admission in evidence, over objection, of the articles thus seized, violated said defendant's rights guaranteed by the Fifth Amendment to the United States Constitution and section 10 of article II of the Illinois Constitution. Haywoody's motion to suppress should have been allowed."

Then, noting that "although there was other evidence tending to establish Haywoody's guilt," Haywoody's conviction was reversed and the case returned to Cook County for a new trial. The case was never retried, however, because the illegally seized evidence could not be used. Without it, the state couldn't expect to win a conviction.

The Illinois Supreme Court, commenting on the Haywoody

case, could have been talking about defendants in general, and especially our criminal procedure, when it stated:

"A defendant, whether guilty or innocent, is entitled to a fair, orderly, and impartial trial in accordance with our laws. Under our system of jurisprudence, there is not one form of trial for a guilty person, and a different form for an innocent person."

Amen.

* * *

What lawyer does not dream of arguing a case before the United States Supreme Court?

A case that I took to our highest tribunal was that of Cleburn Woods, who had been convicted of selling narcotics. Our office handled the appeal, just as we have so many cases, when the defendant ran out of funds. The case was first tried by Woods' private counsel and it was on the basis of that record, and the constitutional issues raised in it, that we appealed.

Appeal is expensive. The defendant must provide the higher court with transcripts and he must pay the cost of other expenses, as well. Usually those who are not affluent are tapped out of funds by the time the trial is over. This is what had happened to Cleburn Woods. But there were potentialities in his case that we thought were worth bringing to the attention of a review court. Without the participation of the public defender's office, the case obviously was not going any further.

Although the case and its legal points intimately became a part of my life and work, Cleburn Woods himself was little more than a name to me. The attorney has very little contact, if any, with the defendant whom he picks up as a client for the first time on appeal. He has not had the pre-trial and the daily trial contact, in and out of the courtroom. The reason for this is that on appeal, the client's physical presence is not required in the courtroom. During the trial, the facts of the case were decided by the judge or the jury. On appeal, the arguments come from the trial record and the points of law.

The offense for which Woods was convicted allegedly occurred in a Chicago restaurant on February 28, 1964. He was indicted for selling heroin, "contrary to the statute, and against the peace and dignity of the same people of the State of Illinois." That September, Woods pleaded not guilty before Judge Herbert R. Friedlund and asked for a bench trial. Woods was represented by his private counsel, Walter LaVon Pride, while Assistant State's Attorneys Patrick Tuite and Robert Martwick prosecuted.

After a two-day trial, Judge Friedlund found Woods guilty and sentenced him to ten-to-eleven years in the penitentiary.

A major issue in our appeal was whether the defense has the right to the name and address of a state's witness, in this case the man to whom Woods was alleged to have sold the heroin. We claimed that if a police informer is present at the time of the alleged crime, and therefore is a material witness and a crucial witness, then the defense has the right to that person's true name and address. This kind of informer was distinguished from another kind of informer who merely informed by going to the police station and announcing, "Joe Doakes is selling narcotics at a certain address." We did not argue that *that* informer's identity couldn't be concealed.

But when the informer was physically present, as was alleged in the Cleburn Woods case, we contended that we of the defense should have an opportunity to find out what his background might be. The only successful way this can be accomplished is to know his true name and address. From this, much might be discovered by the defense. We might be able to demonstrate that the witness was not a credible person. He might have a criminal record. He might be facing charges himself in another case, which the defense would certainly wish to bring to the court's or the jury's attention. Or perhaps the informer had planted narcotics on the defendant and then told police a different story. Or maybe the informer had been part of a narcotics ring, happened to get caught, and now was copping a plea, making a deal with the police by informing. These possibilities would all be pertinent to a man's proper defense.

During Cleburn Woods' trial, his attorney had sought to obtain the state's major witness's true name and address, but the trial judge had not allowed it. Our appeal would revolve around this section of the transcript.

Woods was accused of selling a "bag" or tinfoil package of diacetyl morphine hydrochloride, or heroin, to the police informer, in the area between the Union Stockyards and Lake Michigan on the South Side. This is in the northeastern portion of the Chicago black belt.

The police did not actually see the transaction, which occurred in a nearby restaurant under the elevated tracks at Forty-Third, but Woods was paid, police alleged, in four one-dollar bills of which the serial numbers had been recorded and three silver quarters that had been marked. The informer left the scene, after wiping his face outside with a handkerchief to signify to police that the purchase had been made. The state did not claim to have recovered the quarters, but only the bills. The informer had been given seven dollars, consisting of six singles and four quarters; afterward, he returned two dollars and twenty-five cents to the police. The contents of the bag he claimed to have bought from Woods were analyzed and found to be heroin.

The heart of our appeal, of course, was concerned with the testimony of the informer, who identified himself as "James Jordan." On cross-examination by defense attorney Pride, it was established that "Jordan" was a narcotics user. Then Pride pushed on the matter of identification, as shown in this segment of the transcript which we were to scrutinize carefully:

Q. Now, do you use any other names?
A. Do I use any other names?
Q. Yes. If I'm not speaking clearly ask me and I'll attempt to speak more clearly. Do you use any other names?
MR. MARTWICK (assistant state's attorney): I'll object to that.
MR. PRIDE: Q. Do you use any other names except James Jordan?
MR. MARTWICK: Judge, I'm objecting to the question.
THE COURT: What was the question?

MR. PRIDE: I asked him if he used any other names besides James Jordan.

THE COURT: He may answer.

MR. MARTWICK: Judge, in the *People* vs. *Durr,* I don't believe he has to reveal these names for his own safety.

MR. PRIDE: Well, he is here himself.

THE COURT: Well, as far as protection, I can see where it is for his protection that he wouldn't use names because he might be involved in other cases as an informer, so I won't let him answer.

MR. PRIDE: Q. Is James Jordan your correct name?''

MR. MARTWICK: Object.

MR. PRIDE: I have a right to know if it is his correct name.

THE COURT: He may answer if it is his correct name or not.

MR. PRIDE: Q. Is that your correct name?

A. No, it is not.

Q. What is your correct name?

MR. MARTWICK: Object.

THE COURT: I won't have him answer that.

MR. PRIDE: Q. Are you known in the streets as ''Saltpork''?

MR. MARTWICK: Object.

THE COURT: I won't have him answer that.

In delving into Jordan's background, the trial lawyer went into the witness's employment record. He had worked as a janitor for a period. He had also received several hundred dollars as a paid informer from the police contingency fund, at the rate of ten dollars at a time. The trial attorney also established that Jordan was a narcotics user who claimed he had not injected since two days before. Having established that Jordan had received no money from the police or from any other employment for about two weeks, he then moved to questions of Jordan's environment, logical questions if one wishes to lay the basis for attacking a witness's credibility.

Q. Now, where do you live now?

MR. MARTWICK: Objection.

MR. PRIDE: This is material.

MR. MARTWICK: Objection, Judge.

THE COURT: Yes, objection allowed.

MR. PRIDE: Q. Do you pay rent where you live now?

A. No, I don't.

Q. With whom do you live?

MR. MARTWICK: Objection.

MR. PRIDE: I'm not asking him to give the names.

THE COURT: Strike it.

MR. PRIDE: Q. Do you live alone?

A. No, I don't.

Q. Do you live with your wife?

MR. MARTWICK: Object.

MR. PRIDE: This is material; I'm not asking him to give names.

THE COURT: He may answer as to whether he lives with his wife.

MR. PRIDE: Q. Are you married?

A. Do I have to answer that, your honor?

THE COURT: Yes, answer it.

MR. PRIDE: Well, you don't really have to answer any of this if you don't want to.

MR. MARTWICK: Object to counsel's remark and ask that he be directed to just ask questions.

THE COURT: Are you withdrawing the question?

MR. PRIDE: Well, he doesn't — he comes here as a witness and he acts as though it is a very difficult task to answer.

THE COURT: No, he doesn't. He asked me a proper question. He asked if he had to answer that.

MR. PRIDE: Q. Are you married?

A. I haven't made any task out of anything.

THE COURT: Yes, strike that remark about making a big task out of it.

MR. PRIDE: I don't understand you, Judge.

THE COURT: I struck the remark about you saying it was a task.

MR. PRIDE: All right, Judge. Q. Are you married?

A. No, I'm not.

Q. Do you live with your mother?

MR. MARTWICK: Objection.

THE COURT: Strike that.

Whether or not the judge has made an error in this kind of exchange is not easy to establish. No appeal is automatically won or lost. Ultimately, it is always a matter of opinion — the opinions of distinguished justices who have usually had long years of experience in the law. They have seen many other cases like the one at bar. They can be expected to appreciate shadings and nuances. They interpret the constitutions of the state and the nation. In a sense, they are making law. If the case is one that establishes a precedent that will later be cited by other lawyers and judges in other cases, you can say that this is "new law," as lawyers refer to it.

It goes without saying that, in the beginning, we did not know we would wind up at the Supreme Court of the United States with the Cleburn Woods case. There was nothing to assure us that the case would even be reviewed by a higher court. But we took the first step, as we had done with hundreds of other appeals, when two of my assistants — Frederick F. Cohn and James J. Doherty — and Marshall A. Patner, who was assisting the office in this case, prepared the case for appeal before the Illinois Appellate Court.

In the appeal brief, the trial record was cited to show that Woods had denied having made any sale of narcotics, insisting that he was carrying the single packet for his own use. He said he had referred the informer to another man, Harold Anderson, who was also in the restaurant, for a sale. Explaining the money taken from him, Woods had said he had bought a ten-cent cup of coffee in the restaurant, for which he had given a five-dollar bill, receiving four one-dollar bills and coins in change.

We also made note that on cross-examination the informer had been asked if he had ever appeared against Harold Anderson on a charge of selling narcotics on the same date as Woods was arrested. He was reminded that he was under oath. He said he could not remember. We pointed out that the informer not only was an active participant in the purported transaction, he was also the only person who testified that it actually happened.

Our appeal argument cited *Roviaro* v. *United States,* a 1957 decision that also involved a narcotics informer. *Roviaro* had limited the informer's privilege to those situations in which the informer needed to be protected, thereby protracting his usefulness to the state. But in the Woods case, the informer appeared in court and was an active participant in the alleged crime. Without him, there was no case. If the defendant was not allowed the informer's true identity, how could he attack his credibility and determine if the informer actually made a purchase from Anderson — which had been Woods' explanation for Jordan's acquisition of the heroin? Woods would have to know all of the names that Jordan used, in order to learn if the informer had appeared against Anderson in another case.

In previous cases, the Supreme Court had held that the defendant was entitled to all of the information in the state's possession. Thus the state couldn't divulge some and withold part of what the defense requested. Nor, by our logic, could the state put the informer on the stand, divulge his alias, but refuse to reveal his true identity.

The state, of course, argued to the contrary, claiming that the facts were greatly different than in *Roviaro,* wherein the government had refused to identify or produce the informant. They — Elmer G. Kissane and Kenneth L. Gillis from the state's attorney's office — argued that since Jordan was in court and had testified and was cross-examined, the failure to disclose his real identity could not affect the defendant. They further stated that Woods knew Jordan and had recognized him by that name and that, therefore, *Roviaro* did not apply.

In the flurry of briefs and cited authorities, each side brought all its legalistic weapons to bear on the issues, and it was orally argued before the appeals court.

Then on May 9, 1966, the Appellate Court of Illinois announced its decision. It was a setback for the defense. All three justices concurred in affirming the trial court's conviction.

The future for the case looked none too bright, but the next step was taken nonetheless: the filing, on June 30, 1966, of a petition for leave to appeal from the Appellate Court to the Supreme Court of Illinois. Permission was granted.

In the petition to the state supreme court, prepared by Doherty, Cohn, and Marshall J. Hartman, we cited seven cases, including *Roviaro,* as precedents. The argument raised a number of limitations placed on the defense by not knowing Jordan's real name, ranging from our inability to learn of the man's record of prior convictions to whether he was then in jail or out on bond.

A major thrust of our argument was summed up in one of the concluding questions:

"In short, how could defense counsel effectively exercise the right of cross-examination which is guaranteed in the Sixth Amendment of the United States Constitution?"

The six justices of the Illinois Supreme Court considered the petition, along with the trial record and abstract, and on September 22, 1966, denied the petition without an opinion.

Again, a setback.

When a lawyer vows, "I'll carry this case all the way to the Supreme Court!" he is pledging the ultimate fight, and this is what we in the public defender's office decided to do in the Woods case. Why? Because we thought we were right on the law, despite two setbacks from those two higher courts.

By this time, in the fall of 1966, I was deeply involved in the Speck case, which was to be a major drain on my energies for a year or more, but it was only one of many cases in the public defender's office. Despite all else we had to do, the Woods case was high on the agenda. With Marshall Hartman and Jim Doherty, I began making plans to take the case to the nation's highest court — if it would agree to hear us.

A period of intensive legal research began, at a time when we could very easily have used all our energies on the hundreds of other cases awaiting trial or appeal. *Roviaro* v. *U.S.* was a key case and I researched it again for myself. *Roviaro* had also originated in Chicago, in the Federal District Court, and it had also involved a conviction for violation of the narcotics drug act. Pages of ballpoint pen notes on yellow-lined legal pads grew as we sought to compile precedents that would firmly back up our contentions for the indigent Cleburn Woods. In *Roviaro* the case had been reversed and remanded on a six-to-one Supreme Court decision in which two justices did not participate. At the trial, the informer had been referred to only as John Doe and although his presence had been demanded by the defense, John Doe was not produced, identified, or made available. The Supreme Court had considered this an error. There were distinctions between *Roviaro* and the Woods case, but I thought there were more similarities.

Another key case that I personally researched was *Pointer* v. *Texas,* a 1965 Supreme Court decision in a robbery case that had a similar basic issue: Does the defense have the right to have witnesses confront him and to cross-examine them under the Sixth Amendment, and does the Fourteenth Amendment make this obligatory upon the states? The court had answered this double-barreled question with an unequivocable yes by reversing the case.

In the October, 1966, term of the Supreme Court, Hartman, Doherty, and I filed our petition seeking review by the nation's top court.

We singled out two questions for the Supreme Court to ponder: Is the *Roviaro* ruling satisfied when the state brings the informer into open court but then refuses to disclose his identity? The Constitutional provisions involved, we stated, were the Sixth Amendment and the Due Process Clause of the Fourteenth Amendment. In addition to *Roviaro* and *Pointer,* we cited *Alford* v. *United States*[2] wherein a conviction was reversed after the accused was denied the right, on cross-examination, to ask a witness his address.

"But," our petition continued, "at bar the accused was denied his accuser's correct name! Why? The only apparent reason is that the instant case is a narcotics case. Illinois has fallen into the hysteria pattern in such cases."

As is customary, the attorney general of Illinois, through his assistants Richard A. Michael and John J. O'Toole, filed in opposition to our petition for review.

[2]282 U.S. 687.

Then, on May 15, 1967, the U.S. Supreme Court responded in a way we of the defense had all hoped. It granted the petition, and allowed Cleburn Woods to proceed *in forma pauperis*. The Supreme Court would hear us!

The case was not heard until the October term in 1967, when it was placed on the docket, Cleburn Woods versus Illinois. In our brief we noted the Constitutional provisions involved as the Sixth Amendment ("In all criminal prosecutions, the accused shall enjoy the right . . . to be confronted with the witnesses against him . . . .") and the Fourteenth Amendment (" . . . nor shall any State deprive any person of life, liberty, or property, without due process of law. . . ."). In their brief for the state of Illinois, Assistant Attorney Generals John J. O'Toole and Phillip J. Rock cited twenty-one cases and argued that the state had the privilege to conceal the identify of an informant when identity was not essential to an accused's defense, and that the defendant had not been deprived of a full and fair opportunity to defend himself. They pointed out that the informer Jordan had admitted on the stand that he was an addict, had a record for larceny and burglary, presumably had a criminal charge pending against him, and had been paid for informing, so that by his own admission his credibility was called into question. Thus, they argued, how could divulging his true identity further question his credibility? "The disclosure of the informer's true name and present address would be of little, if any, benefit to the petitioner, while on the other hand the benefit to society is obvious." We responded, point by point. The paper work was done.

The day before the big hearing in December, four of us — Doherty, Hartman, my younger daughter Marie Therese who was a secretary in the office, and I — flew to Washington. All the way up, on the plane, we talked about the case. I took Marie Therese along because we needed the services of a legal secretary and also to give her the experience of seeing the Supreme Court — and to see her father argue a case before that august body. Whenever possible, I had always tried to see that my children shared some of the more interesting events of my career.

The night before the case was to come before the court, I rehearsed my argument. Doherty, Hartman, and Marie Therese each had a vital role as I presented the case in practice. In order to lend authenticity to the scene, Hartman even provided the "Oyez! Oyez! Oyez!" with which the Crier opens each day's court session. For the rehearsal, Doherty and Hartman, who had assisted in the briefs and the abstract from the beginning of the case and therefore knew all of the facts, acted as Supreme Court justices. Marie Therese, who was also to serve as critic, timed me to insure that I didn't run over the thirty-minute limit that each side would have.

As justices, Doherty and Hartman were to do anything that a real justice might do. They would stop me, as I was speaking, and ask questions. Any such interruption from the bench tends to throw a lawyer off, but in the Supreme Court it could mean the end of your presentation. The justices can cause your thirty minutes to be used in any way they desire. If they deem it necessary, they might even give you only five minutes; they might question you for twenty-five minutes. The next morning, as I prepared to leave the hotel, I felt I had a flawless presentation that I would be able to give in the proper amount of time.

The U.S. Supreme Court Building, situated near the Capitol, is a very impressive edifice with its great white marble pillars and the thirty or so steps up which you walk to the entrance. The inscription over the pillars tells in four words what it is all supposed to be about, going to the essence of our American judicial theory: *Equal Justice Under Law*.

I registered at the Supreme Court Clerk's office, where I was given a card with instructions.

Issued to: Gerald W. Getty
Counsel in No. 158

1. Display this card to attendant seated at entrance to the Bar.
2. Remain seated at reserved tables behind Counsels' table *throughout* the argument of the case immediately preceding your

case on the calendar, unless special arrangements have been made with the Clerk.

3. Counsel should compute their remaining time during argument. *Do not* make inquiry of the Chief Justice.
4. If you have ordered lunch, you will be escorted from the Clerk's desk at 12:00 o'clock.

When it is in session, the court convenes at 10 A.M. They then hear cases until 12 noon, at which time they recess until 12:30 P.M. for lunch and then reconvene until 2:30 P.M. Each day's session is four hours long. When a case is on the "summary calendar," the presentations are limited to thirty minutes for each side. On other cases, each side will have one hour. Of course, some cases are consolidated, so that one hearing may stretch for as long as eight hours — which was true for one power-rate case that was before the court during the month we were there. That case was finished before we approached the bar.

The courtroom itself is magnificent, but what is really striking is how small, considering the vastness of this country, is this room where so many far-reaching cases are heard and decisions made. As you walk in, you can see the high rostrum where the nine black-robed justices sit. The ceilings are high, something like twenty feet, with tapestry drapes accentuating the formal atmosphere in which some of the greatest legal decisions of the world have been handed down.

The sessions are open to the public and there are seats for visitors with thick, soft-cushioned theater-type seats upholstered in a red velvet that matches the draperies. Just beyond the visitors' section is a railing of polished wood and on the other side are two counsel tables, one for each representative of the two opposing litigants.

It is the most formal court setting in this country. The United States Attorney General and his assistants appear in morning frocks when they are before the court. Although business suits are deemed sufficient for other lawyers, the formality of the environment is not lessened. This alone should be enough to impress attorneys and visitors alike with the deep seriousness of the matters that are to come before the court.

That day, as on all other days the court convenes, the Crier heralded the nine men's entrance in formal, sturdy stentorian style:

"The Honorable, the Chief Justice and the Associate Justices of the Supreme Court of the United States."

Having arisen in preparation for the court's arrival, we remained standing as the justices walked to the bench.

Then the Crier, using the same words Marshall Hartman had used in our rehearsal the night before, announced:

"Oyez! Oyez! Oyez! All persons having business before the Honorable, the Supreme Court of the United States, are admonished to draw near and give their attention, for the Court is now sitting. God save the United States and this Honorable Court!"

I didn't have long to wait, because we were the second case, but I was very conscious of the meaning of that day. In my role as public defender, I was bringing to this, the highest court in the land, the case of Cleburn Woods, a poor black man from Illinois.

Suddenly, I stood before Chief Justice Earl Warren and his distinguished eight colleagues, and I had to make the most of my allotted half hour. I had tried to learn something about each of the justices so that I could answer by name if any one of them questioned me, avoiding the impression that I had never heard of him before.

As the petitioner, I spoke first, allowing twenty minutes for my presentation and saving ten for subsequent eventualities. The clerk of the Court provides a two-minute warning for summing up and then rings a bell when the time is up. When the time is up, that means not a second more. The Chief Justice is quick to cut you off if you run over. The Supreme Court is no place for foot-dragging.

"Mr. Chief Justice, and may it please the Court," I began and therewith I plunged into the argument for Cleburn Woods, outlining the two Constitutional provisions involved and presenting the question that the court would now review:

Should the informer's privilege be permitted to encroach upon the accused's right under the Sixth Amendment to be confronted by the witnesses against him?

Then I explicated the facts of the case. I went into the fact that the state had produced the witness against Woods but had not disclosed his name or address and that the witness had given an incorrect name on the witness stand. I alluded to Jordan's nickname.

"The only thing we knew, or that the defendant knew, was that there was an informant by the name of 'Fishbait.' "

Justice Byron White interrupted me.

"I read that," he said. "It wasn't 'Fishbait'; it was 'Saltpork.' "

"Oh, you're absolutely right, Mr. Justice White," I instantly acknowledged. " 'Fishbait' was in another case I had!"

It was a rare moment of levity that fleetingly changed the somber character of the courtroom. The justices spontaneously roared with laughter.

Court attachés later told me that they had never seen the court explode into a belly laugh like that before.

Then I moved along with my argument. "It is our position that on an issue of guilt, where the informant is a material witness, the interjection of the governmental privilege is unfair and wrong." I cited our authorities to support our reasoning. I pointed out that, more than credibility, we were concerned with determining guilt itself, by possibly revealing if the narcotics purchase may have been made from a person other than the defendant — as Cleburn Woods had insisted. "Finally, the right of cross-examination should not and cannot be balanced, as a matter of public interest, against the rights of the individual." I contended, as we had in the past, that the witness's correct name and current address were essential for a proper cross-examination.

As I had anticipated, some of the justices asked questions during my presentation, including one that we had rehearsed the previous night. "Now, if we decided in your favor, what authority would this court have to order this upon the State of Illinois?"

The obvious answer was the due process clause of the Fourteenth Amendment, which had been construed similarly in the cases I had cited. The Supreme Court had ruled on school segregation, using the due process clause as authority: a state may not deny to any person equal protection under the law. The question now, it seemed to me, was whether it covered penniless, black Cleburn Woods as well as the wealthiest white, Anglo-Saxon Wall Streeter.

Then O'Toole responded for the State of Illinois, meeting my argument with his own arsenal of logic and cited authorities, and it was over. The long months of preparation had climaxed, for both sides, in one hour of argument.

Two months later the decision was announced in a written opinion. The first news I had of it was when members of the Chicago press called me, to ask my reaction.

The Supreme Court had decided in our favor, in an eight-to-one decision. The conviction was reversed, and remanded to the lower courts for retrial.

It was not a great publicity case. In fact, many people never knew of the successful fight for Cleburn Woods all the way to the nation's highest tribunal. But certainly for me it was a feeling of accomplishment and all of us who had taken part in it were overjoyed. Not that we had time to celebrate. By then we were deep into other cases, in the midst of a job that never ends — defending the poor. Since that time, however, our own appellate division in Chicago has cited the decision and I assume it has been cited in other cases throughout the country. It had become another small, but not unimportant, brick in our legal edifice of Constitutional rights.

What happened to Cleburn Woods? He was never retried and thus was freed by the decision. He never came by to thank me and I never looked him up. Which was par for the course.

Whatever his fate thereafter, he had lent his name to one small portion of our legal mosaic, to be cited as I found it recently in a notation contained in a book of Supreme Court decisions. The case established that "the constitutional right of an accused to confront the witnesses against him prohibits an informer from hiding behind an alias and refusing to supply his correct address while undergoing cross-examination at trial."[3]

Behind those words lay a much larger point: that Cleburn Woods, who probably had never before dreamed of being heard by the Supreme Court, was entitled to the full protection of the Constitution — and had received it, just as a millionaire might have.

[3]*The Criminal Law Revolution, 1960–1968* (Washington, D.C., The Bureau of National Affairs, Inc., 1968).

CHAPTER 17

The Defender Rests

I ENJOYED my years dedicated to defending the poor.

There is no better way to say it. I was doing work I liked to do and I felt I was doing it well. The job, in return, gave me that which can never be bought — a sense of social usefulness, a deep feeling of having served my fellow man in a way that was basic and vital.

What more can you ask of a career?

After the Speck case, as I became known outside Cook County and Illinois, I was steadily offered defense cases that would have brought me substantial fees. Several times I considered leaving the public defender's office; in all fairness to myself, I was compelled to give serious thought to it. I was also interested in real estate and other areas of civil law; in private practice, I could embrace these interests, as well. But I had devoted my life to defending the indigent and I wanted to continue. As public defender, I hoped to contribute even more than I had in the past. I turned down the lucrative offers.

Because the job had brought me honors, I felt I owed it a few more years. While vice president of the National Legal Aid and Defender Association, I also had been chairman of its Defender Section. For three consecutive terms I was president of the

Illinois Public Defender Association, which in 1970 named me Public Defender of the Year. DePaul University, my alma mater, also awarded me an honorary Doctor of Laws degree.

But it wasn't all roses. In 1969 I was a candidate for delegate to the Illinois Constitutional Convention. On the day before election, someone distributed leaflets all over our suburban district attacking "Boss Daley" and describing me as "the hand-picked stooge of Daley." Indeed! Anyone who knew the relationship between Mayor Daley and me would have laughed. But this last-minute political smear appeared when it was too late for me to reply. It worked. I lost the race. Being associated with Daley in Chicago was an asset, but in the suburban area outside of Chicago it was deadly.

As criminal law changed in the mid-sixties, requiring more and more lawyers to provide the expanded legal services to the indigent that Supreme Court decisions dictated, I found my administrative duties increasing and my courtroom activity decreasing. Most persons would consider this an improvement in status. Interviewing defendants in the bullpens close by the courtrooms or in the overcrowded jail was always like a descent into hell. There was no privacy. There might be fifteen other prisoners in the bullpen while I was counseling my client; the room hummed with conversation. The jail was only slightly better. Nor did the clients always follow advice. Some clients had tuberculosis and were told by the jail doctors to wear special masks that would protect anyone who might come in contact with them. Sometimes they wore them, sometimes they didn't. Working under conditions like these, with clients in volume, was enough to cause you to wonder how you maintained your good humor and mental balance through the years.

Even so, in the late-1960s and into the 1970s I kept my hand in as an active trial lawyer. If an assistant was ill or if a lawyer was overburdened on a particular day, I would fill in for him. Other cases I chose for myself at the beginning; still others had novel appeal issues that I handled personally. I remained on the firing line and maintained an open door policy in the office so that any assistant would feel free to walk in and informally discuss any personal or legal matter.

Each year seemed to bring new responsibilities and challenges, as Supreme Court decisions strengthened the constitutional rights of criminal defendants. The public defender's workload could only grow. The landmark *Gideon* v. *Wainright* decision in 1963 extended the right of counsel to all indigents facing felony charges, and *Douglas* v. *California* required that the state provide appeals for indigents. The *Escobedo* (378 U.S. 478) ruling of 1964 extended to the criminal suspect the right of counsel at the police station, during interrogation. (*Escobedo* was a Cook County case.) In 1966, *Miranda* v. *Arizona* (384 U.S. 436) took it a step further: The police must inform the prisoner of his right to remain silent and that anything he says may be used against him and that he has the right to have the advice of an attorney before interrogation; if he wants an attorney, he must be told the police will call an attorney for him; if he can't afford an attorney, the state will get one for him. These are called the warnings of *Miranda*. In 1967, the *Gault* decision established that the rules of evidence must be applied in juvenile cases. This ruling extended to juveniles the rights that adults had in criminal proceedings. As Justice Abe Fortas wrote in the opinion, "Under our Constitution the condition of being a boy does not justify a kangaroo court." *Gault* was an Arizona case, but the National Legal Aid and Defender Association filed an *amicus curiae,* or "friend of the court," brief that was collaborated on by L. Michael Getty, my son, who was then with NLADA, and Marshall Hartman and Jim Doherty, from my office.

These decisions made even more clear the vital significance of the defendant's constitutional guarantees in the overall picture of what we think of as "law and order." Traditionally, there are five disciplines that, working together, bring about the final product. They are:

1. Police and all law enforcement bodies
2. Courts

3. Prosecution
4. Defense, whether a public defender or private counsel
5. Corrections

The defense attorney is every bit a part of the larger law enforcement pattern as is any of the other four disciplines. Unless the defendant is well-represented, so that the stature of the defense is equal to that of the prosecution, there can be no equitable law and order; instead, there may be a miscarriage of justice.

The statistics of the public defender's office from the mid-1960s on are staggering. In 1964, when the new Illinois criminal code and the Supreme Court rules authorized an appeal of all penitentiary sentences in which the defendant had not been granted probation and had not pleaded guilty, the appeals handled in our office jumped overnight from about fifteen a year to an average of 200 cases per year. The defendant had the right to a court transcript and the public defender was appointed by the court. We had to supply court transcripts and appeal briefs. Twenty lawyers were assigned to writing appeals alone. And while we manned the twenty courts on the seven floors of the Criminal Court Building, the suburban courts required the services of from four to five assistant public defenders. Another lawyer was needed for the Mental Health Hospital. Eight manned the Juvenile Court. In 1971, there were seventy-eight lawyers in my office and that wasn't nearly enough.

One result of *Gault* was that the defender in Juvenile Court now tried his case virtually the same as he would in a criminal court. In addition to the runaway and truancy cases, the Juvenile Court heard murders, rapes, robberies, and burglaries committed by young offenders. If convicted, the indigent juvenile had the right to a free transcript and the public defender on appeal. A defendant's age no longer precluded his being protected by the Constitution.

Just as essential was the public defender's role at the Cook County Mental Health Clinic. I had argued that all patients were entitled to be represented at commitment proceedings. During a thirty-day experimental period in 1963, an assistant saved thirty persons from being committed to an institution. Most of them were elderly, whose relatives were using this building of unfortunates as a dumping grounds. Some of the victims were eccentric, senile, or unwanted; others were just underfoot or perhaps not keeping themselves as clean as they might. Husbands or wives would sign their mates of a lifetime into institutions. Children would attempt to commit their parents.

The County Board had consistently turned me down for funds for this purpose, so I sent an assistant to the clinic anyway and finally the County Board gave in and authorized me an extra lawyer. Although most of these hearings are extremely brief, lasting no more than a few minutes, our 1968 statistics give some idea of how busy that lawyer was. That year, we represented 4,008 patients, of whom 983 were dismissed or withdrawn, 361 were discharged, and 340 were placed in care and custody of the court. About once or twice each month, a rare jury trial would be held in the clinic, in an area provided for such legal hearings.

Despite our always overburdened staff and our anemic budget, we had a fine showcase in Cook County. Our public defense of the underdog gave Chicago an image of enlightened, humane leadership that attracted visitors to our office from Japan, England, Canada, Formosa, West Germany, Czechoslovakia, and Puerto Rico, with an eye to implementing the system in their countries. Our statistics alone were impressive. A 1971 comparison of public defender and private counsel dispositions in Cook County told much of the story. The public defender had 27 percent of all jury trials and won not guilty verdicts in 45 percent of them; private counsel had 73 percent of all jury trials and won not guilties in only 20 percent. As for bench trials, the public defender had 55 percent of them and won not guilties in 67 percent; private counsel had 45 percent and won not guilties in 30 percent.

Statistics, of course, do not tell the whole flesh-and-blood story. They are only the dry, aggregate result of individual actions and struggles. The same is true of the financing of the public defender's office. In Cook County, the public defender's office has always been a stepchild of the county. Beginning in the mid-1960s when Judge John S. Boyle became chief judge of the courts, a position he was to hold until the 1970s, the financial predicament of the public defender's office grew more acute. In 1971 our budget amounted to $1,433,000; of our 102 employees, there were seventy-eight lawyers, seven investigators, and seventeen stenographers. By contrast, offices serving comparable population areas — Los Angeles with 146 attorneys and an $8 million budget, and the state of New Jersey with 111 lawyers (sixty-one fulltime) and an appropriation of $5½ million — had more to operate with. I felt we had received about one-third of what we needed.

That year, including all cases, ranging from the most serious charges at the indictment level down to those of juvenile delinquencies and the very brief hearings in the Mental Health Clinic, our office represented a total of 44,500 persons.

Enough to prove a point.

Judge Boyle was not easily impressed. He did nothing about providing more attorneys for the office. In my 1972 budget request I asked for $2,067,000, by no means an unreasonable figure. He personally ordered $573,909 cut from it, leaving $1,493,000, scarcely more than the year before.

One item illustrates the depth of the problem. I had estimated we would have 7,621 misdemeanor appeals to add to our already heavy appeal caseload. An Illinois Supreme Court decision now allowed indigents to appeal misdemeanor or minor convictions. For this additional work, I requested six more lawyers. Judge Boyle disagreed entirely. But the handwriting was on the wall. The backlog in appellate cases was already large; it would rapidly grow. A lawyer can only write so many abstracts and briefs in a month; as a creditable number, one should handle three or four cases a month before the Appellate Court of the Illinois Supreme Court. To insure a quality product, no heavier caseload should be placed on one appellate lawyer.

Many Circuit Court judges were sympathetic to me but were in no position to materially help. Officials of the Chicago Bar Association wrote letters to the County Board, recommending increases in salaries and larger office facilities; these had no effect either.

The problem grew decidely worse. In the past I had gone before the County Board personally to explain my budget requests. Now Judge Boyle, claiming that the judges were responsible for the office of public defender, began going before the County Board instead of me. By then he had also taken over the Probation Office and the Jury Commission, contending they were parts of the Circuit Court. Then, in a letter dated January 26, 1972, he announced that, thereafter, employment applications, changes in staff, and payroll control, as pertained to my office, would be handled by his office.

These were basic administrative functions of the public defender. I was required to send lawyers I wanted to hire as assistants to Judge Boyle's office, where they were to be interviewed by a committee. This action in early 1972 was the last straw in a long series of moves that could only sap the independence of the public defender's office — which should remain as independent as the state's attorney's office.

My protest fell upon deaf ears. The Chicago chapter of the American Civil Liberties Union joined me in complaining of Judge Boyle's action, but he nonetheless carried it out. As I saw it, it damaged the cause of justice everywhere. Others saw it the same way. Soon afterward, a class action suit was filed against Judge Boyle by the Legal Aid Bureau, Businessmen for the Public Interest, and ACLU, on behalf of the indigents of Cook County.

A private practice became an even more attractive idea now and I seriously began reconsidering my earlier decision. Out of the public defender's office I would have more time to devote to a variety of interests. Gracia and I owned property in Michigan which had a lovely lake on it. In late 1971 we had begun planning to build a house at this cool retreat from crowded Chicago. It was close to the small town of Irons, Michigan, far from the pressures of the city. As a lawyer in private practice I would be able to have more leisure time with my family, even when in the city. The afternoon rush in Chicago was so mad that I habitually remained at the office until 6 P.M.; by then the traffic was reasonable on the Dan Ryan Expressway as I drove south to Dolton. Certainly I expected to be busy, but I would have better control over my hours and how busy I would be.

I was proud of my record as public defender. Of the many clients I had represented who had been charged, none had gone to the chair. Only Speck had received a death sentence; this was later reversed. Since December, 1954, when I was named public defender, some assistants had heard the death verdict in murder cases, but nobody represented by my office had actually gone to the chair. Considering the cases that we had, this was a creditable performance.

For twenty-eight and a half years I had defended the indigent. For eighteen of those years I had been head of the office. I had made my contribution. I could now leave with a feeling of achievement and satisfaction.

I resigned, as of April 1, 1972. As I walked out of my office for the last time, a great responsibility lifted from my shoulders. It was as if, at last, I had closed in a tough, long-running jury trial.

A new phase of my life was beginning. I eagerly looked forward to exciting new vistas.

It was an ending with a beginning.

* * *

In December, 1972, the Illinois Defender Association and the Cook County Public Defender's office honored me with a testimonial dinner, open to anyone who wished to attend.

The month before, my son, L. Michael Getty, an assistant state's attorney, had been elected a state representative to the General Assembly. Gracia and I had built our house up in Michigan. Speck had been resentenced; although no longer public defender, I had represented him without fee, closing the case. My private practice was flourishing. It was as if all the loose ends of my career had been wrapped up for the occasion.

Associate Circuit Court Judge Thomas Cawley, who had once been my first assistant, served as master of ceremonies. He lauded me for not having a grey hair after twenty-eight and a half years of defending the poor. U.S. District Court Judge Abraham L. Marovitz, Illinois Appellate Court Justice Thomas A. McGloon, Judge Joseph A. Power, and Acting Public Defender James J. Doherty all made brief speeches. Ed Rooney from the Chicago *Daily News* was there. In all, several hundred friends and colleagues attended.

Not one of my former clients was there.

It told a lot about the nature of the job.

Going beyond the personal honors that I enjoyed, it also told a lot about the future of the public defender system, proving that the more fortunate of us believe in protecting the rights of the underdog. The dinner was another affirmation of faith in the system's permanence, not only in Cook County but in the nation. As the states and counties pay to apprehend and prosecute, they must also, when the defendant is indigent, pay to defend. Each of these disciplines must function, if our system of justice is to function properly.

I am sure that everyone at the dinner that night felt, as I do, that the system can only expand in the years ahead. Consistently, the decisions of the courts have pointed in this direction. Now a criminal defendant must be represented by counsel even at the misdemeanor level. This alone will account for a sizeable expansion in public defender services over the country.

Perhaps in rural areas it will still be possible to appoint lawyers for particular cases and pay them by the case, but in the urban areas this is no longer a feasible policy. As the cities continue to explode in both population and crime, the burden on the courts will be staggering. As always, most of the defendants will be poor and the courts will have to provide them legal counsel. The existing public defender offices will be forced to enlarge, and the system inevitably will spread to other states and cities.

Having given so many years to the public defender system, I can generate a lot of sentiment about it. I can extol the high idealism that the office symbolizes. But in assessing its future, only hard, proved facts are needed or useful. The facts are in its favor. As a system, it works. It is efficient. It is the most economical solution we have yet designed for this burgeoning problem. An independent public defender, free from political control by county board, judges, or other such bodies, is the surest guarantee we have that the poor will receive fair and equitable treatment in our criminal courts.

It's the best system that we have for defending the poor. Its growth in the years ahead can only deepen our appreciation for its vital role in man's pursuit of justice for everyone.